The Collier Quick and Easy Guide to

CHESS

IMPROVE PRACTICAL OR VOCATIONAL SKILLS
SUPPLEMENT YOUR FORMAL EDUCATION
GET MORE FUN OUT OF HOBBIES

This Collier guide is designed to offer concise, authoritative information in a clear, readable manner. Carefully prepared with the latest, up-to-the-minute material, it is also valuable as a source for permanent reference. Titles in this series include—

AMERICAN HISTORY
Robert Sobel, Ph.D.

ARITHMETIC
Simon Dresner

BOOKKEEPING
Morton D. Bluestone, M.A.

BOWLING
Hal and Jean Vermes

BUSINESS LETTER WRITING
Abraham Ellenbogen

CARPENTRY
Clarence Herisko

CHESS
Richard Roberts

DRIVING
Edward A. McInroy, M.A.

ECONOMICS
George G. Dawson, Ph.D., and Russell H. McClain, Ph.D.

EFFECTIVE SPEAKING
Bernice Loren

ELECTRONICS
Jesse Dilson

ETIQUETTE
Dorothy Sara

GOLF
Robert Scharff

HOME MAINTENANCE
Martin Sara

HUNTING
Robert Scharff

INSURANCE
Martin Cornwall

LAW
Jesse Raphael, LL.B.

MAGIC
Hal G. Vermes

MOTOR BOATING
Robert Scharff

PHYSICAL FITNESS
Justus Schifferes, Ph.D.

PLAYING THE GUITAR
Frederick M. Noad

RAPID READING
Myron Q. Herrick, The Reading Laboratory, Inc.

RUNNING A MEETING
Jack T. Parker

SALESMANSHIP
Hal G. Vermes

SEWING
Dorothy Stepat De Van

SKIN AND SCUBA DIVING
Robert Scharff

TENNIS
Robert Scharff

TV WRITING
George Lowther

WATER SKIING
Glen E. Anderson

WORLD HISTORY
Edwin Dunbaugh, Ph.D.

The Collier Quick and Easy Guide to

CHESS

A SELF-INSTRUCTION GUIDE
TO BASIC AND ADVANCED PLAY

BY RICHARD ROBERTS

Collier Books, New York, N.Y.
Collier-Macmillan Ltd., London

A COLLIER BOOKS ORIGINAL

First Edition 1962

Acknowledgment is made to David McKay Company, Inc., for permission to quote from the following:

Kenneth Harkness, The Official Blue Book and Encyclopedia of Chess
Emanuel Lasker, Common Sense in Chess

The Macmillan Company, New York
Collier–Macmillan Canada Ltd., Toronto, Ontario
Printed in the United States of America

CONTENTS

Chapter One

A HISTORICAL INTRODUCTION TO CHESS

On Guard

BEFORE YOU EVEN START to study chess you should be warned:

Chess, like cigarettes and alcohol, can become habit-forming. And the habit can be just as noxious as it is with chain-smokers or dipsomaniacs.

Taken in moderation, chess is a wonderful and stimulating activity; overdone, it can lead to the breaking up of homes and the wasting of fortunes. Even in the near-addiction stage chess can be a difficult thing to live with, especially for wives. You are advised, then, to take the plunge in easy steps and, when you have finished the book, to move into the world of chess gradually.

Ignore this advice and you may find yourself alone and friendless in a world peopled only by Knights, Bishops, Queens, Kings, Rooks and Pawns and shaped —like the world of the Middle Ages—like a square (an eight-by-eight square). The walls of your home will be lined with chess books—all others having been given away to make room for them—and chess sets. After a while you will have only the books, the walls having been taken away after you lost your job because you couldn't concentrate on anything but chess.

It is one thing to be a professional chess player and to spend all your waking hours, and many of your sleeping hours, working out chess moves. In a professional this is forgiveable. But if you intend only to make chess a hobby, a pastime, a source of relaxation and endless enjoyment (all of which it can be), then take it with the proper attitude:

For all that has been said about chess, it remains, first, last and always, only a game.

Legend and Fact

You have been duly advised. Now come in and join the fun.

Chess players are in illustrious company. Napoleon was an avid, if miserable, player. Benjamin Franklin and King Ferdinand of Spain were chess enthusiasts. So were Sergei Prokofieff, Charles Dickens, Abraham Lincoln and Humphrey Bogart. And Edgar Allan Poe, who apparently never managed to win and therefore wrote some scornful sour-grapes things about chess and chess players.*

Non-chess players, of course, are also in illustrious company. King Tut and Socrates didn't play, possibly because the game hadn't been invented in their days. There is no record of Beethoven's having played. Nor is it known that General Eisenhower, Galileo, Jean Harlow or Casey Stengel ever played. It would, in fact, be quite reasonable to assume that more famous, near-famous, infamous and unknown people have not played chess than have.

But that is neither here nor there. Obviously, having bought this book (or have you borrowed it? or are you leafing through it at the bookshop?), you want to learn to play chess and you don't particularly care whether Kings Ferdinand or Tut, Beethoven or Humphrey Bogart played. Still, chess has an interesting, if vague-ish, history. When, for example, was it invented? And where and by whom? And why?

Unfortunately, the origins of chess are not nearly as easy to pin down as the origins of, say, Monopoly or baseball or goldfish-swallowing. This had led many chess authors to dismiss the entire subject with something like: "The beginnings of chess are veiled in the thick mists of time," which is poetic and, to a great extent, true—but which doesn't really say much.

Actually, the history of chess begins with . . . with . . . well, the beginnings of chess are veiled in the thick mists of time, but the earliest written references date to 600 A.D. These early references occur in Sanskrit works, which gives the lion's share of credence to the theory that chess originated in India. (Claims also have been made for the Greeks, Romans, Hebrews, Egyptians, Chinese, Japanese, Arabians, Irish, Welsh and Moors, among others.)

Who devised the game? There are dozens of stories and legends—many preserved in the literature of India, Persia and Islam—about how the game came to be: this or that King or Emperor or Shah was bored

* See *The Murders in the Rue Morgue.*

one day and this or that Wise Man dreamed up the game; or one King challenged another to concoct a game that couldn't be deciphered—and so on. The legends are charming, but they are no more than fantasy.

However, Donald M. Liddell, the author of *Chessmen,* a book tracing the history of chess pieces, has presented an interesting theory that, if it doesn't fix a time or place or person for the origin of chess, does make a case for its antiquity. Liddell notes that the Hindu name for chess is chaturanga, meaning the four sections (anga) of the army. They are represented on the chessboard as elephants, horses, chariots and infantrymen. The chariot, Liddell points out, became obsolete and was dropped from the Indian army when it proved useless during the Alexandrian invasion, which took place in 326 B.C. Therefore, says Liddell, chess must have been invented prior to that invasion.

A nice theory, but it stands or falls solely on its own merits; there is no documentary evidence to support it. There is documentary evidence, though, for the theory that the game was introduced from India into Persia, where the name was changed to chatrang, or shahtrang. The Moslem world apparently was introduced to chess when the Arab-Persian wars began in 527 A.D. The Arabs, who changed the name of the game to Shatranj, became chess zealots, despite Mohammed's injunction that a man should concern himself with only three things—his horses, his weapons and his wives.

Devout but chess-playing Moslems got around this by maintaining—and chess-playing Moslem lawyers backed them up—that chess was not a recreation but an exercise in war tactics and strategy. The lawyers, however, specified that the game had to be played with no stakes; that it not be allowed to interfere with prayers; that no foul language be used while playing, and that it not be played in public places (Moslem potentates used to circumvent this last rule by wearing disguises when they played in the market place).

Legends abound about the chess activities of the Caliphs. One Caliph, al-Mamun, apparently had more enthusiasm than talent, for he is said to have lamented: "Strange that I who rule the world from the Indus in the East to the Andalus in the West cannot manage thirty-two chessmen in a space of two cubits by two." (That two-cubit-square chessboard, which would be about 36 inches square, would be a monster by today's standards. But then the old-timers, it is said, used to make their boards out of solid gold, too. And one King—so the story goes—became enraged at a chess opponent who tried to cheat and promptly did him in with one blow of a chess piece. You could hardly do a man in with the chess pieces they make nowadays.)

Caliph Harun al-Rashid, of Arabian Nights fame, was the first to openly promote chess. He subsidized strong players and arranged matches. Apparently al-Rashid was not too strong a player himself, for he was beaten three times in a row by a slave girl. Duly impressed by her skill, he asked her to name her own reward. She chose amnesty for her boy friend, and the Caliph granted the request.

Possibly the first recognized chess master was a Moslem named al-Adli, who wrote a book on technique. Al-Adli went undefeated until shortly before his death, when he lost to one al-Razi in a match arranged by Caliph al-Mutawakkil. The greatest of the Moslem chess masters was al-Suli, a Baghdad historian who investigated the underlying principles of sound chess technique and who was the first person to set up a system for classifying players according to strength.

After the Caliphates died out, toward the end of the Twelfth Century, the center of chess activity moved to Syria, Turkey and Egypt; the game also became popular among the Moguls. The Mogul Emperor Timur (1336-1405), better known as Tamerlane, was a skilled player and a patron of the game. It is said that he was playing chess one day when two messengers arrived, one to announce the birth of a son, the other the completion of a city Timur had ordered built. Timur had just executed a chess maneuver known as a shahrukh (in modern parlance a double attack against King and Rook), so he named both the son and the city Shah-Rukh.

From the Near East the game spread slowly to and through Europe and had already become popular among the upper classes there before the end of the Caliphates. By 1061, in fact, chess was popular enough to be banned by the Church. Even a high churchman —a Bishop—was caught playing the game. His superior, St. Pietro Damiani, Cardinal-Bishop of Ostia, imposed a penance and reprimanded him. The reprimand is reproduced in a letter St. Pietro sent to Pope Alexander II:

"Was it right, I say, and consistent with thy duty, to sport away thy evenings amidst the vanity of chess, and defile the hand which offers up the body of the Lord, and the tongue that mediates between God and man, with the pollution of a sacrilegious game?"

One of the objections the Church may have had to chess was that, at that time, it could be played with a throw of dice determining which piece was to be moved (that form of the game died out shortly before the Renaissance). Then again the Church may have looked with a baleful eye upon the practice of permitting a Knight (the live kind, not the chess piece) to visit a lady in her room if chess were the object of his call.

In the French romance "Huon de Bordeaux," written around 1200, Huon and the daughter of King Ivoryn agree to play chess with these stakes: if he wins he is to spend the night with her; if he loses, his head is to be lopped off. The dialogue runs this way:

HUON: "Lady, which game will you play? Will you have it with moves or with dice?"
LADY: "Let it be with moves."

As we said, chess was quite popular. And its popularity grew despite the ban. By 1400 the Church, seeing the futility of it all, lifted the proscription. That gave the lower classes a chance to enjoy the game, too.

In his book *The Adventure of Chess* Edward Lasker relates that a game of chess played a role in getting King Ferdinand to put his O.K. on Columbus' trip Across the Ocean Blue. Ferdinand, Lasker says, was engrossed in a game when the Archbishop of Toledo dropped in at the Royal Palace to ask the King whether he had come to a decision about Columbus: would he or would he not grant "the Genoese" the title of admiral?

Ferdinand was in a tight spot on the chessboard and not in a very good humor. "Speak to me no more of this Genoese," he said. "I shall lose a splendid game." Then, frowning, he added: "Your Genoese shall not be an admiral." So much for oddballs who thought the world was round—and for Archbishops who interrupted chess games.

The game continued and the King's opponent, rubbing his hands, gloated that "the battle will soon be decided . . . and if I mistake not, this game, at least, is mine." Ferdinand squirmed and looked gloomy. Fortunately the Archbishop was either persistent or thick-skinned, for he hung around.

As the game went on, a friend of the royal family edged over to the board, studied the positions and then whispered to the Queen: "If his highness plays correctly, he wins." Isabella took the hint and stayed her husband's hand as he was about to make a losing move.

"Do you not win my Lord?" she asked.

"Win?" Ferdinand asked, putting down the piece and going back to his calculations. After a while the light dawned, Ferdinand saw the winning move and his mood changed. As for Columbus, he said, "little harm can come from appointing him admiral."

And so it was that Ferdinand won his game, Columbus got his title, the U.S.A. was on its way to being discovered and everyone lived happily ever after.

A Touch of Morality

We'll skip a few centuries now and move up to Benjamin Franklin's time. Franklin, who had a good deal to say about almost anything, didn't omit chess. And a sizable part of his chess writings may be found

in his little essay "The Morals of Chess," * from which the following are excerpts.

Chess is not merely an idle amusement; several very valuable qualities of the mind, useful in the course of human life, are to be acquired and strengthened by it: for life is a kind of chess, in which we have often points to gain, and competitors to contend with and in which there is a vast variety of good and ill events that are, in some degree, the effect of prudence, or of the want of it. And this we may learn by playing at chess.

He goes on to list these "valuable qualities of the mind" as:

1st, Foresight, which looks a little into futurity, and considers the consequences that may attend an action. . . . "If I move this Piece, what will be the advantage or disadvantage of my new situation?" . . .

2d, Circumspection, which surveys the whole Chessboard, or scene of action. . . .

3d, Caution, not to make our moves too hastily. . . .

And, lastly, we learn by Chess the habit of not being discouraged by present bad appearances in the state of our affairs; the habit of hoping for a favourable change, and that of persevering in the search of resources. . . .

And a Little Immorality

Franklin advised chess players to lose or win gracefully and not to gloat over an adversary's mistakes. This gentlemanly approach differed sharply from that of the Spanish Bishop, Ruy Lopez (you'll find, in Chapter 8, an opening named for him), who had this advice for chess players:

"If you play by day, place your opponent facing the light, which gives you a great advantage. Also, try to play your adversary when he has just eaten and drunk freely."

Other authors, essayists and chess players have, through the centuries, offered advice on all aspects of playmanship as well as on the game itself. B. H. Wood, in the Illustrated London News, 1949, for example, offered sage counsel on the art of making excuses for losing. Your loss, he said, can be attributed to:

. . . interference by spectators, the noise of traffic, toothache, headache, backache, the foulness of your opponent's pipe, his constant humming or finger-drumming on the table, bad light, blinding light, defective chessmen, a board too large, a board too small, an atomic explosion in Siberia [unfortunately that one can no longer be looked at so lightly], the Government, the Inland Revenue, or a bluebottle blundering across the fairway.

It is odd that Wood should have omitted from his list several of the more commonly offered excuses. Such as:

* In *A Treasury of Chess Lore,* edited by Fred Reinfeld (New York: Dover, 1951).

"I got bored because he played so badly it wasn't a challenge."

OR

"I like to lose now and then just to remind myself what it feels like."

OR

"I always do that—you know, I get impatient and just make any old move."

As for the art of winning gracefully: first you will have to learn to win. And that is one object (but not THE object) of this book.

The Champions

Before closing this introductory chapter, we will introduce you briefly to some of the names you are going to run across later on; names that appear later but not here can be assumed to be those of chess players of rank and status. But they were also-rans, because the following is a list of world champions.

HOWARD STAUNTON: An Englishman who was unofficial world champion from about 1843 to 1851. But from what is known of his readiness to meet challengers, he may have retained his "title" more by footwork than by talent.

ADOLPH ANDERSSEN: Unofficial champion from 1851 to 1866. An Old-World gentleman who had kind words for the man who defeated him, namely . . .

PAUL MORPHY: The boy-wonder of chess. Born in New Orleans in 1837, he won the first big American tournament, the American Chess Congress, in 1857. The following year he went to Europe and defeated all comers. Staunton, however, refused to grant him a match. He went back to the States determined to forget chess and pursue a career in law. Numerous setbacks and frustrations aggravated what probably was a heavy predisposition to mental instability, and he died at the age of 47. He was the subject of the 1961 best-seller *The Chess Players,* by Frances Parkinson Keyes.

WILLIAM STEINITZ: An Austrian who became the first official world champion. He held the title for 28 years against all contenders, finally meeting defeat at the hands of . . .

EMANUEL LASKER: A mathematician, philosopher and one of the most profound and original thinkers in chess. He held the title for 27 years, losing it, at the age of 52, to the brilliant, handsome and urbane young Cuban . . .

JOSÉ RAUL CAPABLANCA: Like Morphy, Capablanca learned chess as a child, reportedly by watching his father and uncle play. At 23 he cajoled his way into the International Masters Tournament at San Sebastian, Spain, and surprised the chess world by coming out on top. Shortly after his picture appeared in newspapers around the world a surge of interest in chess among women was noted. Capablanca held the title from 1921 to 1927, when he was defeated by a White Russian émigré named . . .

ALEXANDER ALEKHINE (pronounced ool-YAH-keen): Here was a man who lived for nothing but chess (though he held a doctorate in law). Even his friends conceded he was a cad, an opportunist and a megalomaniac. And even his enemies conceded he was probably the greatest chess player who ever lived. He was also an alcoholic, and his loss of the title in 1935 to Dr. Max Euwe of Holland has often been attributed to his having been rather under the weather during their match. He regained the title in 1937 in a return match. Alekhine died in 1946 on the eve of a scheduled match with . . .

MIKHAIL BOTWINNIK: To determine Alekhine's successor, six of the top players of the world (Max Euwe of the Netherlands, Reuben Fine and Samuel Reshevsky of the United States, and Paul Keres, Vassily Smyslov and Mikhail Botwinnik of the Soviet Union) were invited to a tournament. Botwinnik won, thus becoming champion of the world. He lost the title, for a year, to Smyslov and, for another year, to . . .

MIKHAIL TAL of the Soviet Union. After regaining the title from Tal, Botwinnik lost it again, in 1963, to . . .

TIGRAN PETROSIAN of the Soviet Union, and decided to retire from championship competition.

And now—on to the game of chess.

Chapter Two

THE BOARD AND THE MEN

Familiarity Breeds Sense

AN OLD ENGLISH (or is it German?) recipe for rabbit stew advises the would-be cook: "First, go out and shoot a rabbit."

The same sort of advice applies to the would-be chess player:

First, go out and get a chessboard and a set of chess men. You'll find many diagrams in this book. Look at them, study them—and translate them into real set-ups of real chess men on a real chessboard. In this way you will not only get to know the feel of chess pieces, but you will also develop the ability to visualize the board, the men and the moves when you see a printed diagram.

Trying to play chess without having the feel of the game is like trying to learn to act without ever walking across a stage. It's possible—but a thousandfold harder to do. After a while you will get to feel at home with a chessboard; the pieces will become familiar figures to you. And you will, if you give yourself half a chance, grow to love this fascinating "royal game."

Chess has often been called a game of war, and there probably is more than a grain or two of truth in this. But the comparison cannot be carried too far (although one chess master actually won many games basing his strategy on the principles of military operations). Chess has remained essentially unchanged for a thousand years or more; war, on the other hand, has not.

Where wars were once decided by the clash of men on well laid-out fields of battle, they are now fought by entire populations in an arena that outreaches the world. Chess is still played on the same four-sided battlefield used by its earliest exponents. That battlefield is the chessboard; let's examine it.

The Board

The chessboard is eight squares wide and eight squares long, a total area of 64 squares. In any row the light and dark squares alternate; in any diagonal the squares are all one color.

Colors are far from standard; they range from straightforward black and white to such off-beat combinations as green and blue or gold-flecked and silver-flecked. By convention, however, the lighter squares are called white and the darker ones black. And by convention, too, the board is placed between the players (who alternate in moving) so that each player has a white square in his lower right-hand corner. The rows that point from one player to the other are called files; the crossing rows are called ranks.

So much for the board. Now let's look at the forces —the chess pieces.

The Men

THE KING

The most important piece—the one around which the whole game revolves—is the King. He is the largest piece and, in most traditionally designed sets, can easily be recognized by the cross he wears on his crown. The symbol for the King is ♔ for White and ♚ for Black; his abbreviation is K.

THE QUEEN

The strongest piece is the Queen. She is the power behind the throne, and her status is indicated by her size; she is just a hair smaller than the King, who still outranks her in importance. Unlike him, however, she wears a coronet, not a crown, and there is no cross to top her off. Her symbol is ♕ for White and ♛ for Black; her abbreviation is Q.

THE ROOK

Next, in order of power, is the Rook, the piece that in standard sets looks like the tower of a castle. Many casual chess players, in fact, call this piece the castle. But, as you will soon learn, this can be confusing. The true name is derived from the Persian word rouk, which means elephant. You can see evidence of this origin in chess sets made in the Far East—or designed to look as though made in the Far East. In these exotic sets the Rook is, in fact as well as in name, an elephant, often carrying a howdah on its back. In standard sets, which are called the Staunton Pattern after the English chess master, the piece looks something like the symbol ♖ for White and ♜ for Black. And the abbreviation—casual players notwithstanding—is R.

THE BISHOP

The Bishop is the piece with the slit in its head. Supposedly, this represents a Bishop's mitre. But it might also represent a court jester's hat (the French call this piece le Fou, the fool, or jester). The English abbreviation, however, is B. And the symbol of the piece is ♗ for White and ♝ for Black.

THE KNIGHT

The Knight is probably the most fascinating piece for beginners and grandmasters alike (though beginners seem to mix their fascination with a touch of fear). It has not changed its appearance since chess was invented (some might say discovered), or so we are led to believe by historical findings. It is true that in many old chess sets, and in some modern ones, the piece is a knight on horseback. But though the knight himself may disappear, his horse does not. For this reason the casual player is at odds here, too, with official rules. He calls this piece the Horse. But he would have trouble following a printed score or a chess book, because the abbreviation is not H. It is, in most modern chess books, N. This is not a case of poor spelling; the convention was adopted because the old abbreviation (Kt) frequently was confused with K, the abbreviation for the King. When game scores appeared in agate (that miniscule type so handy for hidden clauses in legal documents) the chess enthusiast, trying to distinguish K's from Kt's, often as not ended up in an optometrist's chair. The symbol is unmistakable. It is ♘ for White and ♞ for Black.

THE PAWN

We come now to the last piece, the Pawn, often—but mistakenly—called the lowly pawn. In all sets, no matter what their origin, no matter how radical their design, the Pawn is the smallest piece on the board. As though to make up for stature, though, there are more of them than of any other piece. The Pawn is at the bottom of the power ladder but he can and often does hold the big guns at bay. And, he can be the decisive factor in a game. The symbol for the White Pawn is ♙ and for the Black Pawn ♟ The abbreviation is P.

How the Board Is Set Up

Having learned what the board and pieces look like you can now get the forces set up. Remember to place your chessboard so that a white square is at the lower right-hand corner.

Put one White Rook (use the White pieces only for the time being; we'll get to the Black shortly) on the lower right-hand square and the other White Rook in the dark square at the lower left. Now, on the same rank (horizontal row), place a Knight next to each Rook, then a Bishop next to each Knight.

Only the two center squares of the bottom rank should now be unoccupied; these are for the King and Queen. The Queen always stands, at the start of the game, on a square of her own color. Thus, the White Queen should be placed on the left-hand center square. The King stands next to her.

The principal pieces now fill the bottom rank. The Pawns come next. Set them up on the rank immediately in front of the principal pieces, one Pawn in front of each piece. This completes the starting line-up for White.

Now turn your board around (or walk around to the other side of the board if you enjoy that split-personality feeling of playing both sides) and set up the Black pieces. They are arranged precisely the way the White pieces are—Rooks occupying end squares, Knights next and then Bishops. Notice, however, that because the Queen always starts life on a square of her own color she will, from Black's point of view, stand on the right-hand center square.

And notice, too, that as a result King faces King and Queen faces Queen across the board.

Your board is now set up for the start of a game. For a picture of how it should look, see page 13.

Using the symbols for board and men, the starting position looks like this:

DIAGRAM 1

Everything is ready. But the action can't begin (unless you care to make it poker, using the pieces for

chips) until you learn how the pieces move, how they capture, how powerful each is and what each one's weakness may be.

How the Pieces Move and Capture

THE ROOK

Clear your board of all pieces. Now take a White Rook and put it in the following position on the board:

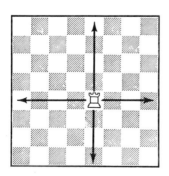

DIAGRAM 2

The Rook moves in straight lines, along the ranks and files, as indicated by the arrows in the diagram. As long as his path is unobstructed there is nothing to stop

him except the edge of the board. Any enemy piece within his range can be captured. The piece that is captured is removed from the board and the capturing piece takes its place. To illustrate the Rook's powers of capturing, let's add some pieces to the board.

DIAGRAM 3

The Rook can capture the Black Queen, who is within his range on a file. The Black pawn lies along the Rook's rank, but it cannot be captured because the White Bishop blocks the way. The Rook cannot jump over any piece, his own or the enemy's. Thus, the Black Bishop is safe. But the Black Knight may be captured. Note that word "may." Capture is not compulsory.

If the Rook were to capture the Queen, the board would look like this:

DIAGRAM 4

Notice that the Black Queen has disappeared from the board and the White Rook has taken her place.

Clear your board again and put a Rook down on any square. Now count the number of squares swept by the Rook's lines of fire along ranks and files. Not counting the square on which he stands, the Rook commands 14 squares. Now change the Rook's position. He still commands 14 squares.

This is one of the Rook's great powers; he always commands 14 squares, no matter where he stands. Of course, if he is blocked by his own men his great range of fire does him no good. And this is his big weakness; he can be all-too easily hemmed in by his own allies. He needs open lines along which to exert his strength.

THE BISHOP

Clear your board again and, this time, put a White Bishop on it as shown below:

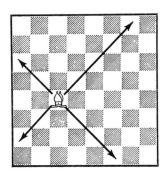

DIAGRAM 5

The Bishop, as you see, moves along diagonals and is confined to squares of one color. It can command as many as 13 squares, but as few as 7 (try putting the Bishop where the lower left-hand arrowhead is in the diagram; you will see that the Bishop's range has been cut down to 7 squares). Like the Rook, it can capture any enemy piece that stands in its line of fire. And, like the Rook, it cannot jump over any pieces.

Let's add a few pieces to the board to see how the Bishop captures:

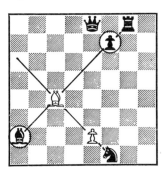

DIAGRAM 6

Two Black pieces can be captured—the Bishop and the Pawn. The Rook is safe because the Black Pawn blocks him from the Bishop's line of fire; the Knight is immune because one of the Bishop's own Pawns obstructs it. The Black Queen is out of the Bishop's range.

Once more, let's see what the board would look like if a capture were made. The White Bishop captures the Black Bishop. The board then looks like this:

DIAGRAM 7

The Black Bishop is gone and the White Bishop has taken its place. Notice that the Bishop is still in a position to capture the Black Pawn.

And now . . .

STOP!

How well do you know the material you've studied so far? Test yourself before going on.

Self-Testing Quiz No. 1

(a) What's wrong on the following diagram of the starting line-up?

DIAGRAM 8

(b) Which Black piece, if any, can be captured by the White Rook in the following diagram?

DIAGRAM 9

(c) Put a White Bishop into the following diagram so that it will be in position to capture the Black Rook.

DIAGRAM 10

(The answers are at the back of the book.)

If you passed (you did, didn't you?), you're ready to continue.

THE QUEEN

This is, as you already know, your most powerful fighting unit. What makes her so strong? Look at the way she moves.

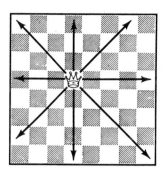

DIAGRAM 11

She moves along the ranks and files as well as along the diagonals—combining the powers of Rook and Bishop. She commands a total of 27 squares in this position. And any enemy pieces that stumble into her far-sweeping line of fire can be captured. Let's take a look at how the Queen captures.

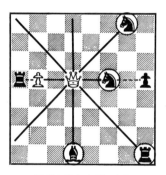

DIAGRAM 12

The Queen can capture either of the Black Knights; one lies in her range along a diagonal, the other on a rank. She can capture the Bishop, which is in her line of fire on a file. And she can capture one of the Black Rooks along a diagonal. The Black Pawn is saved because the Black Knight blocks the way. The second Black Rook is safe because the Queen's own Pawn stands in the way. (The Queen, despite her mighty power, cannot jump over pieces.)

If the Queen were to capture the Rook, the board would look like . . .

STOP!

Self-Testing Quiz No. 2

Set up the board as it would look if the Queen were to capture the Rook. Then look in the back of the book to see if you were right.

Can the Queen possibly have a weakness? Indeed she can. Her weakness (as wise men long ago learned of women) is her strength. She is so valuable that she can easily be harried by lesser pieces. No player would want to give up his Queen in return for a Bishop or a Rook. So, when the Queen is attacked by a lesser piece that is protected she cannot afford to capture the attacker. She must beat an ignoble retreat.

THE KNIGHT

The Knight is known in German as der Springer—the jumper or vaulter. This is because the Knight, unlike other pieces, has the power to jump over his own and enemy pieces. He does not jump in the sense that a checker piece does; that is, he does not capture what he jumps over. He captures the piece that occupies the square on which he lands. He is a great one for operating in close quarters; he can literally leap into the middle of things and, if the going gets too rough, leap right out again. Let's examine the way the Knight moves:

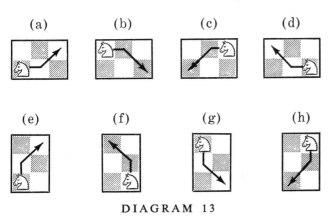

DIAGRAM 13

As you see, the Knight moves one square along a rank or file, then one square along a diagonal. This gives him eight ways to move: right and up (a); right and down (b); left and down (c); left and up (d); up and right (e); up and left (f); down and right (g), and down and left (h).

In the following position the Knight can capture any of the Black pieces by moving to the square occupied by that piece:

DIAGRAM 14

Notice that in the preceding diagram the Knight has a choice of eight different captures, corresponding to the eight squares to which he can move. When the Knight captures he, too, replaces the captured piece.

THE PAWN

The Pawn is the foot-soldier of the chess army. Like any soldier, he plods slowly along while the cavalry and artillery charge ahead on wheels and the generals move overhead in jets. He is limited to moving straight ahead (not being allowed to retreat), except when he encounters the enemy. And, except for his first move, he can travel only one square at a time.

On his first move—and then only—he is permitted the option of moving two squares forward. In the following diagram, for example, the White King's Pawn, on his first move, can go to either A or B.

DIAGRAM 15

The Pawn, unlike the other pieces, does not capture the same way he moves. Though he moves straight ahead, he captures diagonally. In the following diagram, then, the White pawn can capture either the Black Rook or the Black Pawn. It would, of course, take the place of whichever piece it captured.

DIAGRAM 16

Though the Pawn's lot seems a weary one, the end of its journey can mean glory. If it reaches its last rank —the one on which the enemy's principal pieces stood at the start of the game—it becomes a Knight, a Bishop, a Rook or even a Queen. For this reason games are often decided by the loss of a single Pawn. And for this reason, too, the "lowly" Pawn has the power to throw the generals of the opposing army into confusion.

STOP!

Don't continue until you are sure you have mastered the material presented thus far.

Self-Testing Quiz No. 3

(a) Which Knight—Black or White—in the following diagram can capture an enemy Bishop?

DIAGRAM 17

(b) If it were Black's turn to move in the diagram above, in how many ways could he capture a piece?

(c) Are there any pawns in the diagram below able to capture anything? If so, which piece can the Pawn capture?

DIAGRAM 18

THE KING

We have saved the King for last because he is, after all, the heart and soul of chess. You can lose every other piece you have and still play on (for a while, anyhow). You cannot lose your King. (He cannot, in fact, be captured, but more about that later.)

The King can move in any direction, along a rank, file or diagonal, forward or backward. But he can move only one square at a time, except under special circumstances, which we will discuss soon. He can capture any piece within his range. But—and this is a big "but"—he cannot move into the line of fire of any enemy piece.

In the following diagram the King can move to any of the squares numbered 1 to 8. If an enemy piece occupied one of those squares the King could capture it and take its place—provided that in doing so he did not move into the range of any enemy piece.

DIAGRAM 19

Now, keeping the White King in the same position, let's add some Black pieces to the board.

DIAGRAM 20

Now the King cannot move to square 1 because he would be moving into a position where the Black Pawn or Black Rook could capture him. That square is controlled by the Rook and Pawn and the King cannot move to a square controlled by the enemy. Square 2 is controlled by the Black Knight. Squares 3, 4 and 5 are controlled by the Black Queen. Squares 5, 6, 7 and 8 are controlled by the Black Rook.

Is the King immobilized? No—he can capture the Black Rook. If he did so, the board would look like this:

DIAGRAM 21

The King has replaced the Rook and he is not in the line of fire of any Black pieces.

Putting the King in Check

A king under attack by an enemy piece is said to be "in check." If the King is attacked everything must be subordinated to the job of getting the King out of check; no moves can be made by the attacked King's side until the King's safety is attended to. There are three ways in which the King can be gotten out of check. These are:

1. By moving the King to a square not controlled by a hostile piece.
2. By placing one of the King's men between the attacking piece and the King, thus blocking the hostile's piece's line of fire.
3. By capturing the attacking piece.

Let's examine those three ways.

DIAGRAM 22

In the diagram above the Black King is attacked by the White Bishop. Can he or one of his men capture the Bishop? No. Can a Black piece be moved between the Bishop and the King to shield the King? No. But the King is not doomed. He can move to a square that is not under attack—the squares marked with X's. He cannot, of course, move to the back rank because that rank is in the White Queen's line of fire. And moving along the diagonal to the square marked with a cross is futile (as well as illegal) because that square is controlled by the attacking White Bishop.

Here is another position.

DIAGRAM 23

The White King is attacked by one of the Black Rooks. The possible escape squares are occupied by the King's own men—he cannot flee to them. The squares marked with X's are controlled by the second Black Rook. And there is no White piece capable of placing itself between the attacking Rook and the King. But White's Bishop can save its King by capturing the attacking Rook.

And a third example.

DIAGRAM 24

The King is attacked by the Black Rook. The two escape squares are occupied, one by the White Bishop, one by the White Pawn. There is no way to capture the Rook. But the King can be saved by interposing— by moving a man between himself and the attacking piece. The Pawn, of course, able to move forward only, is of no use. But the Bishop can be moved to the square marked X, shielding the King from the Rook.

When the King is attacked by a Pawn or a Knight there can be no interposing, of course. In the case of such an attack the King can be saved only through the capture of the attacking piece or by moving out of the attacking piece's range.

STOP!

Have you learned thoroughly all the material up to this point?

Self-Testing Quiz No. 4

(a) In the following diagram the White King is in check. How can you get him out of check?

DIAGRAM 25

(b) In the following diagram the Black King is being attacked by the White Bishop. Can he capture the Bishop to get out of check?

DIAGRAM 26

(c) In the following diagram the Black King is attacked twice, by the Rook and by the Queen. How can you get him out of check?

DIAGRAM 27

Long Live the King

When the King is attacked and it is impossible to get him out of check the game is over. The King has been "checkmated" and his side has lost. (The word "checkmate," like the word Rook, comes from the Persian. It is derived from "Shah Mat," which means "the King is dead.")

In the following position, for example, the White King is attacked by the Black Queen. He cannot move to another point on the bottom rank because that entire rank is swept by the Black Queen's line of fire. He cannot flee diagonally to the possible escape squares on the rank above because those squares are occupied by his own Pawns. And he cannot move to the White square directly above him because he would still be in check—this time by the Black Bishop. There is no way to interpose a White piece between the King and the attacking Queen. And the Queen cannot be captured.

DIAGRAM 27A

Thus the King has no way out of check. He has not been captured—that is, he has not been removed from the board—but he has no way to avoid capture on Black's theoretical next move. The move remains theoretical because the game ends at this point.

The Special Powers

The last moves to be considered are the "special circumstance" powers referred to briefly earlier. One of those special powers involves Pawns, the other involves the King and Rooks. First, the Pawn's specialty.

PAWN CAPTURES EN PASSANT

A Pawn, you remember, has the option, on his first move only, of going forward two squares instead of one. And Pawns, remember, capture on a diagonal instead of capturing the way they move. With this in mind, look at the following diagram:

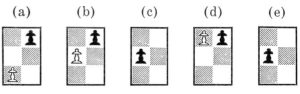

DIAGRAM 28

Box (a) represents a section of the chessboard; the White Pawn is standing on home base, on the rank just in front of the principal White pieces. If the White Pawn moves forward one square on his first move the position will be as it is in box (b); the Black Pawn would then be able to capture it and the result would be (c). If, however, the White Pawn moves two squares on his first move the position will be as it is in (d) and the Black Pawn will have been deprived of a possible capture.

The Black Pawn (as any Pawn in similar circumstances), however, has a special prerogative. He can treat the White Pawn as though it had moved only one square forward and he will then be able to capture it. The result, of course, is the same (e) as when the White Pawn actually moved only one square and was captured (c).

This power is called capturing *en passant* (French: in passing). The power, however, must be exercised by the capturing side on its very next move following the two-squares-forward Pawn move. If the capture is not made then the pawn positions as shown in (d) stand and the privilege of capturing that Pawn en passant (abbreviation, e.p.) has been forfeited.

CASTLING

The special-circumstance power involving King and Rooks is called castling. When a player makes this move, he castles (remember? we said the casual player's use of this word could be confusing).

Because the King's safety is of prime concern it can be dangerous to leave him in the middle of the board on or near his original square. Once the pieces start moving into action a King in the center can be easily exposed to attack. He must be moved to a safer spot (to the security of his "castle"). Basically, the castling move is made as shown below:

DIAGRAM 29

The King is moved two squares toward his Rook and the Rook goes to the square over which the King passed to get to his new position. The combination King-Rook move is counted as one move (it is the only time in the game a player is permitted to move two pieces at once). The diagram above shows the

King castling on his own side of the board. He can also castle on the Queen's side, as follows:

DIAGRAM 30

Once again the King has moved two squares toward a Rook (this time toward the Queen Rook) and the Rook has moved to the square through which the King passed. This is called Queen-side castling, or castling long. King-side castling is also called castling short.

It may have occurred to you that castling is a great way to get out of check. Alas, you'll have to forget it (unless, like some players, you make your own rules to suit your convenience); it is illegal to castle when the King is in check. There are some other provisos, too. You cannot castle if:

1. The King or the Rook has been moved before. (If only the King Rook has been moved it is still legal to castle on the Queen's side with the Queen Rook. Likewise, if only the Queen Rook has been moved it is legal to castle on the King side.)
2. One or more squares between the King and Rook are occupied by pieces of either color. (If a square between the King and Queen Rook is occupied it is legal to castle King-side.)
3. The King, in castling, has to pass through a square controlled by an enemy man. (Naturally he could not castle if the square he ended on was under attack; he would then be moving into check which, remember, is illegal.)

Let's examine castling more closely. Look at this position:

DIAGRAM 31

In the preceding diagram the White King can not castle on his Queen's side because the squares between him and the Queen Rook are not clear; the White Knight occupies its home square. He cannot castle King-side, either, because in doing so he would have to pass through a square which is in the Black Queen's line of fire. Thus the White King, in this position, cannot castle.

The Black King cannot castle King-side because his own Bishop is in the way. But there is nothing to stop him from castling long.

Have you got the special powers and checkmate down pat? Let's see.

Self-Testing Quiz No. 5

(a) In the following diagram which King can castle and on which side? What keeps the other King from castling?

(b) In the following diagram Black has just made a Pawn move. Is White in a position to capture en passant?

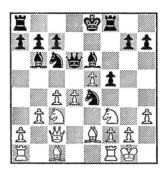

DIAGRAM 33

(c) In the following diagram can either side make one move and checkmate the opposing King? If so, make the move and show the final position.

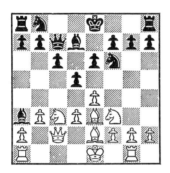

DIAGRAM 32

DIAGRAM 34

Chapter Three

NOTATION

The Shorthand of Chess

THE LITERATURE OF chess, like its origins, is a subject upon which there has been much speculation. Who wrote the first chess book? Your guess is almost as good as the most learned chess historian's. There is, however, general agreement on this: the first printed English chess book—actually a translation of an earlier work in Latin—was brought out in 1474.

Since that time the literature of chess has grown tremendously. More than 20,000 books have been devoted to the game and the number of magazine articles is beyond reckoning. This vast output, which increases every day, would have been next to impossible were it not for chess notation, the shorthand systems used to describe the board, the pieces and the moves.

Without notation, a book of collected chess games, for example, which ordinarily would run to about 250 pages, might require 700 pages. Publishers would be understandably reluctant to put out a book of that size, and chess enthusiasts would think twice about paying its justifiably high price. Chess books, in fact, would be rarities.

The basic principles of descriptive notation—the system most commonly used, despite its drawbacks—were known and used as far back as the Tenth Century. It was only in the last hundred years, however, that abbreviations came to be used and standardized. And abbreviations are the keystones of notation. Let's see how it works.

Set up your pieces for the start of a game. Notice that, because King faces King and Queen faces Queen, an imaginary line can be drawn down the center of the board, separating the King and his pieces from the Queen and her forces. Reading across the bottom rank from the Queen's side to the King's we have the following lineup:

Queen Rook (abbreviated QR), Queen Knight (QN), Queen Bishop (QB), Queen (Q), King (K), King Bishop (KB), King Knight (KN) and King Rook (KR).

The Pawns are named for the pieces that stand behind them. Thus, reading along the second rank, again from the Queen's side to the King's, we have the Queen Rook Pawn (QRP), Queen Knight Pawn (QNP), Queen Bishop Pawn (QBP), Queen Pawn (QP), King Pawn (KP), King Bishop Pawn (KBP), King Knight Pawn (KNP) and King Rook Pawn (KRP).

The files, too, are named for the pieces that initially occupy them. White's extreme right-hand file, then, is the King Rook (KR) file. This is also Black's KR file, though it is, of course, on Black's extreme left-hand side. White's extreme left-hand file is the QR file; it is also Black's QR file, though Black—again—sees it as his extreme right-hand file.

The files, as you see, have the same names from both the Black and White points of view. The ranks, however, do not. White's first rank is Black's eighth and vice-versa. Suppose, for example, that you want to describe the following squares:

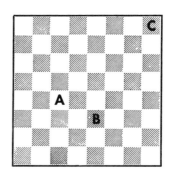

DIAGRAM 35

We know that square A lies on the Queen Bishop file for both White and Black. From White's point of view (by custom, White is always at the bottom of a printed diagram) the square is four ranks from the bottom. For White, then, square A is Queen Bishop 4 (abbreviated QB4). From Black's point of view, however, it is five ranks from the bottom (to see this more clearly, turn the diagram around). And thus square A is Black's Queen Bishop 5, or QB5.

Square B is on the King file for both White and Black. Looked at from White's side, it is three ranks from the bottom, making it K3. Looked at from Black's side, it is six rows up, making it K6.

Square C is on White's last, or eighth, rank and therefore is White's KR8. But it is on Black's first rank, making it Black's KR1.

You see, then, that every square on the board has two designations, one for White and one for Black. The board, with each square given its two designations, looks like this:

BLACK

QR1 QR8	QN1 QN8	QB1 QB8	Q1 Q8	K1 K8	KB1 KB8	KN1 KN8	KR1 KR8
QR2 QR7	QN2 QN7	QB2 QB7	Q2 Q7	K2 K7	KB2 KB7	KN2 KN7	KR2 KR7
QR3 QR6	QN3 QN6	QB3 QB6	Q3 Q6	K3 K6	KB3 KB6	KN3 KN6	KR3 KR6
QR4 QR5	QN4 QN5	QB4 QB5	Q4 Q5	K4 K5	KB4 KB5	KN4 KN5	KR4 KR5
QR5 QR4	QN5 QN4	QB5 QB4	Q5 Q4	K5 K4	KB5 KB4	KN5 KN4	KR5 KR4
QR6 QR3	QN6 QN3	QB6 QB3	Q6 Q3	K6 K3	KB6 KB3	KN6 KN3	KR6 KR3
QR7 QR2	QN7 QN2	QB7 QB2	Q7 Q2	K7 K2	KB7 KB2	KN7 KN2	KR7 KR2
QR8 QR1	QN8 QN1	QB8 QB1	Q8 Q1	K8 K1	KB8 KB1	KN8 KN1	KR8 KR1

WHITE

DIAGRAM 36

The bottom figure in each square is the White designation; the top figure (which should be looked at "upside-down," from Black's point of view) is Black's. This is one of the principal drawbacks of descriptive notation. There are others, and we will . . .

STOP!

Before going further, make sure you know the board thoroughly.

Self-Testing Quiz No. 6

(a) In the following diagram, on what square (from White's point of view) is:

1. *The White Bishop?*
2. *The White Rook?*
3. *The Black Queen?*
4. *The Black Knight?*

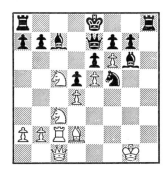

DIAGRAM 37

(b) Name those same squares from Black's point of view.

(c) Set up your board with the White King at KN1, the White Queen at QB3, White Rooks at K1 and K2 and White Pawns at KB2, KN3 and KR2. Put the Black King (set up the Black pieces from Black's point of view) at QR1, Black Rooks at Q1 and QB1, Black Bishops at QN3 and QB3, a Black Knight at Q5 and Black Pawns at QR2, QN2 and QB2. Compare your board with the diagram in the answer section.

Abbreviations and Ambiguities

You now know the symbols for the pieces and for the squares. There remain only a few more basic abbreviations, the most important of which are the following:

The symbol — means "is moved to." Thus P—K4 means "Pawn is moved to the square King 4" or, more simply, Pawn to King 4.

The symbol × means "captures." Thus B×N means "Bishop captures Knight."

The symbol O-O means castles King side.

The symbol O-O-O means castles Queen side.

The abbreviation ch means "check."

The abbreviation N×P ch, therefore, would mean "Knight captures Pawn and gives check."

The double designation for each square is not, alas, the only weakness of the descriptive notation system. Because each side has eight pawns, two Knights, two Bishops and two Rooks, a move can be, if the notation is not done carefully, ambiguous or misleading. In the following diagram, for example, the move B—N5 for White can be interpreted two ways: it can mean QB to KN5 or KB to QN5.

If we want to make the move clear, we must specify which Bishop is doing the moving. If we want to move the King Bishop to QN5 we would notate the move as B−QN5 or as KB−N5. It is not necessary to write KB−QN5 because once we specify either the piece or the square to which it goes we have made the move clear. We want clarity, not complexity.

Now look at the following diagram.

DIAGRAM 39

The only difference between this position and the one in the previous diagram is that now Black's QP is at Q3 instead of Q2, his KP is at K4 instead of K3 and his KB is at KB1 instead of at K2. But what a difference! Now if we see B−N5 for White it can mean only one thing: Bishop to King Knight 5.

Why? Because Bishop to Queen Knight 5 would check the Black King and the move would be written B−N5 ch. The abbreviation ch—or the lack of it—makes the move clear. Only the QB can move to N5 without giving check.

Sometimes, as you see, moves can be written quite simply. An even better example is the move P−K4. At first thought you might be tempted to ask "which Pawn moves to K4?" But set up your board for the start of a game and notice: only one Pawn—the KP—can move to K4. Therefore it's not necessary to spell out he whole move. P−K4 speaks for itself.

Now set up your board in the following position:

Suppose you, as Black, want to move a Knight to KB5. You cannot write N−B5 or even N−KB5, because both Knights are in a position to move to KB5. You must specify which Knight is to make the move. One Knight is at KN3, the other at Q4. To clarify your move you must specify which of the two Knights makes the move. If you move the Knight from KN3 to KB5 you notate it as N/3−B5; if you move the Knight at Queen 4 the move becomes N/4−B5. Notice that you don't have to specify King B5, because it would be impossible to move either Knight to Queen B5. Again, the object is to keep it as simple as possible.

Let's alter the positions again, to the following:

DIAGRAM 40

DIAGRAM 41

Now if you, as Black, want to move a Knight to K4, you must be even more specific than in the previous example. Last time, you got away with N/3 or N/4 as identifications. This time both Knights are on the third rank; therefore N/3 could be either one. The Knight that moves must now be identified either fully (as N/N3) or by his file (as N/N). Moving the Knight at N3 to K4, then, would be written as N/N3−K4 or as N/N−K4. Moving the Knight at QB3 to K4 would be written as N/B3−K4 or N/B−K4.

In the following diagram both Black Knights are in a position to capture a White Bishop. If, therefore, we wrote N×B for Black, the move would be ambiguous.

Which Knight? And which Bishop? Here, again, clarification is needed.

DIAGRAM 42

If Black captures a Bishop with his Knight at KN3 the move is written as N/KN3×B. (Notice that N/N3×B will not do because both Knights are at N3 —one at KN3, one at QN3.) If the capture is made with the Knight at QN3 the move is written N/QN3×B.

Sometimes the piece that is captured, instead of the capturing piece, needs further identification. Look at the following diagram.

DIAGRAM 43

Playing Black, you capture a Pawn with a Knight. In writing the move, you must make clear which Knight captures which Pawn. The Knight at QN3 can capture the Pawn at QR5 or the one at QB5; the Knight at KN3 can capture the Pawn at K4 or the one at KR5. Thus, if the Knight at QN3 captures the Pawn at QR5 the move is written as N×QRP or N×P/QR5 (Notice—you don't have to specify which Knight makes the capture; only one of the Knights can capture the Queen Rook Pawn. You do, however, have to specify that the captured pawn is the QR Pawn; if you wrote simply N×RP it could mean N×KRP, too.)

The object of descriptive notation, then, is to make each move as clear as possible with as few complica-tions as possible. For a while—until you get used to the system—this may seem like trying to make Aristotle look as easy as McGuffey's Reader. With a little practice, though, you'll find that descriptive notation, despite its drawbacks, is really quite capable of doing its job.

Before notating a move, consider:

(a) Are there two similar pieces that can make the same move?
(b) Are there two similar pieces that can be captured by one piece?
(c) Are there two pieces that could possibly be confused with each other?

If the answer to any of those questions is yes you will have to notate the move with care to avoid ambiguity.

How well do you think you'd do in . . .

Self-Testing Quiz No. 7

(a) Set up your board in the starting position. Now make the following moves (White, who always moves first, is in the left-hand column; Black's moves are in the right-hand column).

1	P—K4	P—K4
2	N—KB3	N—QB3
3	B—N5	P—QR3
4	B—R4	. . .

Now consult the diagram in the answer section. Your board should correspond to the diagram. If you were right, continue from there with the following moves:

4	. . .	N—B3*
5	O—O	B—K2
6	R—K1	P—QN4

(b) Consult answer section again to see whether your board corresponds with the position reached. If there's a difference start again with move 1.

(c) In the following diagram White captures the circled Black Pawn with a Bishop; Black replies by capturing the Bishop with the circled Knight. Write these moves in descriptive notation.

* When only a Black move is given it is preceded by three dots to denote the absence of the White move. Thus . . . Q-R4 means Black plays Queen to R4.

DIAGRAM 44

(d) In the following diagram Black makes the move B×P/B5. How does the board look after that move?

DIAGRAM 45

The Algebraic System

Now that you know how descriptive notation works you can take a look at a system that's a lot more efficient and many times simpler. This is the algebraic system, and you are likely to encounter it only in records of international chess tournaments—maybe. It is as understandable to a Russian or a Greek as it is to an American or an Englishman. And, like many really good things, it is having a hard time becoming accepted. For this reason—and this reason only—this book uses descriptive notation. We could become crusaders for the algebraic system, but where would that leave you? Almost any chess book or periodical you pick up will be written in descriptive notation.

Under algebraic notation the ranks of a chessboard are numbered from *1* to *8*, as they are in descriptive notation, but the files are designated by letters, *a* to *h*. The board looks like this:

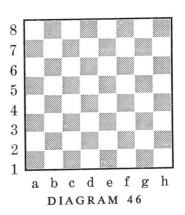

DIAGRAM 46

Thus any square is designated by a combination letter-number. White's QN5, for example, is *b5*. Black's QN4 is *b5,* too. A move is recorded simply as a starting square and a finishing square—the square from which the piece moves and the square on which it lands. Thus, in the following diagram, the White move N/QN3−Q4 is written as *b3−d4*. No further clarification is needed.

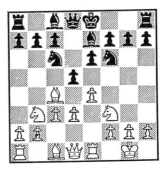

DIAGRAM 47

The opening move P−K4 is written simply *d4* (no ambiguity here—there is only one piece on the board that can move to K4 at the start of a game). Even captures are designated in this simple way.

If you think algebraic notation is the answer to the chessplayer's prayers you are free to use it. You are also free to try to convince other chess players, book and magazine publishers and authors to try to use it. And good luck to you.

Chapter Four

THE ELEMENTS OF CHESS

Introduction

CHESS, LIKE MUSIC, can be an immense source of satisfaction and delight. It would be ridiculous, of course, to say a man has to be a Doctor of Musicology or a front-rank virtuoso to be able to appreciate a Beethoven sonata. And it would be just as ridiculous to say he had to be a grandmaster to enjoy or play a game of chess.

But there is no doubt that, in chess as in music, the greater your understanding the greater your enjoyment (and the better you can play, of course). The tone-deaf listener hears nothing but noise; for him a great symphony might just as well be an air-raid siren. The man who can tell the difference between a clarinet and a bass fiddle is in a better position, but not much better; he can derive some pleasure from the interplay of orchestral timbres, but the niceties of form are lost on him. The amateur who understands some basic principles of harmony and construction can delight in following the development of themes. And the music lover who has taken the trouble to study, in addition to harmony, counterpoint, finds endless sources of beauty where the untutored listener hears only meaningless notes.

So, too, in chess. The man who understands nothing about the game sees only two players pushing pieces of wood (or plastic or ivory) around on a checkered board. The man who "knows the moves"—as some twelve-million-odd Americans do—understands *how* the pieces are moved, but not *why*. The chess player who has learned half a dozen basic rules (such players are known among the experts as "woodpushers") can see the more obvious threats, the more glaring errors.

And the amateur who has taken the trouble to study tactics and strategy and fundamental principles can follow the course of the game, can see the slow but sure development of a plan, can understand the execution of that plan. And he can derive endless enjoyment from the subtle shifts of power on the chessboard.

The Stages of a Chess Game

A chess game, like a classical sonata, is divided into movements. Unlike most sonatas, though, the movements of a chess game are not clearly defined; they merge gradually and imperceptibly into each other.

The first movement is the opening. In this phase the pawns and pieces (strictly speaking, a chess player works with sixteen "men"—eight pawns and eight pieces) are moved from their initial squares to positions from which they can exert their powers. Pawns are moved forward to give the pieces room in which to operate. Defense formations are set up. The groundwork is laid for the skirmishes that are sure to follow and, usually, the King is castled into safety.

The second phase is called the middle game. Here both sides maneuver for position. Here, too, White—who, having the first move, has had the initiative—strives to maintain his slight edge, to increase it if possible and to capitalize on it. Black, on the other hand, tries to wrest the initiative from White. (Sometimes, if White has played poorly, this can be done in the opening.) Frequently, attacks are launched. If they have been carefully planned and carried out they can succeed, leading to the capture of material, a superior position or in some cases, to victory then and there. If the preparation or execution is faulty the attack may peter out and lead only to a disastrous counter-attack or even the loss of the game.

When most of the pieces have been removed from the board by capture and exchange and only a few remain, the game has entered the final phase—the end game. Many players never learn to conduct an end game properly (or even improperly) because they feel there is no adventure to be found in the cautious, logical movements of only a few pieces or pawns. Many players, in fact, are never faced with the need to learn end-game techniques because they always choose to do or die in the middle game.

The end game, though, can be and frequently is the most fascinating part of a chess game. Its logic is inexorable. Technique of the highest order is needed and —though it seems to be easy to look ahead with so few men on the board—the least slip can lead at once to crushing defeat. A well conducted end game is a delight not only to the winner, but to the loser as well. Here, truly, is the battle of wits that chess at its best can be.

Strategy and Tactics

Anyone who has been in service during wartime knows that he is sometimes given orders to do what seems to be meaningless. He and his company, or his squad, are told to capture this hill or that outpost; to retreat when they are apparently in a solid position. A bomber squadron is given an objective that appears to have no significance.

The orders come from field commanders who, in turn, have been given the word from their superiors. And far from the scene of the action, in mahogany-paneled offices, sit the men whose decisions trickle down through channels, eventually to be translated into the sometimes apparently meaningless orders. These men at the top devise the over-all plans, the "big picture." These are the men who formulate strategy.

Those who put the plans into action, who make the raids, the thrusts, who carry on the skirmishes, who retreat and advance—these are the men involved in tactics.

Strategy, then, is the plan, the conception. Tactics are the means by which the plan is carried out.

In chess, the careful player bides his time, playing cautiously until, perhaps, his opponent makes an error. The error need not be a great one; a good chess player can spot the most subtle, almost imperceptible mistakes. The error is enough to give the man who has seen it an idea—a plan. The problem then is to make sure there are means for carrying out that plan.

Richard Teichmann, one of the world's greatest chess masters, once said "Chess is 99 per cent tactics."

Developing the Pawns and Pieces

At the beginning of a chess game, with all pawns and pieces standing on their starting squares, neither side is in a position to do much, strategically or tactically. The Rooks, for all their power, are helplessly locked in behind their own men. The Bishops command only the squares they stand on. The Queen has nowhere to go, can capture nothing, can threaten nothing. The King, monarch of all he surveys, surveys nothing more than the back of a Pawn's head.

The process of moving the pawns and pieces to positions where they can act, offensively and defensively, is called development. Properly carried out, development can give a player a strong position, a chance to act forcibly and decisively and an opportunity to plan and carry out attacks. Properly carried out, development also means security. Improperly carried out, it can spell quick defeat.

Set up your board and notice that only the Pawns and Knights, which can hurdle obstructions, are able to move; all other men are hemmed in.

The King Knight can go to KB3 or KR3; the Queen Knight can go to QB3 or QR3. Each of the Pawns can move one or two squares; the King Pawn can go to K3 or K4, the Queen Pawn to Q3 or Q4, the King Knight Pawn to KN3 or KN4, and so on. This gives you a choice of twenty possible opening moves.

How do you decide which one to make?

Before you can make that decision you must know what your goal is—not your ultimate goal, which is checkmating your opponent, but your immediate goal. What do you want to accomplish in your first few moves?

You want, first of all, to free your locked-in pieces, to give them space in which to operate. At the same time, you want to keep your opponent, if possible, from freeing his pieces.

You want (if you are playing White) to maintain the initiative. If you are playing Black you want to win the initiative.

You want to control as much of the board as possible and to keep your opponent from seriously contesting that control.

The key to all these objectives is the center.

The Center of Power

The center means the squares K4 and Q4 and, to a lesser extent, KB4, QB4, K3 and Q3 (for both sides). He who controls the center controls the game. In the diagram below the central squares are heavily shaded; the "outer ring" squares of the center are less heavily shaded.

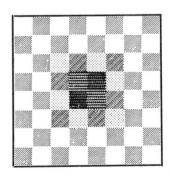

DIAGRAM 48

One of the axioms of chess is that an attack on a wing—that is, an attack launched at the King's or Queen's flank—is best met by a counter-thrust in the center. It is also axiomatic that only a player who doesn't want to win or who doesn't know how to, would launch an attack without having control of the center.

The center can be controlled either directly, by occupying it with pawns or pieces, or indirectly, by keeping it "under observation." In the next diagram (49A) White controls the center through occupation; he has a

Knight posted strongly at K5, he has Pawns at K4, Q5, KB4 and QB4. In "B" Black appears to have the stronger possession of the center, but that possession is illusory. Actually, White has the center well under control through the two Bishops, which sweep the center squares, the Queen and the two Knights, who exert their power across the crucial center squares. This is indirect control.

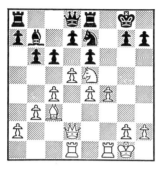 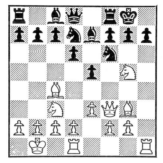

DIAGRAM 49A   DIAGRAM 49B

Though the principles of indirect control were known a hundred years ago or more, the system has been thoroughly analyzed and elaborated only in the last fifty-odd years. The proponents of indirect control came to be known as the "hypermoderns" because their theories apparently refuted all the old classical concepts of development. We'll get back to the hypermoderns and their system later. Meanwhile, we'll concentrate on the fundamental principles of development —and get back to that question of which move to make first.

Before trying to answer that question, take a closer look at what happens to a piece as it moves in toward the center.

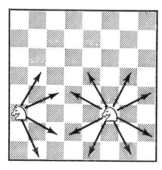

DIAGRAM 50

In the diagram above, the Knight at QR3 (one of the two squares to which the Queen Knight can move from its initial position) controls a total of four squares —QN1, QB2, QB4, and QN5. The Knight at KB3 (one of the two squares to which the King Knight can go on its first move) controls eight squares— KN1, KR2, KR4, KN5, K5, Q4, Q2 and K1.

The Knight at the edge of the board, then, is deprived of half of its possible squares of control. The Knight that is closer to the center controls its full complement of squares.

The position shown above could not, of course, occur in an actual game; it is only a demonstration position. Now look at this position:

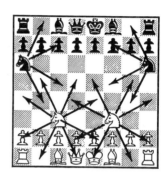

DIAGRAM 51

This position actually could come about in a real game. Notice that Black's Knights, posted at the edge of the board, command a total of eight squares. White's Knights, more centrally posted, command a total of sixteen. Some of those sixteen are occupied; this does not mean they are valueless. On the contrary, it means the Knights are protecting the Pawns or pieces that occupy those squares.

Notice, too, that White's Knights are in command of the crucial center squares; the Knight at KB3 commands the important squares K5 and Q4; the Knight at QB3 commands the other vital squares K4 and Q5. Black's Knights, on the other hand, command only two semi-central squares—QB4 and KB4.

Black, by posting his Knights at the edge of the board, has given up his rights to the center. White monopolizes control of the middle of the board.

It is obvious, then, that the closer the Knight gets to the center, a) the more squares he commands, and b) the more powerful is his control of the vital squares.

Now let's see what happens to a Bishop as it approaches the center.

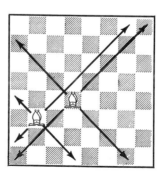

DIAGRAM 52

The Bishop at QN3 sweeps a total of nine squares. The Bishop on the central square Q4 sweeps thirteen. The difference between central placement and sideline placement is not as marked as it was with the Knights and the reason is simple: Bishops can operate at long range, whereas Knights are close-range pieces. Frequently, in fact, Bishops are posted at QN3 or KN3 and, although they are far from the center, these posts are strong ones for the Bishops, who can "observe" the central squares from the flanks.

The Queen, too, exerts greater power from the center than from the sides. Look at the difference in scope between the Queen in diagram A below and the one in diagram B.

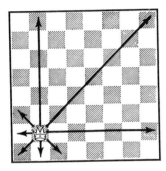
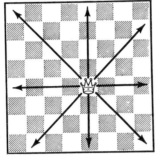

DIAGRAM 53A   DIAGRAM 53B

The Queen in diagram A, posted near the edge at QN2, commands twenty-three squares; the Queen in diagram B, centrally posted at K4, commands twenty-seven squares. Again, because the Queen is a long-range piece, the difference betwen the centrally and non-centrally located pieces is not as dramatic as with the short-range Knights. But it is, nevertheless, a significant difference.

Strength Through Mobility

There is an aspect of this centralization business that hasn't been touched on yet. That aspect is mobility.

It stands to reason that a piece that is free to move around on, say, ten squares, is more mobile—and hence of more value—than a piece that is confined to three or four squares. The free piece can be shifted for aggressive or defensive purposes; it can threaten and parry; it has room to retreat, if necessary. The restricted piece is more a handicap than an asset. It gets in the way of its own men, instead of cooperating with them, because it cannot be moved out of the way.

The more centrally a piece is placed the more squares it commands; the more squares it commands the more room it has in which to move about; the more room it has in which to move the greater its mobility; and the greater its mobility, the more its value.

If you should ever get to a master's chess tournament you will notice that, quite frequently, a lot of backing and filling goes on behind the lines, so to speak. Pieces are shifted around without engaging the enemy directly. This apparently meaningless jockeying for position is characteristic of what is called positional play—chess in which the moves are quiet, rather than dramatic; in which changes in position are subtle; and in which the violent thrusts, if they come at all, are made only after all this maneuvering has been going on for some time.

You may notice, too, that little by little one of the two players seems to get more and more room in which to maneuver, while his opponent gets less and less. Eventually, one man's control of the board becomes overwhelming; the other man's pieces have no room in which to breathe. Then, and only then, does violence —in the form of crushing attacks—break out.

How does this apply to centralization and mobility? And to the opening moves? Its relevance can be formulated this way:

The more centrally a player's pieces are posted and the greater their mobility, the more his opponent's pieces are deprived of good squares and the more their mobility is diminished. Look at the following diagram:

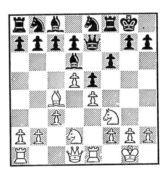

DIAGRAM 54

White effectively occupies and controls the center. He has Pawns at K4 and Q5, a Bishop at QB4 and Knights at KB3, Q2. Black is helpless; he cannot play his Queen Knight to its best square, QB3, because the White Pawn at Q5 controls that square. Black's Queen Bishop is hemmed in by its own pawns and is useless. The Black King Knight, having been poorly placed, now has nowhere to go. The Black Queen has only two squares available to which to move.

Black, in short, is cramped; his pieces are stepping on each other's toes; he commands almost no space.

The White pieces, on the other hand, have room in which to maneuver; they are aggressively posted and ready for action. In such a position it is only a question of time (and not much time at that) until White smashes through to victory. Black can do nothing to stop it.

Black, obviously, has played the opening poorly. He

has failed to develop properly. White, just as obviously, has played well, developing properly, capturing the center and forcing the poorly placed Black pieces farther and farther into a cramped position.

How to Lose Quickly

Let's follow the opening moves of a fictitious game (it may actually have been played somewhere, sometime, but it is hard to imagine anyone playing as badly as Black does here) to see how, by failing to develop properly, one side hands control of the board—and the game—to the other.

1	P–K4	P–KR3

DIAGRAM 55

Position after 1 . . . P—KR3

White has posted a Pawn in the center; Black has done nothing to contest that control and has made a useless and (as you will see) dangerously weakening move.

2	P–Q4	N–QR3

DIAGRAM 56

Position after 2 . . . N—QR3

White now occupies the central squares Q4 and K4 and his two central Pawns control the four squares in front of them. Black continues to waste time, posting

a Knight where it is valueless to contest White's growing strength in the center.

3	B–QB4	P–KB3

DIAGRAM 57

Position after 3 . . . P—KB3

Another useless and dangerous move by Black. White now has cleared the way for action by both Bishops and the Queen and has, in fact, posted one Bishop aggressively already. Black has shut his pieces in, has wasted time, has failed to fight for the center. The time is now ripe (so quickly? yes—so quickly because Black has played so badly!) for White to take advantage of Black's foolishness.

4	Q–R5ch	

DIAGRAM 58

Position after 4 . . . Q—R5ch

The beginning of the very sudden, but more than justified, end. Black's King cannot move out of check; the White Queen cannot be captured. Black has only one move at his disposal; he must interpose with the KNP.

4	. . .	P–KN3

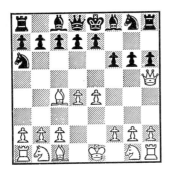

DIAGRAM 59

Position after 4 . . . P—KN3

And now the end.

5   Q×NP mate

DIAGRAM 60

The End: Position after 5 QxNP mate

The moral of this sad tale is: he who develops properly gets a strong game. Or, put the other way, he who develops badly weakens his game.

Intelligence Conquers Rigidity

Before continuing it would be well to warn you that you may run across books in which "rules for development" are laid down. You may be told, for example, that you should always develop your Knights before your Bishops (that is, that you must move your Knights off their original squares before you move your Bishops) or that you should never move your Queen in the early stages of the game. Or that once you move a piece you must not move it again until your other pieces are developed.

Such rules were laid down by no less a chess player than Emanuel Lasker. In his book *Common Sense in Chess,* Lasker tells the would-be chess player, among other things:

1. Do not move any Pawn in the opening of a game except the King and Queen Pawns.

2. Do not move any piece twice in the opening, but put it at once upon the right square. (In my practice I have usually found it strongest to post the Knights at B3, where they have a magnificent sway, and the King Bishop somewhere on his original diagonal, if not exposed to exchange, at QB4.)

3. Bring your Knights out before developing the Bishops, especially the Queen Bishop.*

Basically, there is nothing wrong with these rules, if you adopt the proper attitude toward them. And that attitude must be one of flexibility.

Chess, as far as rules go, is like driving a car. Most of the time the rules are valid and serve you well. But whether you stick to them or not often depends on what the other fellow does. It is quite true that you should always keep to the right on the road. But do you stay there when another driver, coming from the opposite direction, disobeys the rules and heads straight for you? In such a case, adhering to the rules is, to put it conservatively, foolish. And though the law says you may go when the light turns green, would you go if a ten-ton trailer-truck started across the intersection against the light?

And so it is with chess. By and large it is better to develop Knights before Bishops. But it ain't necessarily so all the time. Depending upon what you have in mind and—even more important—what your opponent does, it may well be better to develop your Bishops first.

It is also true that moving the King or Queen Pawn is an excellent idea. Moving the Queen Pawn opens a diagonal for the Queen Bishop and gives the Queen a little space in which to get around; moving the King Pawn opens diagonals for the King Bishop and the Queen. Ordinarily, other Pawn moves tend to weaken your position.

Nevertheless there are many quite valid openings in which neither the King Pawn nor the Queen Pawn is moved. And there are many in which other Pawns are moved. (We will consider opening play and opening systems in much more detail in Chapter 8.) Again, what you do depends on your objectives and your opponent's replies.

Another great chess master, Aron Nimzovich, the quixotic and brilliant exponent of hypermodern play, had this to say about development in his famous (or notorious) book, *My System:*

By development is to be understood the strategic advance of the troops to the frontier line. [Nimzovich defined the frontier as the line dividing the board in half horizontally.]

The process is analogous to the advance on the outbreak of a war. Both armies seek to reach the frontier as

* Emanuel Lasker, *Common Sense in Chess* (New York: McKay, 1946).

quickly as possible in order to penetrate into enemy territory.

Development is a collective conception. To have developed one, two or three pieces does not mean that we are developed. On the contrary, the situation demands that *all* pieces be developed. If I may so put it, the period of development should be inspired by a democratic spirit. How undemocratic, for instance, it would be to let one of your officers go for a long walking tour, whilst the others kicked their heels together at home and bored themselves horribly. No, let each officer make one move only, and . . . dig himself in.*

So now we have Lasker, Nimzovich and Common Sense telling us not to move a piece twice while other pieces are undeveloped. It must be a valid rule. Still—to use an extreme example—in the short game illustrated above, White not only moved his Queen early, but he also moved it a total of three times. And the Bishop was developed before the Knight. The result? The player who disobeyed all these rules won handily.

Bear in mind, however, that the other player—Black—disobeyed rules, too, and he did so to the extent that White was able to make "mistakes" and cash in on them.

The point is that there is really only one inflexible rule in chess. That rule is:

There are no inflexible rules.

There are, rather, guideposts, general principles that, under normal circumstances, should be followed. If White and Black play well, both will follow, generally, these principles. If one side goes wrong the other is justified in breaking the rules to take advantage of his opponent's errors.

General Opening Principles

With all this in mind we can now formulate the basic principles of development, as follows:

1. Make only those Pawn moves that are necessary to open lines for your pieces. Other Pawn moves (such as P–KR3 and P–KB3 in the game above) can weaken your position and leave you wide open to assault.
2. In general, it is better to develop your Knights before your Bishops, because the Knights, as we demonstrated before, are short-range pieces, whereas the Bishops can sweep the board. However there are times when developing Bishops (or a Bishop) first is justified and even desirable.
3. Unless you have good reason to do so, it is better not to develop your Queen too early in the game. You will only lose time if your Queen is attacked by lesser pieces or by Pawns and has to retreat.

* Aron Nimzovich, *My System*, trans. by Philip Hereford (London: Bell and Sons, 1957).

4. Castle early (one wit, paraphrasing an equally witty student of politics, said: "Castle early and castle often."). But be sure, before you castle, that you will not be walking into a trap. Be sure, too, that you don't have a better move at your disposal.
5. Get each piece out and well posted before you start to maneuver. This is the old don't-move-a-piece-twice rule, but put in a less dogmatic way. Certainly if you see a chance for a gain of material, without loss of position, or for a good attack, you are justified in moving a piece twice or more often. If your opponent has played decently, however, this opportunity is not likely to arise early in the game.
6. Above all, strive to control the center and to see that your opponent doesn't get that control.

So much for general principles. Now . . .

STOP!

. . . to make certain you understand them.

Self-Testing Quiz No. 8

(a) White has begun a game with P—Q4. What are some good moves for Black and what makes each of these good?

(b) A game begins as follows:

1	P–K4	P–K4
2	N–KB3	N–QB3
3	B–N5	N–Q5
4	N–B3	

Which side has made an error, and what was the error?

(c) In the following diagram which side has the stronger position?

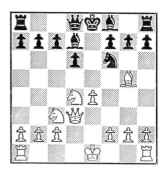

DIAGRAM 61

(d) In the following diagram it is White's turn to move. He is about to capitalize on Black's poor play.

What fundamental defensive measure has Black neglected that has helped White to achieve such a deadly attack?

DIAGRAM 62

(e) It is Black's turn to move in the following diagram. What move would be good? Why?

DIAGRAM 63

Don't Aid the Enemy

If you have done reasonably well in this quiz you are in a position now to answer that question posed back on Page 28. You know which of the twenty possible first moves accomplish something and which do not. And, knowing this much, you can actually sit down with a real opponent for a game of chess. A final word of warning, though, before you do:

Don't make moves that help your opponent as much as, or more than, they help you.

This kind of error is frequently made by beginners because, unless the move is carefully considered, it may not appear to be a bad one. It may even look like a good one. Don't let appearances fool you.

In the next diagram, for example, Black, wanting to develop his King Bishop—and doubly tempted because of that alluring "check!"—may jump to the conclusion that B—N5ch is a good move.

DIAGRAM 64

If Black does play B—N5ch, White can reply P—B3, forcing the Bishop to retreat and making Black waste time. Or White can reply B—Q2. If White does reply B—Q2, Black will have to make a decision: he must either retreat or capture the White Bishop (protecting the Black Bishop with N—B3 is useless; White simply plays P—B3 and again Black is forced to retreat).

Assuming that White replies B—Q2 and that Black then captures the White Bishop—what then? White simply recaptures with the Queen and the board then looks like this:

DIAGRAM 65

It is true that White has had to bring his Queen into play early. But the Queen is in no danger and is, in fact, quite mobile and ready for action. (White, incidentally, had the option of recapturing with either of the Knights.) Black made two moves with his Bishop and what does he have to show for them? Nothing. The Bishop has disappeared from the board. Not only did he waste time, but he also helped White to develop.

Here is another example of the kind of play that succeeds only in helping your opponent to develop. For the first four moves both sides play "by the book," making the standard moves in what is called the Classical Variation of the Nimzo-Indian Defense.

1	P—Q4	N—KB3
2	P—QB4	P—K3
3	N—QB3	B—N5
4	Q—B2	P—Q4

So far all according to Hoyle. The board looks like this:

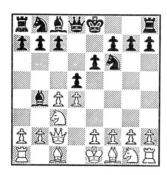

DIAGRAM 66

Position after 4 . . . P—Q4

Now White blunders. He thinks (perhaps his trouble is that he doesn't think; he only acts) he can capture the Black Bishop at N5 by attacking King and Bishop at the same time. He moves his Queen a second time, playing 5 Q—R4ch.

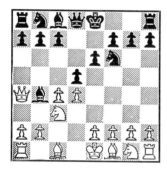

DIAGRAM 67
Position after 5 Q—R4ch

Black's reply is simple and logical. He plays 5 . . . N—B3, developing a piece, blocking the check and protecting the Bishop.

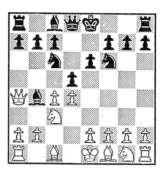

DIAGRAM 68
Position after 5 . . . N—B3

White's little misadventure has come to naught—or less than naught. He retreats his Queen, moving it a third time, back to B2. Black has been given, in effect, a free move, and he uses it to develop further. He now plays 6 . . . O—O.

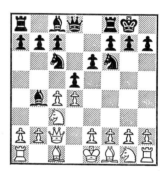

DIAGRAM 69
Position after 6 . . . O—O

Black has developed both Knights, one Bishop and has castled. White, who has wasted time, has developed the Queen and one Knight; he has not castled and will not be able to do so until he moves his Bishop off QB1 (to castle Queen's side) or until he moves his King Knight and King Bishop off their initial squares (to castle King's side).

White has played well—for Black.

Chapter Five

ELEMENTARY TACTICS

The Basic Weapons of Chess

IN OUR DISCUSSION of tactics and strategy in the preceding chapter we compared (as we had done before and will do again) chess to war. In war, we noted, strategy is the province of the upper-upper echelons, the four-star generals and their aides. Their decisions are translated into action by the lower echelons, eventually becoming questions of tactics, which is the province of field officers and, in the long run, the ordinary G.I.

In war, if the strategy is faulty, it is more likely than not that the low man on the totem pole—the infantryman—will feel its effect hardest. The generals and their aides, having suffered damage only to their egos and status, will live to make new and perhaps more effective strategic decisions.

If the tactics are faulty, again it is the private, not the general, who gets it.

But in chess, you—the player—are all things to all men. You are the commander in chief, the four-star general, the field officer, the noncom and the private. If you, the general, make a mistake, you, the private, will know it. And if you, the private, err, you, the general, still will be affected.

You and you alone are responsible for strategy—the big picture, the broad conception—and for tactics—the skirmishes, the maneuvering and the hand-to-hand (or piece-to-piece) fighting. It is up to you, then, to make correct decisions on all levels of play. You cannot expect to devise good strategy when you don't have the tactical means to carry out that strategy. And you cannot expect tactics to cover up your poor strategic planning.

Because strategy involves rather complicated decisions, which, in turn, are based upon deep knowledge of positional play, we will not discuss the principles of strategy. (After all, the recruit is not called in to confer with the generals about policy; if he has it in him, he works his way up through the ranks, learning and absorbing as the years go by, as his experience broadens, eventually reaching the general staff. Then, and only then, does he work on the big picture.)

But even the greenest recruit—and that is what you

still are at this stage—must learn how to handle his weapons; must learn to take apart a rifle, must learn to aim, must learn to use other basic weapons—the submachine gun, the mortar, the grenade; must learn how to infiltrate, camouflage; must learn, in short, the way to survive in battle.

And so must you.

You're now going to meet the basic weapons of chess. You're going to learn how they work and when they can and can't be used. You're going to learn to attack and to counter-attack, to thrust and defend. You are going to become intimately acquainted with the arsenal of chess.

The Pin

Probably the most commonly used weapon in a chess player's arsenal is the pin, a device that is beautifully simple and wonderfully effective. It is, in fact, so basic a weapon that it plays an important role in many opening systems. Here's how it works:

DIAGRAM 70

In the diagram above it is White's turn to move. He sees that the Black King and the Black Bishop are in line with each other along the Queen file. This is the key to what follows. White plays 1 R—Q1!

DIAGRAM 71

Position after 1 R—Q1

The Black Bishop is paralyzed. It cannot move because in doing so it would expose its King to check. It is pinned down, helpless. No matter what move Black now makes with his King (the only piece he can move) White will capture the Bishop on his next move.

Simple? Quite. And powerful? Very!

The essential principle of the pin is this: When the King and any other piece or Pawn are in line with each other along a rank, diagonal or file, the piece or Pawn can be immobilized by forcing it to become the shield against a check. Thus paralyzed, it can easily be attacked again and captured. (In the example above there was no need to attack the pinned piece again; the pinning piece itself was in a position to capture it without trouble.)

The pinning can be done by any piece that moves in a straight line. Bishops can pin along a diagonal, Rooks along a rank or file, Queens along diagonals, ranks or files.

Here is an example of a pin by a Bishop.

DIAGRAM 72

It is White's move. He sees that the Black Knight and its King are in line with each other along the diagonal QR1–KR8. (Always be on the alert for this kind of set-up; all sorts of possibilities present themselves when your opponent allows two pieces to be in line with each other—especially when one of them is the

King or Queen.) The Knight can be pinned, and White does the pinning with 1 B—N2.

DIAGRAM 73

Position after 1 B—N2!

The Knight is paralyzed. He cannot move without exposing the King to check. Black, however, thinks he sees a way out. He plays 1 . . . P—B4, giving Pawn protection to the Knight. He is willing to exchange his Knight for White's Bishop. But White caps the pin, attacking the immobilized Knight a second time, with a Pawn. He plays 2 P—K3.

DIAGRAM 74

Position after 2 P—K3!

Now the Knight is dead. He still cannot move, and no matter what Black does the Pawn will capture the Knight on White's next move. And if Black retakes with the Pawn the White Bishop will then capture the Pawn, too.

Never underestimate the power of the pin. Or, as Fred Reinfeld (one of the most prolific modern writers on chess) said:

"The pin is mightier than the sword."

Now let's see how the Queen goes about pinning a piece. Obviously, combining as she does the powers of Rook and Bishop, she should be a formidable weapon. Remember, however, that the Queen's weakness (Chapter Two, Page 16) is her strength; she is not to be lightly parted with, and when she is attacked by a lesser piece or by a Pawn she must retreat. The only time you give up your Queen voluntarily is when, by so doing, you get an overwhelmingly powerful position.

DIAGRAM 75

In the diagram above it is White's move. He notices that Black's King is in line, not with one piece, but with two. It is in line with the Bishop on the King file and in line with the Rook on the diagonal QR4–K8. White, then, has a choice—he can pin the Bishop or the Rook.

If White chooses to pin the Bishop he will gain nothing. The play would run this way:

1   Q–K2   R–K4

By playing 1 . . . R–K4 Black protects the pinned Bishop. White, therefore, correctly decides to pin the Rook (there is another reason for White's choice: the Rook is more valuable than the Bishop—but more about this in a later chapter).

White plays 1 Q–R4.

DIAGRAM 76

Position after 1 Q–R4

The Rook is lost. Black has no way of protecting it. Black could try 1 . . . B–Q5ch or B–Q7ch. But either of these foolish moves would only mean the loss of the Bishop, too, and would bring an end to the game that much more quickly.

Sometimes a pin can boomerang, as it does in this next example.

DIAGRAM 77

White, who has the move, sees that the light-squared Bishop and the King are in line with each other on the Queen file, thus making a pin possible. Black would have no way to protect the Bishop so White sees no difficulty. He plays 1 R–Q4, pinning the Bishop.

DIAGRAM 78

Position after 1 R—Q4

White has made a first-class blunder—the kind that makes a chess player wonder why he didn't take up poker or butterfly-collecting instead. Black's reply to the pin is 1 . . . B–B4!

DIAGRAM 79

Position after 1 . . . B—B4

The pinner finds himself pinned, and decisively, too. White cannot capture the Bishop at Q5 now because he cannot move his Rook. And, since his Rook is immobilized, he can now move only his King. No matter where he moves the King the Rook will be captured on Black's next move.

The Relative Pin

The pins we have discussed so far have been "absolute" pins. The pinned pieces could not be moved because this would have exposed the King to check. But there is another kind of pin, sometimes called a "relative" pin and sometimes a "permissive" one. In these pins the King is not involved and the pinned piece can legally move, though it probably would be disastrous for it to do so.

Here is an example of a relative pin.

DIAGRAM 80

It is Black's move. White threatens to play KN×P, so Black plays 1 . . . B—KN5, pinning the Knight at KB6. It is not illegal for the Knight to move—he would not be exposing the King to check—but if he does move, the Black Bishop will capture White's Queen. Such a loss is usually tantamount to losing the game.

DIAGRAM 81
Position after 1 . . . B—KN5

The pin effectively prevents White's playing KN×P. As you see, not all pins are designed for or lead to captures; sometimes they are used—as here—for defensive purposes. They can also be used to keep an enemy piece away from the scene of a coming skirmish.

Here is another relative pin.

DIAGRAM 82

Black has the move. He sees White's Rook and Knight in line with each other along the King Knight file—a natural for a pin. So he plays 1 . . . R—N1.

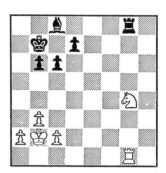

DIAGRAM 83
Position after 1 . . . R—N1

The White Knight is pinned. Relatively, of course; there is nothing in the rule book that says he can't move it. If he does, though, the Rook will be lost. There is little White can do on that side of the board, so he undertakes a mild sort of counter-play on the other side, playing 2 K—B3. Black follows through with 2 . . . P—Q4!

DIAGRAM 84
Position after 2 . . . P—Q4

The Pawn move released the Bishop's power along the diagonal QB1—KR6, and the helpless Knight, unable to budge, is hit again. Whatever move White makes he will lose his Knight.

Even a "relative" pin can be absolutely effective.

Not all pins are obvious. Sometimes it takes more than a casual glance at the board to discover one. As in the following example.

DIAGRAM 85

White has the move. He is a Rook down and his Queen is attacked. He could retreat his Queen—but he has a better move at his disposal. He plays 1 N—B6ch!

DIAGRAM 86

Position after 1 N—B6ch

The Queen, of course, cannot capture the Knight, who is protected by the Bishop. But—and this is the important but—the Knight Pawn cannot capture the Knight either. It is pinned; it must stay where it is to protect the Black Queen. If Black were to play 1 . . . P×N White would reply 2 Q×Q! The Knight, then is quite safe where it is, and Black must get out of check by moving his King. White can then play Q×Q, breaking up Black's Pawn position, and follow this through with N×R.

Unsticking the Pin

The pin, quite obviously, is a deadly weapon. Can there be a defense against it?

Yes—and you have already seen one defense. You saw how a counter-pin worked. And a counter-pin is just one way of coping with the pin. It is an example of the best defense known: offense.

Here is another example of the way a pin can be broken by a successful counter-attack.

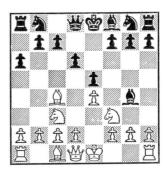

DIAGRAM 87

In the diagram above White's Knight at KB3 is pinned. But the pin is the only thing in Black's favor. It is obvious that Black has played poorly; he has developed only one piece—the pinning Bishop—and has spent the rest of his time making Pawn moves.

White, who has developed superbly, takes advantage of Black's weak position, ignoring the pin and launching a winning counter-attack. He plays 1 N×P!

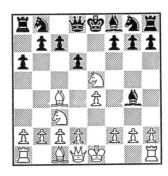

DIAGRAM 88

Position after 1 NxP!

Black's best move would be 1 . . . P×N. Even this would not help, though, because White would reply 2 Q×B, giving White a plus of one Pawn in addition to the much more important plus of a superior development. Black, however, fails to see this; he plays 1 . . . B×Q? and White's devastating reply is 2 B×Pch!

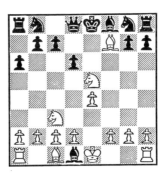

DIAGRAM 89

Position after 2 BxPch

Black now realizes he has fallen into a trap. But it is too late to get out of it. He has only one move at his disposal, 2 . . . K—K2. And this leads straight to the coup de grace, 3 N—Q5 mate.

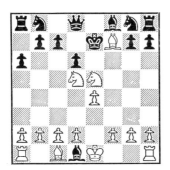

DIAGRAM 90

Position after 3 N—Q5 mate

Not all counter-attacks are as final as this one. The moral might be: a pin is only as strong as the position of which it is a part. Black's pin was strong, but his position was fatally weak.

Other defenses against pins are less spectacular, but they all serve their purpose. There is, for example, interposition.

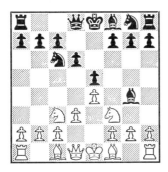

DIAGRAM 91

White's Knight at KB3 is pinned. The simplest way to break the pin is to interpose a piece between Queen and Knight. White therefore plays 1 B—K2.

DIAGRAM 92

Position after 1 B—K2

The Knight is now free to move. If it does, and Black captures the Bishop, White simply recaptures.

Another way to break a pin is to drive off the pinning piece.

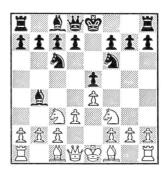

DIAGRAM 93

Here White could interpose, playing B—Q2. Instead, planning a later attack on the Queen's wing, he decides to accomplish two things at once: drive off the pinning bishop and advance his Queen's side Pawns. He plays 1 P—QR3. Black, wanting to keep the pin, replies 1 . . . B—R4. And White pursues his objective with 2 P—QN4.

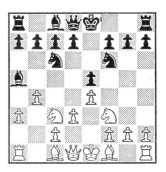

DIAGRAM 94

Position after 2 P—QN4

The Bishop must now leave the diagonal. White has broken the pin by interposing a Pawn; has driven the Bishop off the diagonal and has advanced his Queen's side Pawns.

A pin can be broken by moving the shielded piece.

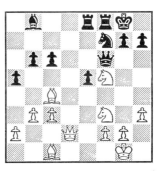

DIAGRAM 95

In this position White's Bishop at QB4 pins the Black Knight. Black can unpin the Knight by playing 1 . . . K—R1.

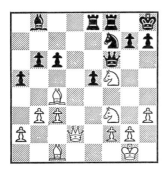

DIAGRAM 96

Position after 1 . . . K—R1

The King, having moved off the diagonal along which the Knight was pinned, has freed the Knight and broken the pin.

A pin can be broken by exchange.

DIAGRAM 97

Here White's Rook seems to be effectively pinned. But White can break the pin by ignoring it! He plays 1 R×R.

DIAGRAM 98

Position after 1 RxR

If Black now captures the Queen, White will play 2 R×R and end up with a Rook against Black's

Bishop, a strong end-game advantage. If Black, on the other hand, plays 1 . . . R×R, White replies 2 Q×B and winds up with an even greater balance of power— Queen against Rook.

Double Attacks

Another often-used weapon is the double attack. This tactical device can be executed by any piece or Pawn and sometimes, because of the nature of the attack, it is known as a fork (no—this doesn't mean picking up a table fork and stabbing your opponent; it is far more subtle than that, though just as effective, from a chess point of view).

The following illustrates the basic principle of the double attack, executed, in this case, by a Pawn.

DIAGRAM 99

It is White's move. He plays 1 P—Q6.

DIAGRAM 100

Position after 1 P—Q6

The Pawn now attacks two Black pieces simultaneously. If the Knight moves off, the Bishop falls; if the Bishop moves, the Knight falls. Because the Pawn is supported by a Rook, capture doesn't help. 1 . . . B×P would simply be followed by 2 R×B.

A Pawn need not be supported to carry out a double attack—or a "pawn fork." In the following example the unsupported Pawn packs as big a punch as did the supported Pawn in the previous example.

DIAGRAM 101

Black is somewhat behind in material, having a Rook and Bishop to White's two Rooks. He can more than equalize with 1 . . . P—Q5.

DIAGRAM 102
Position after 1 . . . P—Q5

The Pawn attacks both Rooks at the same time. One will fall. White can make a desperate attempt to wriggle out of his troubles, by playing P—B5ch. This can cause a few delays, but nothing more. White will still lose a Rook.

Double attacks, like pins, are particularly effective when one of the pieces involved is the King. The Bishop's double attack in this next example is successful because the enemy King is attacked. The "priority of check"—the necessity to get the King out of check before anything else is done—ensures the success of the Bishop's venture.

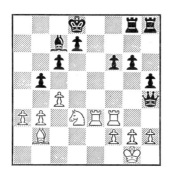

DIAGRAM 103

White is in trouble. Black has an attack aimed directly at the King. He threatens to play Q×RPch and follow this up with an advance of the King's-side Pawns, which are backed up by the Rooks. In addition, Black has a tremendous material superiority—a Queen, two Rooks and a Bishop against White's two Rooks, Bishop and Knight. But White, in one crushing move, destroys the attack, eats into the King's-side Pawns and restores material equality. He plays 1 B×Pch!

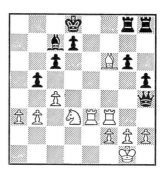

DIAGRAM 104
Position after 1 BxPch

White, in capturing the Pawn, gives check and attacks not only the Black Queen, but one of the Black Rooks as well. Black's dangerous threat has become an idle boast.

Had the move not attacked the King as well as other pieces—or had it attacked Queen, Rook and, say, a Knight—Black could have saved the Queen (or the Rook) and might well have continued with his original plan. The fact that Black had to attend to his King before all else gave the double (in this case, triple) attack additional, and decisive, power.

The Rook, too, as might be expected, is versatile when it comes to double attacks. Here is an example of a double attack as executed by a Rook.

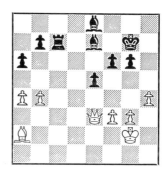

DIAGRAM 105

Black, like White in the previous example, is behind in material and needs to do something to even things

up. The "something" is a double attack. He plays
1 . . . R—B7ch.

double attack can bring victory closer in spectacular
fashion. He plays 1 Q—Q4.

DIAGRAM 106

Position after 1 . . . R—B7ch

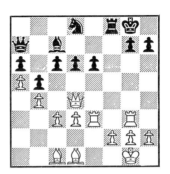

DIAGRAM 108

Position after 1 Q—Q4

The Rook attacks King and Bishop simultaneously. Because of the priority of check, the King must be attended to. If he is moved out of check, Black will capture the Bishop. White could interpose, playing 2 Q—B2, but he would, of course, lose his Queen by doing so. Better to lose the Bishop.

The Queen, whose power extends along ranks, files and diagonals, is a virtuoso at double (and triple and quadruple, etc) attacks. However, the old admonition about using the Queen applies here, too: make sure there is no reply available that will mean retreating the Queen or, worse yet, losing her. Study the position carefully before launching a Queen attack.

Here is a good example of the Queen's ability to attack in several directions at once:

With this move White threatens mate at KN7. He also threatens Black's Queen. Black cannot cope with both threats at once. He must attend to the mating threat, which he can do by playing 1 . . . R—B2 (protecting the threatened Pawn at N2) or P—K4 (cutting off the Queen's attack on the Pawn at N2). But in so doing he must lose his Queen. Faced with this prospect, Black's best move is 1 . . . resigns. He could, it is true, play 1 . . . Q×Q. But this would be equivalent to resigning, since White's material advantage only increases with each exchange.

Though the Queen is the most powerful piece on the board, she is not the most powerful piece for double or multiple attacks. That honor belongs to the Knight, who is without a peer when it comes to attacking several pieces at once. It is the Knight's peculiar ability to jump or hurdle obstructing pieces—his own as well as the enemy's—that gives him his unique effectiveness in multiple attacks. In addition, he can attack from positions from which he himself is not exposed to capture.

Here are some examples of double and more-than-double attacks by Knights.

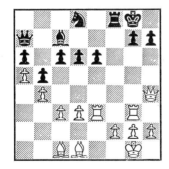

DIAGRAM 107

White is ahead materially and this alone is ordinarily enough to insure victory. But in this position a deadly

DIAGRAM 109

Black's Rook at N1 is attacked by the Knight. Unthinkingly, Black plays 1 . . . R—QR1. White's reply is a triple attack—a fork—by the Knight. White plays 2 N—B7ch, attacking King and both Rooks.

DIAGRAM 110

Position after 2 N—B7ch

One of the Rooks must fall.

This next example will serve not only as a demonstration of the power of the Knight fork, but also as an introduction to a subject you will be learning about much more extensively—and intensively—later in this book: combinations.

DIAGRAM 111

White is behind materially, having a Queen, Knight and Pawns to Black's Queen, Rook and Pawns. In addition—and more vital—Black threatens mate starting with Q×Pch. White looks for a way out.

He could try a Knight fork at once, playing 1 N—B4. But Black's reply would more than meet the challenge; Black would simply play Q×Pch. The King would have to retreat, the Knight would be captured and the mating attack would roll on unobstructed.

What White does have is a brilliant combination that begins with the sacrifice of his Queen. He plays 1 Q×Rch.

DIAGRAM 112

Position after 1 QxRch

Black's best move is 1 . . . K—B1. He is now a piece down, but at least he would have a fighting chance. (The tables, as you see, have turned, and Black is on the defensive.) Instead, Black plays 1 . . . K×Q and White replies 2 N—B4ch.

DIAGRAM 113

Position after 2 N—B4ch

Black must lose his Queen and the best he can hope for after recapturing the Knight is a draw.

Sometimes a double attack can be used to win material. As it does in the next example.

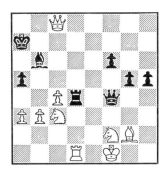

DIAGRAM 113A

White is two pieces ahead. He also threatens mate on the move (Q—QN7 mate). Things look grim for Black. But are they really that grim?

If the White King were at White's KB2 instead of

at KB1, a crushing double attack would be possible. Is there a way to get the King to that square?

There is. Black plays Q×Nch.

White has no choice in the matter. He must play K×Q.

DIAGRAM 113B

Position after 2 KxQ

Black, by sacrificing his Queen, has forced the King to move to his KB2. The giveaway has set White up for a powerful discovered check. Black now plays 2 . . . R—Q1 dis ch, getting back the Queen he had parted with, at interest. (He wins a Queen and a Knight for a Queen, ruining the mating threat and giving himself a good fighting chance to win the game.)

This technique of forcing an opponent into a position where tactical tricks—pins, forks and others (still to come)—can be used in decisive ways is called combination. What appeared, in the example above, to have been the throwing away of a Queen led, in reality, to a salvaging of an otherwise lost game.

Combinations, like quail in the underbrush, are often there when we don't see them. They have to be searched for. But, as we said, more about that later. Meanwhile . . .

STOP!

Can you spot a pin, a fork, a double attack? Try to in:

Self-Testing Quiz No. 9

(a) It is White's move. His Rooks are forked by the Knight. How can he get out of his difficulties and win material at the same time?

DIAGRAM 114

(b) In the following position, Black sees a chance for a double attack on White's Queen and Knight. He plays 1 . . . R—K4. Can White do something about this double attack? If so, what?

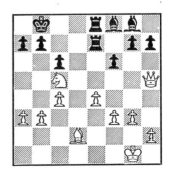

DIAGRAM 115

(c) White has the move. Is there a winning move for him in this position?

DIAGRAM 116

(d) Black is a Rook down. How can he do something about it?

DIAGRAM 117

(e) The Black Knight at QB3 is pinned. What moves will break the pin?

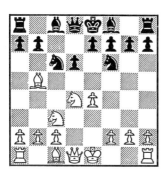

DIAGRAM 118

If you answered Question (a) then you already know the "secret" of escaping from a fork. It is the same "secret" method that was so useful in breaking a pin: counter-attack.

In this next position, White's Queen and Rook are forked by the Knight.

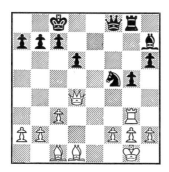

DIAGRAM 119

The "secret" in this case is the application of another tactical device—the pin. If White plays 1 B—N4 the Knight will be pinned. If Black then breaks the pin by 1 . . . K—N1, White can solve his problem neatly with 2 B×N. Suppose, however, that no pin was possible, that the Black King had been at QN1 to start with. What could White have done then? Well, he could have tried R—B3, "pinning" the Knight against the Queen. But Black could then have played N×Q and, in the ensuing exchange, Black would have wound up capturing a Queen and a Rook; White would have captured a Queen and a Knight.

The moral of this is: sometimes there just is no way out of a fork—just as there are pins that are unbreakable. And the further moral is: be on the lookout for such maneuvers by your opponent; don't let yourself get into a position from which there is no escape. That is the challenge of chess.

The Skewer or Hurdle

Look at this position:

It is Black's move. His Queen is attacked. He can-

DIAGRAM 120

not capture the Bishop because the Bishop is protected. If he moves the Queen the Rook will fall (and a Rook, you remember, is more valuable than a Bishop). Black has been skewered, so to speak. The Bishop, attacking the Queen, has his sights on the Rook as well.

There is nothing Black can do except move his Queen out of the way and watch his Rook die.

The skewer (sometimes called a hurdle, for obvious reasons) is sort of a reverse pin. Instead of attacking the less valuable piece by forcing it to become the shield for the more valuable one, it does just the opposite; the more valuable piece must move off, out of the line of fire, and the less valuable one must fall.

As with the pin, the skewer can be carried out only by a piece that moves in straight lines—by a Bishop, Rook or Queen. Needless to say, though, you would not skewer a Rook with a Queen, or a Bishop with a Rook if either of the skewered pieces could be protected. The object of this tactical device is to gain material—and exchanging a Queen for a Rook or a Rook for a Bishop is not, ordinarily, the way to go about winning a game.

Don't, in skewering a piece, skewer yourself instead.

And again, as with the pin, the double attack and the fork, the skewer takes on added deadliness when one of the pieces involved is the King. As in this example:

DIAGRAM 121

Black is a Pawn ahead. He could turn this into victory with long and careful play, but it would be a difficult end game; one slip and victory could become a draw or, worse yet, defeat. But Black has a way to insure victory, and the key to that way is the skewer, brought about through a small combination (you will, as you already know, be meeting more elaborate combinations later on; but it's well to get yourself on a first-name basis with them as you go along).

Black plays 1 . . . R×Pch. White has no choice but to recapture with the King. If he retreats the King the second Pawn will fall and his end game will be absolutely worthless. So White plays 2 K×R.

DIAGRAM 122

Position after 2 KxR

Black's forceful move has set White up for a skewer. The King and Rook are in line along a diagonal. Black now plays 2 . . . B—B3ch. The King must move and Black will capture the Rook. Black has won a Pawn, gotten the Rooks off the board and given himself a guarantee of victory in the end game.

The skewer is a powerful counter-attack device and can often save the day when things look lost. As in this next example.

DIAGRAM 123

Black is in a desperate situation. White threatens mate on his next move (with Q—R6). But Black sees an escape by way of a skewer. He plays 1 . . . B—K3ch, attacking the King and, through him, the Queen.

DIAGRAM 124

Position after 1 . . . B—K3ch

White's King must retreat and the Queen will be lost. It will do White no good to interpose with 2 B—B5. Black simply captures, B×Bch, and again White's King must flee, leaving Black free to capture the White Queen. The two Knights and the Bishop will be more than enough to stop the White Pawn from Queening and to win the game for Black.

Here is another combination involving a skewer.

DIAGRAM 125

Black's Knight at K2 is under attack. Black could protect it with 1 . . . N/R2—B1 or with P—B3. He could also play 1 . . . N—B4, forking a White Rook and Pawn. But he sees a better way. If White's Queen could be forced to play to White's Q5, a skewer of Queen and Rook would become possible. Is there a way to force the Queen to that square? Indeed there is! Black plays 1 . . . N—Q4ch, forking Rook and King. White's hand is forced. He plays 2 Q×N.

DIAGRAM 126

Position after 2 QxN

The Queen has been led to the slaughter—of the Rook. Black now plays 2 . . . B—B3, skewering the Rook through the Queen, who must get out of the way (if she captures the Bishop, the Knight recaptures her and White has thrown away his game). White has the option, of course, of keeping the damage to a minimum by playing K—Q3 as his first reply and then simply recapturing after 2 . . . N×R. He loses either way.

What is the defense against the skewer?

It would simply be repetitious to go into the ways in which counter-attacks, pins, counter-skewers, forks, double attacks and other tactical devices can be used to defend against the skewer. The point is the same as for other weapons: defend or counter-attack as well as you can. If there is no counter-attack, you will lose material. Which brings us back to the old axiom that the best way to defend against the skewer or any other device is to make sure you don't leave yourself open for the use of such weapons.

It may sound like hollow moralizing, but the best advice ever given to chess players is this: make every move as though victory depended on it; in that way you will always make the best move, and the best move will not leave you exposed to tactical tricks.

Overworked Defenders

Some truisms (you can call them platitudes if you prefer) of life seem to have peculiar aptness when applied to chess. Such a truism is the one that you can't be in two places at the same time. Applied to chess, it can be put this way:

One chess piece can't defend two points (or two pieces) at the same time.

Here is an illustration of that principle:

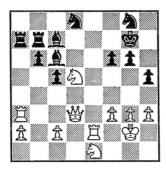

DIAGRAM 127

White's Queen guards the Knight at Q5, which is attacked by the Black Bishop. But the Queen is doing double duty; she is also protecting the Rook at R3, which is under attack by Black's R/R2.

Black notices this and takes advantage of it. He plays 1 . . . B×N. White recaptures with 2 Q×B.

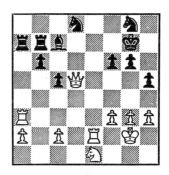

DIAGRAM 128
Position after 2 QxB

Now the Rook is unguarded. Black can play R×R with impunity, coming out a full Rook ahead.

Taking advantage of overloaded pieces—pieces that are trying to do or protect too much at once—is one of the most important elements in combinational play. It can lead to delightfully unexpected (to your opponent) maneuvers. Like this:

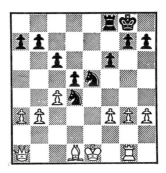

DIAGRAM 129

Black, having the move, notices there is a beautiful knight fork available—. . . N×Pch, forking King and Rook. Alas, the Bishop guards the crucial Pawn. He looks again and sees another knight fork in the offing —N-B7ch, forking (even better) King and Queen. Alas, here too the crucial square is guarded by that same Bishop.

Alas, that is, for White. Because the Bishop—to stretch a metaphor—being only human, cannot do both jobs at once. Something has to give. Black makes sure of the giving with 1 . . . N/K4×Pch. White replies 2 B×N.

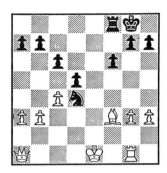

DIAGRAM 130

Position after 2 BxN

Black has given up a Knight for a Pawn, but the loss is very temporary. With the Bishop out of the way he can now play 2 . . . N—B7ch, capturing the White Queen.

Score: Black's loss (after recapture by White)—two Knights; White's loss—Queen and Pawn.

And all because the Bishop was overworked.

A piece does not always have to be protecting two other pieces (or Pawns) to be overworked. If one of its jobs is preventing the opponent's carrying out a threat that is enough to overload it. As in the following example.

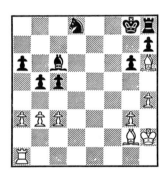

DIAGRAM 131

It is White's move. He sees that it is possible to mate if he can play R—B8. He also sees that only one Black piece—the Knight—is in a position to defend against that threat. But the Knight, at the moment, is defending the Bishop. So—if the Knight can be forced to do two things at once, which he can't do . . .

White plays 1 R—KB1.

Black's only valid move now is 1 . . . resigns.

If he plays N—K3 to stop mate, he loses the Bishop and it's all over but the shouting. If he tries B×B White simply continues with R—B8 mate.

Even the threat of piling the work on an overloaded piece can accomplish much. And this is the essence of a principle you will meet again and again in chess: threats can be as effective as action, and sometimes

DIAGRAM 132

Position after 1 R—KB1

even more effective. They force your opponent to take steps to meet the threat; such steps can be weakening or worse.

Again the best defense against such tactics is not to get into a position where they can be applied. And if you do get into such a position your best bet is counter-attack. If no counter-attacking possibilities present themselves, and if defense seems impossible—resign. You can't always win (and you will learn a good deal in the losing, too).

False Protection

You have already become acquainted with the principle of false protection, though the principle has not been labeled as such. You met it in the section on the pin, in the play that began with Diagram 85. The Black Queen was protected by a Pawn, but it was really false protection; when the Pawn was needed it could not do its job. You met it, too, in the preceding section on overworked defenders. The Bishop in Diagram 132 had false protection.

Here is what might be called a classic example of false protection. It is not as simple and clear-cut as the earlier examples, but it illustrates the point perfectly.

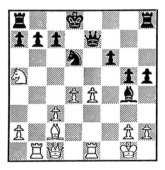

DIAGRAM 133

White's Knight could—if it were not for Black's Pawn at QN1—play to B6 and fork King and Queen. The Pawn is attacked twice, by the Knight and the

Rook/N1, and is defended only once, by the Knight. Black could protect it a second time by either R—N1, or B—B1 or K—B1. He must take into account, however, the function that the threatened Pawn performs. The Pawn, as we already mentioned, keeps the Knight from playing to B6 and forking Their Majesties. Protecting it with R—N1 will not work because a Rook at QN2 will not be able to do the work of a Pawn in the same spot. A Bishop, which captures on the diagonal just as a Pawn does, could replace the Pawn if it were captured by White. So, B—B1 would be a valid move.

Watch what happens if Black protects the Pawn with 1 . . . R—QN1.

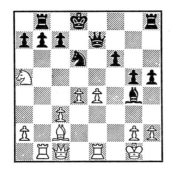

DIAGRAM 134

Position after 1 . . . R—QN1

White now plays 2 R×P. And whether Black recaptures with the Knight or the Rook, White's next move will be N—B6ch, and the Black Queen will fall.

Had Black protected the Pawn with B—B1 and had White then captured, the Bishop would have been in a position to prevent N—B6.

Protection with the Knight and Rook was false protection.

Illusory protection often results from a pin. As in this next case, where the pin, though not apparent, is very real.

DIAGRAM 135

There seem to be no pins here. And yet the White Rook is not only pinned to the first rank, it is glued

there. The Pawn at QN3 is falsely protected. Here's what would happen if White failed to realize his Pawn was, despite appearances, unprotected:

Black plays 1 . . . B×P.

DIAGRAM 136

Position after 1 . . . BxP

The Bishop is as safe as a lion in a den of mice. If the Rook leaves the first rank to capture it, Black replies R—K8ch, and, if White interposes with N—B1, checkmate next move.

The Pawn had false protection. (And this again was a case of a piece trying to do two things at once: protect against mate and cover a Pawn. Though there was no pin in the formal or technical sense of the word, there was a pin as powerful as any.)

Naturally, a real pin can lead to false protection.

DIAGRAM 137

The Black Bishop is vulnerable here because the Pawn that protects it is pinned to its station by the White Rook at R1. Black, in this situation, can retreat the Bishop to B2, unpin the Pawn by playing the K to N1, or give the Bishop added protection with Q—B2. The Pawn alone, because it cannot function, is no protection.

Always look twice at the protection you have given to a Pawn or piece. What may seem, on a superficial glance, to be adequate protection may turn out to be totally inadequate. A piece's protection is only as good as the mobility and security of its guards. Send an overloaded piece to protect something and the something will fall. Permit a guardian to become pinned and the guardian is worthless.

You will find out later, too, that unoccupied squares may need protection as great as or greater than that required by pieces. A vulnerable square, like a vulnerable piece or Pawn, can fall; and when a square falls to the enemy, infiltration and, eventually, defeat, are almost certain to follow.

Discovered Attack

And now we come to a weapon that is always a delight to beginners because of its element of surprise—discovered attack.

The word discovered, in this case, bears its original meaning of uncovered, or revealed (which is, of course, the source of the surprise element). Its effect is somewhat akin to telling your boss, who has summoned you to his inner sanctum to hand you your walking papers, that you want to resign to take a position with a rival firm at twice your present salary.

Here, in a simplified example, is how it works:

DIAGRAM 138

Black has an overwhelming material superiority here —a Queen and Rook against a Bishop and Rook. But Black makes the mistake of playing 1 . . . Q—B5ch.

DIAGRAM 139
Position after 1 . . . Q—B5ch

This move has set Black up for a discovered attack of the most powerful kind—discovered attack with check. White now plays 2 B—K2 dis ch.

DIAGRAM 140
Position after 2 B—K2 dis ch

By moving the Bishop (which he did to block the check) White uncovered the Rook, which now checks the Black King. In this case—which is hypothetical in the extreme; few players would make the blunder Black has made—the discovered attack not only gives check, but it skewers Queen and Rook.

White has turned a sure loss into, at worst, a draw.

The three pieces that move in straight lines—Queen, Rook and Bishop—can do the attacking in a discovered check or discovered attack. Any piece, including Pawn, Knight or King, can mask the attack and then discover it by moving out of the way.

Here is how a Pawn can discover an attack:

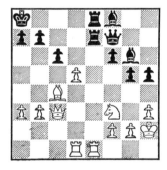

DIAGRAM 141

It is White's move. His Bishop aims right at the Black Queen, but the Bishop's attack is masked by the Pawn/Q5. Move the Pawn and the Bishop's attack is discovered. White can play P×P or P—Q6; either move will accomplish his aim of discovering an attack on the Queen.

There is a further advantage, though, to playing 1 P—Q6; this attacks a Rook, as well as the Queen, and it advances a Pawn to a point where Black will have to expend energy, and perhaps, material, in an effort to keep the Pawn from reaching the last rank and becoming a Queen.

STOP!

You now have a mighty assortment of weapons at your command. How well can you handle them?

Self-Testing Quiz No. 10

(a) *In the following position White, who is a Rook down, is in trouble. Black is threatening to play R×Q, winning not only the Queen but the Knight, as well, through a discovered attack. What can White do about it?*

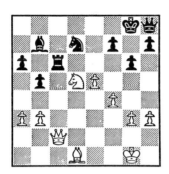

DIAGRAM 142

(b) *In this position Black faces quick destruction. White threatens 1 R—Q8ch; Black's forced answer must be R×R, and White will follow this with Q×R mate. Black, however, has a move available that will call a halt to these threats. What is it?*

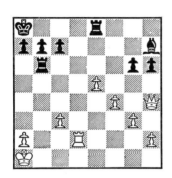

DIAGRAM 143

(c) *It is White's move in the following diagram. He plays 1 N—B6, forking Queen and Rook. What follow-up moves can White make if:*
  1. Black moves his Queen to B1?
  2. Black moves his Queen to B2?
  3. Black counter-attacks with B—R6?

DIAGRAM 144

(d) *In the following position White threatens to discover check, attacking and winning the Black Queen. Black, however, has the move. What moves would prevent the discovered check?*

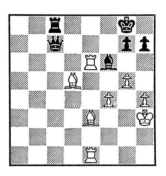

DIAGRAM 145

Double Check

Like a great chef saving his pièce de résistance for the dessert, we have saved for this final section on tactics the most powerful single weapon a chess player can use—double check.

There just is no defense to the double check. It is an overwhelming, psychologically (as well as practically) crushing weapon and—like the triple play in baseball—it comes rarely. But when it does come, the man who employs it feels the taste of triumph and the man on whom it is employed collapses like a punctured balloon.

Reduced to its essentials, the double check works this way:

DIAGRAM 146

To show the power of the double check we have given Black what would normally be an absolutely insurmountable material advantage. We have assumed that Black already has converted a Pawn into a Queen, giving him two Queens and two Pawns to White's Rook and Bishop. The Queen alone, under ordinary circumstances, should be enough to give Black a fairly easy win. A Queen and two Pawns would win with no trouble at all. But two Queens...!

Nevertheless, if White had the move in this position he could win in one stroke, with 1 R—B8 dbl ch and mate.

DIAGRAM 147

Position after 1 R—B8 dbl ch and mate

He has moved the Rook off the diagonal KR3—QB8, discovering a check by the Bishop. And, at the same time, he gives check with the Rook from B8.

If White captured the Rook, the Bishop would still be giving check; if he captured the Bishop, the Rook would still be giving check. To stop the check both pieces would have to be captured at once. Since this is manifestly impossible, the check cannot be countered. It becomes checkmate.

The double check has triumphed over a vastly superior material force.

Notice that, in the position of diagram 147, a simple discovered check would have been insufficient. Had White played R—B4 dis ch or R—KR5 dis ch (in either case, attacking one of the opposing Queens while giving check), the Queen/R5 would simply have captured the Bishop and White would still have had a Queen and two Pawns against a Rook.

The secret of the double check's great effect is that capture or interposition will not work as a defense. The doubly attacked King must move. And, if there is no place to which he can move (as in the example just given) the game is over.

Here is another example of double check bringing a game to a sudden and decisive end.

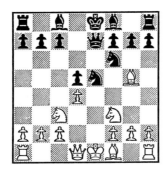

DIAGRAM 148

The position, at a quick glance, looks innocent enough; development is incomplete on both sides; White would seem to have developed more adequately —Black having obviously moved a Knight twice and having moved his Queen in the early stages; an exchange of Pawns has taken place, but little else seems to have happened.

The position is deceptive, though. White must have been asleep at the switch. Despite his apparently superior development he is about to succumb without so much as a by-your-leave. Because Black, having the move, plays 1 . . . N×N dbl ch and mate!

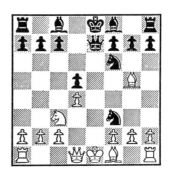

DIAGRAM 149

Position after 1 . . . NxNdbl ch and mate

The attacking Knight cannot be captured; the Queen would still be giving check. And interposing a piece on the King file to block the Queen check would not work; the Knight would still be giving check. The only way out is to move the King, and the King cannot move to an unattacked square—they are all occupied by his own men.

There is more than an example of double check in this illustration. There is also a moral, one that you have been given before and one that will crop up again and again in this book.

That moral is: Don't move mechanically.

Don't "follow the book" slavishly, moving first your King Pawn, then your King Knight, then your King Bishop, then castling, then etc. and etc. Don't make a move simply because it follows a pattern. The only moves to make are the best moves. And if that means breaking the "rules," why then, by all means break them.

Black, as we said, obviously disobeyed rules in the example just given, having moved a Knight twice and having put his Queen into active play before completing his development. White, just as obviously, was intent on following the book to complete his development, paying no attention at all to what his opponent was doing.

Chess is not solitaire!

Your moves must be dictated, not by a book or by your vacuum-packed conception of what should be done, but by what your opponent does in relation to what you have already done. You may fall into the trap of thinking that you are the only one who is planning, scheming and devising. Unfortunately, this is not true. Your opponent, placidly sitting there and staring at the board, is scheming, planning and devising, too.

And unless you take him into account you will get nowhere.

This may sound like fatuous advice. Who, you may say, ever hinted that chess was a one-man game? Everybody knows it takes two to play chess.

The surprising thing is, though, that many chess players—many more than you might suspect—think of chess as a one-sided affair. They get so wrapped up in their own brilliant (or not-so-brilliant) ideas that they fail to realize they have an opponent. They wake up to this disturbing fact only when the opponent's ideas materialize abruptly and present them with difficulties they hadn't dreamed could come about. By then, of course, it is too late—much too late.

As White discovered in the last example.

STOP!

. . . and test yourself before going on to the next chapter.

Self-Testing Quiz No. 11

(a) In the following diagram, it is Black's move. Should he play 1 . . . R×Q?

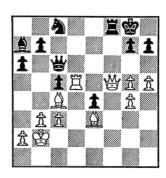

DIAGRAM 150

(b) In the following diagram Black is in check. How would you, as Black, get out of check—(a) by K—R1, (b) K—B1 or, (c) Q×N? What is the best move for Black?

DIAGRAM 151

Chapter Six

END GAME

Introduction

END GAME? Why—you may properly ask—tackle the end game when I haven't even studied the middle game, or even the opening?

A legitimate question, to which there is a legitimate answer. It is quite true that, unless you encounter an opponent who is as much a beginner as you, you are not likely at this stage to get to the end game; chances are you would be checkmated in the middle game or even in the opening.

First, and most obvious, though, is the consideration of sheer numbers. In the end game you will be working with two, three or perhaps four or five pieces at most. It is much simpler to learn to maneuver with a few pieces than with ten or twelve or sixteen. Positions are clearer with an open board; you can learn to visualize more easily, to "see" the coming moves and the positions that will result. To visualize two or three moves ahead when the board is crowded with pieces requires experience (unless you are one of those rare "natural" chess geniuses, in which case you ought to be writing books, not reading them).

But even more important is the fact that end-game positions are goals in themselves. A great deal of middle-game maneuvering, and even of opening play, is dictated by the results that will be found only in the end game. You will find out that much of the work you do in the middle game is directed to bringing about a favorable end game. And how can you do that without knowing what a favorable end game is?

Frequently, too, the essence of an end-game position will appear in the middle game. If you recognize it you will be able to force a gain in material or perhaps even a mate. If you fail to recognize it you will let opportunity slip by and may find yourself losing when, by all rights, you should have won.

And lastly there is the fact that end game, in and of itself, is—despite the sour-grapes attitudes of some players—a delight. Its logic is so strict, its requirements so demanding and its rewards so satisfying that few other aspects of chess can match its appeal.

If these reasons fail to convince you, then, for the time being, take it on faith that "he who masters the end game masters chess."

The Beginning of the End

The end game comes about when most of the pieces have disappeared from the board. Perhaps the single most valid criterion is the functioning of the King. In the opening the best thing to do with the King is to castle him into a secure position; to leave him exposed in the center of the board is to court defeat. In the middle game the King, unless he is forced to emerge from his safe position, remains passive; it is still too dangerous to bring him out because he can be subjected on every side to attack.

In the end game, however, the King's role changes. Not only does he venture forth, but he becomes an aggressive, fighting piece, one of the strongest on the board. He is, in fact, quite indispensable to your offense. Where, in the earlier stages, he remained hidden in his corner of the board, he now strides forth to centralize himself and thus to exercise his commanding powers of attack and defense.

When you can thus convert your King you can be sure you are in the end game.

Another criterion—though this one is not so marked as is the role of the King—is the power of the Pawn. In the opening the Pawns were, so to speak, only in the way; they blocked their own men and had to be moved to give the pieces room in which to operate. They were almost as much a liability as an asset. In the middle game (as you will learn) they become the bastions of defense, guarding pieces that infiltrate the enemy position and that establish themselves in outposts that threaten the enemy. They also, it is true, attempt themselves to penetrate the enemy lines, but in a well played middle game such incursions are not likely to succeed.

Passed Pawns

In the end game, however, the Pawn becomes a powerhouse. It is here that the lowly foot-soldier attacks the enemy brass, driving it into untenable positions. It is here that—as Nimzovich said—the passed Pawn has a "lust to expand"—to push forward to its goal and become an officer.

What is a passed Pawn? Look at the diagram below:

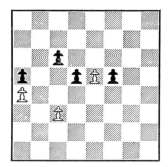

DIAGRAM 152

White's King Pawn and Black's King Bishop Pawn are passed. Neither one will meet an enemy Pawn on an adjacent file in its march towards its last rank. The White and Black Queen Rook Pawns also are passed, but—for the time being—each is blockaded. One of the two united Black Pawns (the Queen and Queen Bishop Pawn) is a potential passed Pawn.

A passed Pawn, then, is a Pawn that is unopposed by an enemy Pawn on its road to the last rank. True opposition comes, not from the Pawn confronting it on the same file, but from a Pawn or Pawns on adjacent files. The Pawn that opposes its counterpart on the same file (as the Queen Rook Pawns in the preceding diagram) can, theoretically, be removed. The Pawn on the adjacent file, however, presents a real difficulty; it can capture the would-be passed Pawn and eliminate it from the picture.

Nevertheless, a Pawn whose road to glory is hampered by opposing Pawns, whether on the same or adjacent files, is not—in function—a true passed Pawn.

It is only when the road is clear that a Pawn becomes truly passed. And then it is a force to be contended with. If it goes on to its goal its power becomes immense. And the closer it gets to its goal, the greater its strength becomes, because the enemy must stop it at all costs. Many a Rook has been sacrificed to halt an ambitious passed Pawn.

What is stronger than a passed Pawn? This is like asking what could be better than having a million dollars (the answer to which, of course, is having two million dollars). And the answer is two passed pawns. Here's what we mean (diagram 153):

The passed Pawns here are united—that is, one can protect the other because they are on adjacent files. In the position given they prevent an enemy piece from occupying any of the four squares on the rank in front of them. If one of them moves forward to the seventh

DIAGRAM 153

rank, the other gives it protection. It is almost impossible to keep one of these Pawns from becoming a Queen (it can be done, but only at the cost of a piece that, under ordinary circumstances, would be far more valuable than a Pawn). If the passed Pawns have the protection of their King they are just about invincible.

Two passed Pawns that are not united can also be a tremendous asset. As here:

DIAGRAM 154

The Black King has more than he can handle. If he pursues the Rook Pawn the Knight Pawn will rush forward to become a Queen. And if he sets his sights on the Knight Pawn the Rook Pawn will go on to Queen. The Black King's problem is a simple one: all he has to do is be on both sides of the board at the same time. Since this is obviously impossible, one of the two passed White Pawns will become a Queen, and the game will then soon be over.

Or they can be weak, as here:

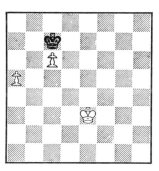

DIAGRAM 155

In the preceding diagram the game is drawn, even if White has the move, because the Black King can pick off the unsupported passed Pawns. Had White's King been there to help out, the Pawns could have triumphed —but he was off fiddling somewhere while the Pawns burned.

Which illustrates a vital point that will be made again and again: The King must be used in the end game as an active, aggressive piece; his help may be the pivot upon which defeat or victory turns.

Critical Timing

You will find, too, that time, in the end game, assumes an importance you might never expect it to have. By time is meant "who has the move?" There are positions (and they arise with frequency in the end game) in which everything but time is equal; the side that has the right (or the obligation) to move finds that this right or obligation spells the difference between a win and a loss.

The following position shows in decisive fashion how valuable time becomes in the end game.

DIAGRAM 156

Each side is about to Queen a Pawn. And whichever side has the move (time) will do it first, thereby winning the game.

In the position given above victory went to the side that had the right to move. In the position given below, however, the reverse is true.

DIAGRAM 157

White, at first glance, seems to have a sure win; his Pawn is about to become a Queen and, in addition, it has the support of the King. But looks are deceiving.

If it is White's turn to move all he can get is a draw. If it is Black's turn, White will mate in short order. Why?

If Black must move, the only square open to him is R2. The play would run as follows:

1	. . .	K–R2
2	K–B7	K–R3 (forced)
3	P–N8(Q)	

And mate follows.

If White has to move he must either abandon the Pawn, in which case only a draw is possible, or he must move to N7, in which case it is stalemate there and then—Black, while not in check, has no moves at his disposal (which is what stalemate is: a side is not in check but can make no legal moves).

The obligation (as opposed to the right) to move— that is, having to move when you don't want to—is called zugzwang.

As you play more and more end games you will learn that zugzwang can be a devilish thing. Just when everything is right, just when all your forces are in the right position to force a win (or prevent one by your opponent) you suddenly find it is your turn to move. If you touch anything your whole set-up collapses. Yet you must move. You are, alas, in zugzwang.

There are all sorts of tricks in the chess expert's bag that can be used to force your opponent into zugzwang. And they are as delightful as any magician's legerdemain. When your opponent, however, pulls one of these tricks on you . . .

We will discuss all these stratagems and devices— the use of the King, the passed Pawn, zugzwang and others—in more detail as we study the various types of end games.

THE MATE WITH QUEEN

The easiest mate is the one in which a lone King faces a King and Queen.

DIAGRAM 158

How do you go about forcing checkmate?

The easiest way is to force the King to the edge of the board. Once he is unable to move further, mate becomes a matter of simple mechanics (indeed, the whole process of forcing a mate with King and Queen against a lone King is simple mechanics; but some beginners, drunk with the power of being able to yell "check" as often as they like, prolong the process indefinitely and, unaware of the few pitfalls that do exist, finally end up stalemating themselves).

From the position of the preceding diagram you can elect to force the White King to any of the four sides of the board. Arbitrarily, we'll pick White's eighth rank, the one nearest the defending King.

Our first move will be 1 . . . Q—N4.

This prevents the King from getting any further away from rank 8 than he is now. He is thus confined to ranks 8, 7 and 6. Now the play runs like this:

| 2 | K—Q6 | K—N7 |

Remember: no unnecessary checks. You must now bring your King up to the opposing King to assist in the coup de grace.

3	K—K6	K—B6
4	K—Q6	K—B5
5	K—K6	. . .

DIAGRAM 159
Position after 5 K—K6

The Kings are now "in opposition": they stand on squares of the same color and are separated by an odd number (one) of squares. When the Kings are in this position the attacking side has a great advantage; it can give check and cut down the defending side's field of operations. Black plays

| 5 | . . . | Q—Q4ch |

DIAGRAM 160
Position after 5 . . . Q—Q4ch

White must either move off the sixth rank or off the King file, in either case getting closer to the edge of the board. The play continues:

| 6 | K—B6 | K—Q5 |

DIAGRAM 161
Position after 6 . . . K—Q5

The Kings are in opposition again. White moves out of that uncomfortable situation.

| 7 | K—N6 | K—K5 |
| 8 | K—B6 | . . . |

Although the Kings are not in opposition, Black uses the position to force the White King further toward the edge.

| 8 | . . . | Q—B4ch |

The King must retreat.

| 9 | K—N7 | K—B5 |
| 10 | K—R7 | Q—B3 |

With his last move, Black cuts down the White King's space even more, depriving him of the sixth rank.

At this point (and even earlier) you must be careful not to do yourself out of a victory by permitting your opponent to stalemate himself. Always make sure when you move that the opposing King has at least one square to which he can go on his next move.

11	K—N8	K—B4
12	K—R7	K—N4
13	K—N8	. . .

DIAGRAM 162
Position after 13 K—N8

Careful! If Black now plays K—N3 in a mistaken effort to bring about the opposition, the game is drawn. White, without being in check, would have no move. The way to bring about the opposition is to force your opponent to walk into it. You may have to "waste time" to do this, but it is the best way.

| 13 | . . . | Q—K2 |
| 14 | K—R8 | K—N3 |

DIAGRAM 163
Position after 15 . . . K—N3

Black has forced the White King to a position in which it must move into opposition.

| 15 | K—N8 | . . . |

DIAGRAM 164
Position after 15 K—N8

This is the position Black has been striving for. The defending King is at the edge of the board, the Kings are in opposition and the attacker has the move.

| 15 | . . . | Q—K1 (or Q—Q1 or Q—N2) mate |

It was possible from the starting position given (diagram 158) to bring about mate in nine moves. But the play we illustrated is more "real"—a nine-move mate would have meant perfect play on both sides, something you are not too likely to encounter. The system, however, and the techniques are the same: you force the defending King to the edge of the board; you do not make useless checks; you cut down the defending King's territory systematically, usually by giving check when the Kings are in opposition; and, finally you force the defending King, when he is at the edge of the board, to move into opposition. Then you mate.

THE MATE WITH THE ROOK

A Rook and King against a lone King is also a fairly simple mate and is similar in many respects to the mate with Queen and King. The big difference is that a Rook can be attacked by a King, where a Queen cannot be. You must take care not to slip and let the defending King capture your Rook.

The goal is the same as with the Queen: force the King to the edge of the board and into opposition and then mate. The final position will be like this:

DIAGRAM 165

The opposition, you see, prevents the defending King from escaping.

The mate can also be brought about without the opposition, as in the following position:

DIAGRAM 166

This is possible because not only is the defending King at the edge of the board, but he is also in a corner. In such a position the opposition is not required. The King has, in effect, mated himself.

To illustrate the mate, let's start with the following position, similar to the start of the Queen-mate position:

DIAGRAM 167

We start by moving our King up. Because the Rook does not have as much power as the Queen, the attacking King will have to be considerably more active in this mate.

1	K—N2	K—Q5
2	K—B2	K—K5
3	R—N5	. . .

With this move White confines the Black King to his fifth, sixth, seventh and eighth ranks. The object, as in the mate with Queen, being to cut down the King's mobility rank by rank and file by file until it is forced into the desired position.

3	. . .	K—Q5
4	K—N3	K—K5
5	K—B3	K—B5
6	K—Q3	K—N5
7	K—K3	. . .

If Black now makes the mistake of playing 7 . . . K—R5 White can reply 8 K—B3. Black then will be forced to play into opposition with K—R6 and White will mate on his next move. So Black plays the only move he really has.

| 7 | . . . | K—N6 |

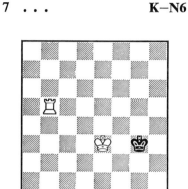

DIAGRAM 168
Position after 7 . . . K—N6

The Kings are now in opposition and a check is called for, to eat into the Black King's space.

| 8 | R—N5ch | . . . |

This forces the Black King to the edge of the board.

| 8 | . . . | K—R5 |

White may have overlooked this; the beleaguered King attacks the White Rook (naturally this would be impossible if the Rook were a Queen). White responds by making a move that not only defends the Rook but further forces the Black King into the fatal corner.

| 9 | K—B4 | . . . |

Black's next move is, like so many others, forced.

| 9 | . . . | K—R6 |
| 10 | K—B3 | K—R7 |

If Black had made the mistake of attacking the Rook with 10 . . . K—R5, White would have retreated the Rook to a safe square along the fifth rank. Black then would have had to go to R6, moving into the opposition, and White would have mated on the following move.

| 11 | R—N8 | . . . |

White could just as well have played 11 R—N7 or 11 R—N6; it is only a matter of deliberately wasting time (from a safe square) to force Black into zug-zwang. An impetuous player might have tried R—N2ch, throwing away the game. Because after Black played K—R8 and White followed with K—B2 or K—N3, Black would be stalemated.

11	. . .	**K—R8**

If Black played 11 . . . K—R6, White would follow with the immediate mate 12 R—R8.

12	**K—B2**	. . .

And now Black is in zugzwang. He must move into opposition.

DIAGRAM 169

Position after 12 K—B2

12	. . .	**K—R7**
13	**R—R8 mate**	

Only 13 moves? And the mate with Queen took 15 moves? Is something wrong here?

Not at all. The mate with Queen and King against King, it was noted, could be accomplished in as few as nine moves with the best of play. The demonstrated mate with Queen was not—repeat, not—the best of play. It was accomplished in the way a non-master might reasonably be expected to accomplish it. The principles were given, which is all that really matters.

In the Rook mate the play was "best." You would not be expected to polish off an opponent as efficiently as this. But, again, the principles do not differ; your object is always to force the King to the edge of the board and then administer the final blow.

MATE WITH BISHOP AND KNIGHT

The mate with a King, Bishop and Knight against a lone King is a long and difficult ending. In addition, to be truthful, you will rarely, if ever, be called upon to use this ending; any opponent who finds himself with nothing but a King is more than likely to resign and save you the trouble of checkmating him.

Why bother with it then?

First, the Bishop and Knight ending is an unparalleled example of the way in which pieces must co-operate with each other to carry out an objective. It is especially so because the Bishop and Knight do not ordinarily lend themselves well to smooth cooperation; the Bishop being a long-range, far-striking piece and the Knight being a short-range, in-fighting piece.

And then there is always the possibility that some stubborn opponent, faced with the odds of a lone King against your King, Knight and Bishop, may challenge you to checkmate him. Knowing this ending is something like knowing how many species of ants are found in Lower Silesia; who knows—you might win a 30-foot cruiser on a quiz program some day because you had that knowledge at your fingertips. (The rules of chess state, incidentally, that a player can challenge his opponent to checkmate him and that if the opponent can't do it in 50 moves the game is a draw.)

Here, then, is the way to mate with Bishop and Knight.

The final position will be this:

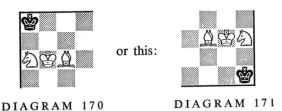

DIAGRAM 170	DIAGRAM 171

or this:

The defending King, as you see, must be driven into one of the two corners of the same color as those on which the attacking Bishop moves. The first objective, then, will be to force the king to the edge of the board; then, gradually, you must force him to the corner—the right corner, of course.

Take the following as a starting point:

DIAGRAM 172

The Black King has stationed himself as centrally as possible; he will try to keep himself in the center and, if forced to the edge, will try to stay out of the white-squared corners. The play might run like this:

1	**B—B7ch**	**K—Q3**
2	**B—B4**	**K—K4**
3	**K—B5**	**K—K5**

The defending King tries to keep maneuvering around the central squares.

4	K–Q6	K–B4
5	B–Q3ch	K–B3
6	N–Q2	. . .

The Knight now maneuvers to get in closer to the action.

6	. . .	K–B2

And the harassed King moves in the general direction of the black-squared corner; if he's going to be cornered, that's where he intends to be.

7	N–B3	K–B3

The Black King, taking advantage of the momentarily open position, heads back for the center.

8	K–Q7	K–B2
9	B–B4ch	K–B3

So far the Black King seems to have been successfully avoiding the edge of the board.

10	B–K6	. . .

The trap, however, is starting to close. With his 10th move White cut the Black King off from Black's B2 and B4. The Knight, having been moved to KB3, cuts off Black's K5 and KN4.

10	. . .	K–N2
11	K–K7	K–N3
12	B–N4	K–N2
13	N–K5	K–R3

At last—the defender has been forced to the edge of the board. Now it only remains to get him to his own R8.

DIAGRAM 173

Position after 13 . . . K—R3

14	K–B6	K–R2

But what's this! The King is going in the wrong direction—wrong, that is, from White's point of view. He is heading for the black-squared corner.

15	N–B7	K–N1

If that's the Black King's game, we can play along with it. We'll force him to his own QR1. And we begin by cutting off his retreat down the King Rook file.

16	B–B5	. . .

He has only one move.

16	. . .	K–B1

From this point on, with the defending King cut off from retreat, the problem becomes a simple one. The White King will move along his sixth rank, toward his final goal of QN6. The Knight will hop around to get to his final position. And the Bishop, who has the job of administering the last blow, will see to it that the Black King does not squeeze out of the trap along the white squares.

17	B–R7	K–K1
18	N–K5	K–Q1

The Black King makes a break for safety, aiming for QB2.

19	K–K6	K–B2
20	N–Q7	K–B3

It looks like the Black King has broken through and is heading back for the center. But the breakthrough is quite temporary.

21	B–Q3	K–B2
22	B–K2	. . .

A waiting move.

22	. . .	K–Q1

And another attempt to escape.

23	B–R5	. . .

Sorry, no escape.

23	. . .	K–B2
24	B–B3	K–Q1
25	K–Q6	K–K1
26	B–R5ch	K–Q1
27	N–B5	K–B1
28	B–B7	. . .

To kill time. Moving the King or Knight now would loosen the net and give the Black King another chance to delay the closing of the trap.

29	. . .	K–Q1
30	N–N7ch	K–B1
31	K–B6	. . .

The White King, as you see, keeps sliding along the sixth rank, preventing the opposing King from creeping away, and getting closer to his final position.

31	. . .	K–N1
32	K–N6	K–B1
33	B–K6ch	K–N1

Almost there.

| 34 | N–B5 | . . . |

The Black King now has only one square to which he can move—and that is the light-colored corner square.

| 34 | . . . | K–R1 |
| 35 | B–Q7 | K–N1 |

| 36 | N–R6ch | . . . |

Only one move left for the Black King.

| 36 | . . . | K–R1 |
| 37 | B–B6mate | |

It is not possible to bring about the mate in much less time than this. But, even if challenged, you should be able to do it within the prescribed 50 moves.

OTHER MATES

The mate with two Bishops almost never occurs. By the time the end game has been reached both sides are almost certain to have lost at least one Bishop. Like the mate with Knight and Bishop it is long and involved—though not quite so involved because Bishops cooperate more easily with each other than with a Knight. The final position would be like this:

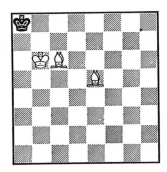

DIAGRAM 174

Because of its rarity we will not bother you with the details of bringing about such a mate. Suffice it to say

that it can be effected in any of the four corners and that the last few moves involve a good deal of "time-wasting" by the attacker—that is, a lot of shifting around on one diagonal by a Bishop. Should you, by some way-out chance, happen to be faced with the prospect of mating with two Bishops, you can do one of two things:

(a) Bluff your opponent into believing you are such an expert that he ought to resign, or
(b) Excuse yourself for a few minutes, run to the nearest bookstore and buy a book devoted to end games.

It is impossible to force a mate with a King and two Knights against a lone King. It is not impossible, however, to mate with the two Knights—only the forcing is impossible. If your opponent slips up and lets himself be mated, it can be done. The final position (to prove that it is possible, despite what many chess books say) would be like this:

DIAGRAM 175

The point to remember is that unless your opponent blunders you cannot bring about a mate with two Knights. It is possible to force a mate when two Knights and a King face a King and a Pawn, but the mate is too tricky to be included in a basic work on chess. Again, you are advised, if you want to learn this mate, to consult a book on end games. (See the list of Further Reading, page 182.

There are some valid conclusions to be drawn from a summary of the basic mates.

¶ A Queen and King can force mate in as few as nine moves.

¶ A Rook and King can force mate in as few as thirteen moves.

¶ A Knight, Bishop and King can force mate in about 30 moves.

¶ Two Bishops and a King can force mate in about 25 moves.

¶ Two Knights and a King cannot force mate.

And the conclusions that can be drawn are:

¶ Try to preserve a Bishop for the end game, because a Bishop is more valuable than a Knight.

¶ Two Bishops are worth considerably more than two Knights.

¶ A Rook is worth more than a Bishop or a Knight.

¶ A Queen is worth more than a Rook.

From these conclusions we can draw up a rough table of values for the pieces. First we will divide the pieces into major and minor pieces. The Queen and Rook, being able to mate alone (that is, with just the King) are the major pieces. The Knight and Bishop, being unable to mate alone, are the minor pieces.

Now if we arbitrarily fix the value of a Pawn as 1, we can say that a Knight is worth about 3, a Bishop about 3½, a Rook about 5 and a Queen about 10. This is, you must remember, strictly a rule-of-thumb kind of reckoning. In certain situations—closed positions, for example—a Knight is worth more than a Bishop. And in other situations a Pawn may be worth more than a Queen.

But for ready-reckoning purposes this scale is valuable. It tells you, for example, not to exchange your Rook for your opponent's Bishop (such a swap is called "losing the exchange" or, simply, "the exchange"). It tells you, also, not, ordinarily, to exchange your Bishop for your opponent's Knight (this is sometimes called "losing the minor exchange").

Do not, though, stick slavishly to this table of values. You might, under some circumstances, be able to bring about a winning position by losing the exchange. Or you might, in other circumstances, be able to create a weakness in your opponent's position by losing the minor exchange.

Now

STOP!

Do you know your basic mates?

Self-Testing Quiz No. 12

(a) In how many moves can White mate in the following position (White to move)?

DIAGRAM 176

(b) It is White's move in the following position. What should he play and why?

DIAGRAM 177

(c) In the following position Black has the move. Should he play 1 . . . B—K5?

DIAGRAM 178

(d) In that same position—the diagram above—how can Black mate most quickly?

(e) In the following position White, with the move, has a mate-in-one. What is it? He also has a "stalemate-in-one." What is that?

DIAGRAM 179

ROOK AND BISHOP vs. ROOK

This mate—where the defending King has the support of a Rook and the attacking King has a Rook and Bishop—is a difficult one for both sides. The defender, if he makes the least slip, is lost; the attacker, if he errs, can easily lose the initiative and the game.

Technically, a mate is possible in this situation only when the defending King has been driven to the edge of the board and into the opposition. The following diagram illustrates what is called Philidor's classical position, that is, the basic situation called for to mate.

DIAGRAM 180

The requirements for mate have been met: the defending King is at the edge of the board and the Kings are in opposition. But Black is threatening to drive the White King out of the opposition by playing 1 . . . R—K2ch. White cannot prevent this by playing B—B6 or B—Q6. Here's what would happen:

1	B—Q6	R—K2ch
2	B×R	. . .

And Black is stalemated.
White therefore plays 1 R—B8ch. Then the play goes like this:

1	. . .	R—Q1
2	R—B7	R—Q7

Even here a pitfall awaits Black. If he had played 2 . . . K—B1 instead or 2 . . . R—Q7, here is what might have happened:

2	. . .	K—B1
3	R—KR7	R—K1ch
4	K—B6	K—N1
5	R—N7ch	K—R1

(and not 5 . . . K—B1; 6 B—Q6ch, for Black would lose his Rook)

6	R—N1	K—R2

(and not 6 . . . R—B1ch; 7 K—K7 dis ch, for Black, here too, would lose his Rook)

7	K—B7

DIAGRAM 181

Position after 7 K—B7

Has White abandoned his Bishop? Not at all. The Kings are in opposition, with the defender against the wall. If Black takes time to capture the Bishop White will play R—R1ch. All Black can do then is to delay mate one move by interposing: 7 . . . R—KR4; 8 R×Rmate.

But back to move 3. Black has just played 2 . . . R—Q7, a waiting move. White, too, now must make a waiting move. He plays 3 R—QN7. (Why all this shuffling around with waiting moves? The object, as you will see, is to force the Black Rook onto a square where White can win by forcing Black to sacrifice his Rook.)

3	. . .	R—Q8
4	R—N7	. . .

White's immediate threat now is R—N8mate. Black counters with

4	. . .	R—KB8
5	B—Q6	R—K8ch
6	B—K5	R—KB8
7	R—KR2	R—B6
8	R—N7	K—B1
9	R—QB7	K—N1
10	R—N7ch	K—B1
11	R—N4	. . .

This threatens B—Q6ch, which will drive the King back into opposition,

11	. . .	K—K1
12	B—B4	

DIAGRAM 182
Position after 12 B—B4

blocking the Rook's path. White now threatens mate at once with R—N8. The only way to stop it—and that is temporary at best —is by sacrificing the Rook. If Black tries to escape by way of K—B1, B—Q6ch can be played and the end is inevitable, for Black would have to move back into opposition and settle for mate then and there or mate after the sacrifice of the Rook.

You see, then, that mate with Rook and Bishop against Rook is a difficult proposition. If White does not pursue his object with precision, the game will be a draw; if he plays with considerably less than precision he can throw the game away altogether.

Black, for his part, must also play with extreme care.

But the interesting thing about this end game for beginners is the way it illustrates a point made earlier: that end game is a beautifully logical part of chess; that with few pieces on the board the moves ahead can be visualized more easily; that each of the pieces that do remain has a role to perform and must perform it accurately; that end game can be a stimulating challenge to the imagination and ingenuity.

ROOK vs. BISHOP

The Bishop alone, as you know, can not, even with the direct help of his King, checkmate a lone King. A Rook, on the other hand, can easily force mate.

Oddly enough, though, the end game in which one King has the support of a Rook and the other the support of a Bishop usually leads to a draw.

When a chess book—this one, for instance—speaks of "usually," it means "usually when the masters play." You will find, for example, that most chess books say the ending Rook vs. Rook and Knight can be won only in special circumstances at the edge of the board. What this means is that when two masters play, the game will in all likelihood be a draw unless one of the players can force the game into the required position. What it does not mean is that when two ordinary, run-of-the-mill players oppose each other the game must be a

draw. No one plays to perfection. But some grand-masters come close, especially in the end game. That is why most games in high-level tournaments and matches end as draws; each side knows (or feels sure) the other will play as well as humanly possible; that no blunders or mistakes will be made, and that, therefore, there will be no chance to exploit errors.

But ordinary players, not having the time to devote to study, cannot possibly play with such near-perfection. They will make mistakes. And their opponents will be able to capitalize on these mistakes. If you should look at a chess book and find, for example, that "the ending Queen against Queen is a draw," don't automatically assume such an ending can't be won. It can be—if one side makes a slip. Thus, though we say the ending Rook vs. Bishop "usually leads to a draw," what we mean is that if you were a master and your opponent a master, the game probably could not be won. But you are not a master, and your opponents will not be masters. So by all means play on.

A win can be forced if the following conditions are met:

1. The Kings are in opposition.
2. The attacking side (the Rook side) has the move.
3. The Kings are on squares of the opposite color to those on which the Bishop moves.
4. The position is not a corner one.

(Again: Notice we said a win can be *forced;* we didn't say a win was not *possible* except under those circumstances.)

The so-called classical position for a win is as follows:

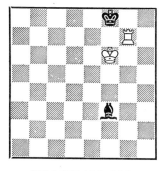

DIAGRAM 183

What makes it "classical?" All the conditions are met—if White has the move. If Black has the move he will take advantage of it to upset the conditions, and he can do this by moving his King out of opposition. (The opposition is always a dangerous position for the defending side.)

White wants to keep the status quo. Not only that, he wants to utilize it to force mate. But if he makes indifferent moves Black will promptly break out of op-position. So White must not give him the chance. He does this by constantly threatening something: mate or capture of the Bishop.

     1   **R—N3** (attacking the Bishop)

Black must make sure his Bishop hangs around the Kings. If he fails to do this it becomes possible to capture the Bishop by threatening mate. For example:

1	. . .	**B—R4**
2	**R—R3**	**B—B2**
3	**R—R8ch**	**B—N1**
4	**K—N6**	

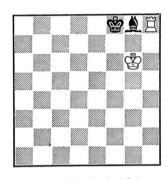

DIAGRAM 184
Position after 4 K—N6

The Bishop, of course, cannot move, being pinned. That means Black can move only his King. And the King can move only to Black's K1 or K2, abandoning the Bishop, which will then be captured.

The results would be similar if the Bishop moved to the Queen file, the Queen Rook file, Queen Knight file or Queen Bishop file. Consequently, it must move to the King file (obviously it cannot move to the King Knight file, which is swept by the Rook). So Black plays

     1   . . .   **B—K5**

White keeps up the attack, playing

     2   **R—K3**   . . .

Now the Bishop can safely move to the King Knight file.

     2   . . .   **B—N7**

White does not let up.

     3   **R—K2**   . . .

The Bishop is being forced to leave the vicinity of the Kings (that is, the file on which the Kings stand or either of the adjacent files).

3	. . .	**B—B6**
4	**R—KB2**	. . .

Now the Bishop must move off the safe files.

     4   . . .   **B—B3**

And White presses his attack.

     5   **R—B2**   **B—Q2**

White has harassed the Bishop into a vulnerable position. He can now bring about a situation analogous to the one in diagram 184, forcing Black to part with the Bishop.

     6   **R—QN2**   . . .

The attack, apparently, has relaxed and Black uses the lull to get out of opposition.

     6   . . .   **K—N1**

But White tops it.

     7   **R—N8ch**

DIAGRAM 185
Position after 7 R—N8ch

The Bishop is lost. If Black interposes White then plays R×Bch. If Black flees to his second rank White follows through by moving the Rook to that rank, pinning and winning the Bishop. Checkmate then follows.

Let's examine the principles behind this play. The object was to force the defending Bishop off the file on which the Kings stood or either of the adjacent files. Why?

Because once off those files the Bishop would be of no value in interposing against a check. If it did interpose, it could be attacked a second time, by the King, and would then have to be abandoned. Or White could kill time, forcing Black to move. And, with his Bishop pinned, Black would have to move away from the

Bishop, thus permitting its capture by White.

And how was the Bishop forced away from the safe files? By constant attack. This constant attack, too, gave Black no time in which to move out of the opposition. Had he taken the time, the Bishop would have fallen at once.

QUEEN vs. ROOK

The same sort of reasoning applies to the end game in which one King is supported by a Queen and the other by a Rook. Here again the less powerful supporting piece must be driven away from the protection of its King. It can then be captured by a series of checks and double attacks.

The general type of position to strive for is the following:

DIAGRAM 186

The Queen, in giving check, also attacks the Rook, which will fall on White's next move.

Here is a simple example of how the Rook can be captured.

DIAGRAM 187

The play is as follows:

| 1 | . . . | Q—Q4ch |
| 2 | K—N1 | . . . |

Any other move loses. 2 K—R3 is followed by 2 . . . Q—R4 mate; 2 K—R1 is followed by 2 . . . Q—R4ch and the loss of the Rook.

| 2 | . . . | Q—B4ch |

This wins the Rook. White cannot play 3 K—B1 because this permits . . . Q—B8 mate. White must therefore move to the Rook file, permitting the double attack on King and Rook.

Sometimes the attacker can use a subtle "trick," as in the following example.

DIAGRAM 188

White plays 1 Q—N1ch. Black cannot go to R3 because this would be followed by 2 Q—R1ch and mate next move. He cannot go to N1 either because White would be able to play Q—N8ch, winning the Rook. So Black plays 1 . . . K—R1. White then plays 2 Q—N8ch, attacking King and Rook. But Black thinks he has a way out; he plays 2 . . . R—N1, parrying the check and attacking the Queen.

DIAGRAM 189
Position after 2 . . . R—N1

An impetuous player might now look at the position and say "Why doesn't White polish him off by attacking the pinned Rook a second time with 3 K—B7?" And if White did, Black's devastatingly simple and simply devastating reply would be 3 . . . R×Q!

No, White has the answer. It is 3 Q—R2mate.

Black, in protecting his King and "saving" his Rook, robbed the King of its only flight square.

Winning with Pawns

Endings in which Pawns are involved are by far the most common, as well as the most difficult, endings. The object in all of them is, of course, to convert a

Pawn or Pawns into higher pieces, usually Queens (though sometimes it is more effective to convert a Pawn into a Rook or even a minor piece). The principles to be learned revolve around the protection and advancement of Pawns, for one side, and the obstruction and destruction of Pawns, for the other.

We will divide this pawn-ending section into three divisions: endings with minor pieces, endings with Rooks (which occur most frequently) and endings with Pawns alone. Each has its problems.

PAWN ENDINGS WITH MINOR PIECES

Except for some unusual circumstances, a Pawn supported by a minor piece can win. Take the following position, for example:

DIAGRAM 190

If Black, who has the move, takes time to capture the Knight, the Pawn will immediately move forward and go on to Queen. If Black, instead, tries to block the Pawn's path with K—N4, White will simply move his King up, relieving the Knight of its guard duty and freeing it to harass and dislodge the enemy King.

The weaker side can force a draw when the stronger side makes the mistake of trying to defend the Pawn with the Knight posted in front of it. In such a case both Pawn and Knight can be attacked; once the Pawn

DIAGRAM 191

is captured, of course, the game is drawn, since the Knight and King cannot mate. In the following example Black can save the game—that is, he can force a draw—by playing K—Q4.

With 1 . . . K—Q4 Black attacks Knight and Pawn. The Knight cannot move to a position from which it can defend the Pawn, and the White King cannot provide protection either. White can save the Knight but not the game. It will be drawn.

The rule then, is: Knight protection for a Pawn should come from behind.

If a hostile King then attacks Knight and Pawn, the Pawn can advance once the Knight has been captured. If, however, the Pawn is protected from in front, it too can be captured.

Try arranging a Knight, Pawn and King on one side and a lone King on the other in several different positions, protecting the Pawn sometimes from the rear and sometimes from the front. You will see that when the Pawn has protection from the rear it is impossible to stop it from Queening if the Knight is captured.

There is, incidentally, an easy way to determine whether a Pawn pursued by a King can reach its eighth rank first. Draw a line diagonally from the Pawn to the rank it is trying to reach; then build a square around the diagonal. If the attacking King is within this square, or has the move and can enter the square on the move, it will be able to overtake and capture the Pawn in time to stop it from Queening. In diagram 192A below if Black has the move his King will be able to enter the square at once; thus he will be able to stop the Pawn from Queening. In diagram "B" the Black King, even if he has the move, will be unable to enter the square in time to halt the Pawn.

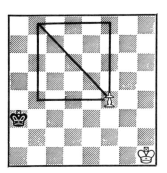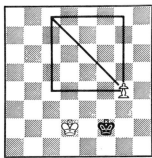

DIAGRAM 192A   DIAGRAM 192B

Two additional factors must be taken into account when using this method: 1. Interference in the path of the pursuing King, and 2. The two-square initial move of a Pawn (that is, if the Pawn is on its second rank the diagonal must be drawn from the third rank).

Back, though, to Pawn-and-minor-piece endings. In the following position Black has an easy win.

DIAGRAM 193

White, of course, will try to stop the Pawn by occupying its Queening square (White's KR1, Black's KR8). Black's object is to get the Pawn to that square. It is, as we said, an easy win—but Black, in his haste, must not push the Pawn to his seventh rank too quickly. Suppose he did:

| 1 | . . . | P—R7ch |
| 2 | K—R1 | drawn |

The Black King must now abandon the Pawn; if it moves in to protect it the position will become stalemated. If Black tries 2 . . . N—B7ch White captures the Pawn.

The correct line of play (from the diagram above) is:

1	. . .	K—N6
2	K—R1	N—B7ch
3	K—N1	P—R7ch

The White King must now go to B1, allowing the Pawn to reach its eighth rank.

Odd things can happen when the roles are, so to speak, reversed—that is, when there is a Pawn and King on one side and a Pawn and Knight on the other. The Knight-side can, for example, win when the Pawn is a Rook Pawn. This is one case in which an advanced Pawn proves to be a liability instead of an asset. Watch.

DIAGRAM 194

The play from the position shown runs as follows:

1	N—N4ch	K—R8 (forced)
2	K—B1	P—R7 (forced)
3	N—B2 mate	

The Pawn prevents the escape of its King.

A Bishop provides more than adequate support for a Pawn and, when the attacking King takes an active role, there is ordinarily no way to stop the supported Pawn. In the following position, for example, the three attacking men—King, Bishop and Pawn—form a solid wedge which the defending King is unable to break.

DIAGRAM 195

The White Rook Pawn cannot be stopped from Queening.

Even when the Bishop moves on squares of a color opposite to that of the Queening square it can effectively clear the way for a Pawn. As in the following example.

DIAGRAM 196

Black's object, of course, is to get the Pawn to R8. Therefore, he plays 1 . . . P—R6. White's reply, 2 K—B2, threatens to prevent this and force a stalemate by bringing the King to QR1 by way of QN1. But Black, using the Bishop effectively, stops this; he plays 2 . . . B—R7.

To get the King to QR1 now, or to stop the Pawn by capturing it, White will have to make a circuitous route, which will give the Black King time to plant himself solidly between his other men. The result will be similar to that of diagram 195, with colors reversed.

ROOK AND PAWN ENDINGS

By far the most frequently occurring endings are those in which each side has Rooks and a Pawn or Pawns, and those in which Pawns alone are on the board.

Before going into the rather complicated Rook-and-Pawn endings, it would be well to get acquainted with two standard positions, one a position in which the weaker side must yield, the other a position in which the weaker side can draw.

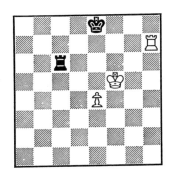

DIAGRAM 197

This is known as Philidor's drawn position; with proper play Black can force a draw although he is a Pawn down. The principle upon which he relies is that the stronger side cannot force a win if the defending King occupies the Queening square.

To carry out his plan the defending side must post his Rook on his third rank and simply shuttle back and forth there until the advancing Pawn reaches that rank. Once the Pawn has reached that point its King can no longer use it as a shield. It is then time for the weaker side to attack from the rear and, by so doing, capture the Pawn.

Thus, the play from diagram 197 might run as follows:

1	P—K5	R—QN3
2	P—K6	R—N8
3	K—B6	R—B1ch

and the position becomes a draw.

Tarrasch has shown that even when the defending King has been forced off the Queening square he can bring about a draw if the defending Rook stands on the larger part of the board, measured from the file on which the Pawn stands, and if he checks the stronger King from the flank at a distance of no less than three files. The weaker King must stand in the smaller part of the board, measured from the file on which the Pawn stands. To illustrate this, let's go back to the position of diagram 197, and have the play run as follows:

1	P—K5	R—B8
2	K—B6	R—B8ch
3	K—K6	. . .

The weaker side, as you see, failed to observe the rule of shuttling the Rook along the third rank until the Pawn had reached that rank. The attacking King can now find shelter behind (or in front of, from his point of view) his Pawn.

DIAGRAM 198

Position after 3 K—K6

White now threatens mate with R—R8. But it is still Black's move. He has a choice of 3 . . . K—Q1 or 3 . . . K—B1. But to follow the principles laid down above he must move his King to the smaller side of the board, measured from the file on which the Pawn stands; therefore he must, to be able to draw, move to B1. The play is:

3	. . .	K—B1
4	R—R8ch	K—N2
5	R—K8	. . .

Now, to carry out the other requisite, Black moves his Rook to the larger side of the board.

| 5 | . . . | R—QR8 |

And, through a series of checks from the flank Black brings about a draw.

The other standard position—the one in which the weak side must yield—is the following:

DIAGRAM 199

This is known as Lucena's Winning Position. It occurs fairly often in play. White's object is to force the Black King away, making room for his own King to move to B7 and support the Pawn as it queens. His secondary object is to prepare to interpose his own Rook safely when Black seeks a draw through check.

The play from diagram 199 might run as follows:

| 1 | . . . | R—R6 |

Black keeps his Rook on the King Rook file to prevent White's occupying it with his Rook and, subsequently, with his King. (If Black moved his Rook off the file the play might be like this: 1 . . . R—K7; 2 R—KR1, R—N7; 3 K—R7, K—B2; 4 R—B1ch and Black must either sacrifice his Rook or permit the Pawn to queen.)

| 2 | R—B5 | . . . |

White plays his Rook to his fifth rank to be able to interpose it safely.

2	. . .	R—R8
3	R—K5ch	K—Q2
4	K—B7	. . .

Object No. 1 apparently achieved.

| 4 | . . . | R—B8ch |
| 5 | K—N6 | R—N8ch |

and now we see why White played 2 R—B5

| 6 | R—N5 | |

Black can do nothing to stop the Pawn now.

From these two standard positions and the play that results we can draw several rather general conclusions that can be applied to Rook-and-Pawn endings. One is that, in most positions, the King must support his Pawns from in front of them; he must, in effect, run interference for them. Another is that Rooks belong behind their own Pawns, supporting them from the rear. A corollary of this is that Rooks must try to stop enemy Pawns by attack from the rear.

In the following position White is a passed Pawn to the good. But his Rook is poorly placed and, as a result, Black should be able to force a draw.

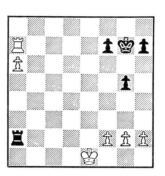

DIAGRAM 200

White's Rook belongs behind the passed Pawn. Posted in front of it, it only holds up the Pawn's progress and leaves it exposed to attack. Black has posted his Rook aggressively. White will try to drive off the opposing Rook—that is, get it off the Queen Rook file. Black will push forward with his Pawns and King, seeking a breakthrough. If White gets too occupied with the Rook-chase, he will soon find himself in a dangerous situation.

The play might run like this:

| 1 | K—Q1 | K—N3 |

(1 . . . R×BP would be followed by 2 R—B7 and White would then be able to improve his Rook's position, well worth the sacrifice of the Pawn.)

2	K—B1	P—R4
3	K—N1	R—R4
4	K—N2	P—B4
5	K—N3	P—B5

DIAGRAM 201

Position after 5 . . . P—B5

At this point White can elect to continue his pursuit of the Rook, in which case Black is sure to break through with a Pawn, or he can break off the attack to protect his King side. In either case the best he can hope for is a draw.

Had his Rook been properly placed the passed Pawn would have insured victory.

Another—and most important—factor to be considered in posting the Rook in the end game is mobility. A Rook that can switch from Queen side to King side with ease is in a much more powerful position than a Rook that is more or less frozen to one side of the board.

DIAGRAM 202

In this position the White Rook is immobile and more a source of trouble than a help. The Black Rook, on the other hand, can swing easily to the opposite wing and help in the coming attack on the White Queen-side Pawn configuration.

When both sides have mobile Rooks each must carefully appraise each change in position and be quick to seize every opportunity for posting his Rook aggressively. In the following position, for example, both Rooks are flexible, each side has a potential Queen in its passed Pawn and the Kings are in analogous positions.

DIAGRAM 203

If it were Black's move he would be wrong to play 1 . . . R—QR1. Passed pawns, remember, must be attacked from the rear. Black's best bet is 1 . . . R—Q7ch, to be followed by R—QR7, posting the Rook behind the passed Pawn. If White had the move he would do well to play 1 R—QR1, stationing his Rook behind and giving support to his passed Pawn.

Before going on to other kinds of end games, let's examine a Rook-and-Pawn end game from actual play, in this case a game between Richard Reti, a formidable master, and Alexander Alekhine. The game was played at the Vienna International Tournament in 1922. The position shown in the diagram below was reached with Black's 30th move. Alekhine played White.

DIAGRAM 204

| 31 | R—K6 | . . . |

With this move White attacks two Pawns at once—the KBP and the QRP. Black cannot protect both at once, so one must fall. But this is chess on a level that few players can ever hope to reach, and Black is not finished yet.

31	. . .	K—N2
32	R×RP	R—QB5
33	R—B3	. . .

White does not try to defend the QB Pawn with 33 R—B2, because this would be followed by 33 . . . R/N2—B2 and the defense would be inadequate.

| 33 | . . . | R×P |
| 34 | P—QR3 | K—B2 |

This keeps White from playing R—N3ch, which would be followed by R—N6 and the loss of another Pawn.

35	R—KN3	R—B7
36	R—KN6	R×BP
37	R×RP	K—N2
38	R—KR4	P—N5

This thrust of the Pawn is a powerful threat. White meets it with counterplay on the opposite wing.

| 39 | R—N4ch | K—B2 |
| 40 | R—N3 | . . . |

The check gave White a chance to bring the Rook to the third rank to defend the Queen's side.

| 40 | . . . | R/B4—QN4 |

The game went on for nineteen more moves and ended as a draw. The position after White's 57th move was

DIAGRAM 205

Position after White's 57th move

Black now played 57 . . . R×P, forcing a draw from what, with less accurate play, would have been a certain loss.

The game ended with

| 58 | R×R | P×Rch |
| 59 | K×P | K–N2 |

The Black King can now stop the White QRP, after first disposing of the KRP.

This end game is an excellent example of how mobility and centralization vitally affect the outcome. You may have noticed that both players apparently broke a lot of rules—such as not posting a Rook behind a passed Pawn. But there are, as has been said before, exceptions to the rules (and, in fact, we noted that the only true rule of chess was that there are no ironbound rules at all).

The important thing to notice is that neither player just waded in blindly, capturing what was obviously capturable and checking when a check was available. Every move had its reason, and both sides tried to keep their pieces as mobile and flexible as possible.

PAWN ENDINGS

Pawns, as you have already seen, are not the lowly things they are often made out to be but are, in fact, the very stuff of which end games are made. The rule of thumb spoken of earlier gave a Knight a value of three Pawns, but in the end one Pawn can be worth far more than two Knights (the one Pawn being a potential Queen; the two Knights being quite incapable of forcing checkmate).

An end game with Pawns alone, then, might well be considered a sort of ideal end game—ideal in the sense that such an end game has been reduced to its barest essentials, to its hard and irreducible core.

The basic problem in a Pawn end game is to force

at least one Pawn through to its eighth rank and to do so before the enemy has had a chance to do the same. With this in mind, consider the following situation:

DIAGRAM 206

White's object is to push the Pawn to B8; Black's object is to stop the Pawn. Naturally Black has no chance of winning, but he can—with improper play on White's part—turn a loss into a draw.

How does White go about ensuring victory?

Not, as you might think, by giving the Pawn a mighty first shove in the right direction. For 1 P–B4 loses (or rather draws) at once. Here is what would happen after 1 P–B4:

1	. . .	K–N2
2	K–N2	K–B3 (or K–N3)
3	K–N3	K–B4
4	K–B3	. . .

DIAGRAM 207

Position after 4 K–B3

The Kings are in opposition. Fine, you say, having learned (and remembered, we hope) that the opposition is usually favorable for the attacking side. The catch is that word "usually"; for this is one of those unusual positions. The opposition works here only when the King stands in front of the Pawn; it is not only useless but also disadvantageous when the opposition is brought about with the attacking King behind or beside his Pawn. As we said before, the King's role is to run interference for his Pawn.

The play continues:

4	. . .	K—B3
5	K—N4	K—N3
or 5	K—K4	K—K3
6	P—B5ch	K—B3
7	K—B4	K—B2

(notice that the Kings are shuffling around the Pawn, one side ready to attack it if the other leaves; the other side ready to push it forward if the defense relaxes)

8	K—N5	K—N2
9	P—B6ch	K—B2
10	K—B5	K—B1

This move by Black just about clinches the draw.

11	K—N6	K—N1
12	P—B7ch	. . .

And this move by White finishes the job.

12	. . .	K—B1
13	K—B6	

Stalemate. Of course White didn't have to make that move; he could have tried, say, K—R2 or K—B5, in which case he would have lost the Pawn and the game would have been drawn anyhow.

Black could have thrown the game away, despite White's faulty play (White's first error was playing 1 P—B4), on his tenth move. Had Black played 10 . . . K—N1 White could have followed through with 11 K—N6 because—

When the attacking King is on the sixth rank, the opposition, even with the Pawn alongside the King, wins.

DIAGRAM 208

Position after 11 K—N6

The play would then continue as follows:

11	. . .	K—B1

(if Black tries 11 . . . K—R1, White, of course, has a free path for his Pawn)

12	P—B7	. . .

This is the key to victory. The Pawn has reached its seventh rank without giving check.

12	. . .	K—K2
13	K—N7	any move
14	P—B8/Q	and wins

This victory was, as you have seen, a result of Black's error on the 10th move. Had Black played correctly, as in the first variation (you might as well get used to this term "variation"; it is used to describe divergent lines of play and is probably the most common word in the chess student's vocabulary), White could have done no better than a draw.

But had White played correctly right off the bat Black could have done nothing to stop the coming checkmate. And what is the correct play from diagram 206?

It is 1 K—N2 and the object of this move is to gain the opposition with the King in front of the Pawn. The play continues as follows:

1	. . .	K—N2
2	K—N3	K—N3
3	K—N4	K—B3
4	K—B4	. . .

The Kings are now in opposition with the Pawn behind the stronger King. In addition, if Black tries to wriggle out of this uncomfortable position by forcing White into zugzwang, White has a time-killing move (known as a waiting move) in reserve: P—B3.

In this position Black has to give way. If he moves to the side, White moves in the opposite direction or straight ahead. If he moves backward White again moves to the side or ahead. This maneuver gains ground for the aggressor.

4	. . .	K—N3
5	K—K5	K—B2
6	K—B5	. . .

Little by little the White King squeezes the Black King into a tighter and tighter bind, gaining space all the while.

6	. . .	K—K2
7	K—N6	. . .

Notice how, when the Black King ducks off to one side, the White King moves forward on the opposite diagonal.

7 . . .   K—B1

White now obtains the opposition again.

8 K—B6   K—N1

And now, with everything secure, the Pawn can proceed.

9 P—B4   K—B1
10 P—B5   K—N1
11 K—K7   . . .

No matter what Black does now he loses. For example:

11 . . .   K—N2
12 P—B6ch   K—N1
13 P—B7ch   . . .

This is possible because the King already stands on the seventh rank.

13 . . .   K—N2
14 P—B8/Q   and wins

Going back to diagram 206, if it were Black's move he could obtain a draw because he would be able to secure the opposition. For example:

1 . . .   K—N2
2 K—N2   K—N3
3 K—N3   K—N4
4 K—B3   K—B4

The Kings are in opposition, but this time White has to move (notice that if the Kings were in opposition on a different file White would have the reserve move P—B3 and would thus be able to force Black, through zugzwang, to give up the opposition), giving up the opposition and letting victory slip away.

5 K—N3   K—N4
6 P—B4ch   K—B4

And we are in the same position that came about when White mistakenly played 1 P—B4.

Time—in the form of the move, the opposition and zugzwang—plays a powerful part in the end game. And it should be obvious, too, that the handling of Pawns is not just a simple matter of pushing them. They must be pushed, true enough, but only at the right moments.

The Rook Pawns, as you may have noticed, seem to have a special life of their own, a rather circumscribed life because of the immovable fence on one side. The fence restricts the movements of the King, who tries to shepherd them to their eighth rank, and therefore makes the reaching of that rank difficult, if not impossible.

A Rook Pawn, in fact, is good for no more than a draw if the defending King can occupy the Queening square at the right moment.

In the following position Black can force a draw if he has the move:

DIAGRAM 209

With 1 . . . K—B2 Black takes the initiative and will be able to scoot into the corner, blocking the Queening and forcing a draw. The play might run like this:

1 . . .   K—B2
2 K—R7   K—B1
3 K—N6
or 3 P—R6   K—N1

and White can do nothing to prevent the stalemate.

If, in the same position, White had the move he could win with 1 K—N7. This would prevent the Black King from approaching the corner and would insure the Pawn's reaching its goal.

When more than one Pawn is on the board the play, naturally, becomes more involved. The goal remains the same, however: Pawn to the eighth rank.

As a rule (that misleading word again!) a Pawn majority can be turned into a passed Pawn. As in the following position (here confined to its essentials):

DIAGRAM 210

White has three King-side Pawns to Black's two. He should be able to force one of them through (whether, subsequently, he sends the lone passed Pawn on to become a Queen is not our concern here; we have already dealt with the problems and techniques of escorting a single Pawn to its goal). The question is: how does White go about it?

White must, first of all, consider which of the three Pawns is most likely to succeed, and he does this by deciding which faces the least opposition. In this case it is the King Bishop Pawn, there being no vis-a-vis opposition on that file. The KBP, then, becomes the spearhead of the drive; he will be supported by the other Pawns.

The play is simplicity itself:

| 1 | P—B4 | P—N3, or P—R3 |
| 2 | P—N4 | |

and the BP must go on to Queen.

| if | 1 | . . . | P—B4 |
| then | 2 | P—B5 | |

Nor will 1 . . . P—R4 work.

Try this play out for yourself, starting first with other Pawn moves and then with 1 P—B4. Try varying Black's answers, too. You will see that 1 P—B4 is the key to success.

Now let's put the Kings into the picture.

DIAGRAM 211

White has the Pawn majority. He also has the advantage of havings Pawns that can protect each other. Black, on the other hand not only has a minority of Pawns, but also they are isolated as well.

Still, turning the Pawn surplus into a victory requires the right approach. And that approach begins with 1 K—B3.

The King plays the most important role. He clears the way for the Pawns, protects them from the enemy King and sees them through to their destination. The play might run as follows:

1	K—B3	K—N3
2	K—B4	K—B3
3	P—B3	K—N3
4	P—R3	K—B3

The Black King, you see, has nothing better to do than shuttle back and forth between B3 and N3, with perhaps an occasional side trip to R3 if White relaxes his observation of the Black BP.

5 P—N4

And White is now ready to break through.

Ideally, an attacking King assaults a Pawn from the front, as follows:

DIAGRAM 212

If, however, such an attack is made impossible by the hostile King, more subtle methods have to be used. As, for example, in the following situation:

DIAGRAM 213

Black's object is the capture of the White Pawn, which blockades the Black Pawn and prevents its reaching the eighth rank. But the direct approach will not work; White will simply counter each move and the result will be a stately, somewhat ridiculous and completely ineffectual (for Black) dance of the Kings.

Black has to go about his job in a roundabout way, using as his weapon zugzwang. The play is:

| 1 | . . . | K—R6 |
| 2 | K—B1 | . . . |

(if 2 K—Q2 then 2 . . . K—N6; 3 K—K2, K—B7
and White must abandon the Pawn there and then)

2	. . .	K—N6
3	K—Q2	K—N7
4	K—Q1	K—B6
5	K—K2	K—B7

DIAGRAM 214

Position after 5 . . . K—B7

White is in zugzwang; he must move and abandon
the Pawn. Black, by constantly forcing the moves,
maneuvered the White King into a position where, with
the Kings in opposition, White had to move. White
tried to avoid this by giving way, but each time he did
Black dexterously took advantage of this by cutting
into White's available space.

The indirect approach is, as you see, often far more
direct than an all-out frontal assault.

STOP!

How well have you digested the food-for-thought
served up in the last few sections?

Self-Testing Quiz No. 13

(a) In the following position it is White's move. If
he captures the Bishop the game will be a draw. How
can he force a win most quickly?

DIAGRAM 215

(b) White has the move in the following position.
How can he capture the Black Pawn and prevent the
capture of his own?

DIAGRAM 216

(c) If it were Black's turn to move in the above position how could he force a win?

(d) In the following position Black, a Pawn up,
threatens mate on the move. But it is White's turn to
move. Can he salvage the game? What is the best he
can expect and how does he go about obtaining that
best?

DIAGRAM 217

(e) Black has the move in the following position.
What is Black's big advantage and what move can he
make to exploit that advantage?

DIAGRAM 218

(f) Black has a winning move in the following position. What is it?

DIAGRAM 219

Mixed Endings

Mixed endings refer to those end games not covered by the basic mates or Pawn-and-piece combinations. All sorts of combinations can crop up from time to time, though the great majority of endings will fall into one of the categories discussed so far.

What do you do, however, when you are faced with an end game in which one side had a passed Pawn and the other a Rook? Can the Rook win, or will the game be a draw (there is no sense in maneuvering for hours on end if it is mathematically impossible to win)?

The side with the Rook can win only if the King on the other side is unable to support the Pawn. Or, put the other way, a Pawn is as good as a Rook when the King gives it support. The following position, for example, is a draw if White has the move; if Black has the move he can win.

DIAGRAM 220

White, with the move, can force a draw. If he plays 1 P—R4 he can push the Pawn fast enough the get it to the seventh rank before Black can capture it with impunity. The moves might be as follows:

1	. . .	K—B6
2	P—R5	K—Q5
3	P—R6	R—KR6
4	K—N6	K—K4
5	P—R7	K—K3
6	K—N7	

The draw is inevitable; Black must sacrifice the Rook to halt the Pawn. The Kings will be alone on the board.

If Black has the move, however, he can win at once with 1 . . . R—KR6. The Pawn cannot be saved and the basic mate with King and Rook follows.

There are, however, some "gimmicks" that can be used by the Rook-side under certain circumstances. If the defending King, for example, is on his third rank, the Rook can fence him off from the fourth rank and, later, pick off the Pawn.

DIAGRAM 221

The Black (defending) King is on his third rank. White therefore plays 1 R—R5, cutting the King off from the fourth rank. Black cannot save the Pawn now. If he pushes it, White simply follows through with R—R3. The play might run this way:

1	R—R5	P—Q6
2	R—R3	P—Q7
3	R—Q3	

and the Pawn falls.

If we alter the position slightly to give Black what looks like more of a fair chance, the system still works.

DIAGRAM 222

The Black King is now somewhat nearer his Pawn. The play would run this way:

| 1 | R—R5 | K—B3 |
| 2 | R—R4 | . . . |

If Black takes time to attack the Rook the Pawn falls at once. If he pushes the Pawn the game continues as follows:

| 2 | ... | P—Q6 |
| 3 | R—Q4 | |

and still the Pawn falls.

Notice that this is a case in which the Rook's place is *not* behind the Pawn; it is one of the exceptions to that general rule.

How about two Pawns—can they win against a Rook? Again other factors must be taken into account. They will win if the Rook's King is not around to join in the attack. As in the following example:

DIAGRAM 223

If White has the move in the position above the best he can do against the protected and united Pawns on the sixth rank is draw. The play might run like this:

| 1 | R×P | K—R7 |
| 2 | R—B6 | ... |

(there is no point in trying to get the White King into action; he is too far away to make it in time)

| 2 | ... | P—N7 |

The Rook must sacrifice himself for the Pawn.

If Black had the move in the same position he would win; the Rook might sacrifice himself for one of the Pawns, but the other would go on to Queen.

Putting the White King into the picture, though, changes everything:

DIAGRAM 224

Even if Black has the move here he cannot win. For example:

1	...	P—B7ch
2	K—B1	K—R7
3	R—R1	K—R6
4	K—K2	K—N7
5	R—QN1	

Black is in zugzwang; he must abandon one of his Pawns; the second will follow into oblivion shortly thereafter.

An end game involving Bishops that move on squares of different colors can be an interesting struggle. If the side with Pawns plays poorly or indifferently, a draw can be forced. But with proper play a win is possible. Philidor laid down a rule for such a play. It states that the Pawns must be placed so as not to interfere with their own Bishop. The side with a Bishop operating on dark squares must try to keep its Pawns on light squares and vice versa. This also serves to give the Bishop room to dislodge enemy men that insert themselves among the Pawns and stop their progress.

Here's an example of the application of this rule:

DIAGRAM 225

Before considering the course of action to be followed by the attacker, let's look at the situation as it stands. White has a far advanced passed Pawn but he cannot immediately push it the one square it needs to become a Queen—it would be captured by the Bishop. Black has two united passed Pawns on his critical sixth rank. But he cannot push them either, at the moment; the White King, supported by the Bishop, guards the area.

By Philidor's rule Black ought to push his Queen Pawn rather than his Bishop Pawn so as not to obstruct the movement of his Bishop. But to get his Queen Pawn to Q7, Black will have to give it protection, by moving his King to K7 or QB7. White can try to delay this by playing K—K1 or B—B6ch. Here is what might happen:

1 . . .	B—R4

(protecting the Queening square)

2 B—B6ch	K—B5

(2 . . . K—K5, of course, loses the Pawn)

3 B—N5	. . .

(the Bishop must get back there to stop P—Q7ch)

3 . . .	K—Q4
4 B—R6	. . .

(the White Bishop can only mark time on the diagonal)

4 . . .	K—K5
5 B—N5	K—KB6
6 K—N1	K—K7

And it's all over but the checkmate.

White could also have tried to get the Black Bishop off the diagonal by sacrificing his advanced Pawn. But after P—K8/Q and B×Q the Black Bishop could easily have swung back or, for that matter, across to the Queen's side, to QR5, where it would be just as effective.

The story is different when the opposing Bishops operate on squares of the same color. In such a case even a single Pawn is sufficient to turn the trick. The way to do it is quite simple: the side with the Pawn confronts the opposing Bishop with his own twice—once from in front of the Pawn, once from a position next to it.

DIAGRAM 226

In accordance with the system, White plays 1 B—B7, confronting the Black Bishop from in front of the Pawn. Black cannot accept the exchange; he must get his Bishop out of there and over to another square from which White's KB7 can be kept under observation. Black, therefore, plays 1 . . . B—K7, preparatory to moving his Bishop to his KR4. White plays 2

B—N8, planning to get his Bishop by a zig-zag motion to his KN6. Black plays 2 . . . B—R4 and White follows with 3 B—R7. Black, trying to put sufficient pressure on the square in front of the Pawn, plays 3 . . . K—K3. White now confronts the Black Bishop the second time, from alongside the Pawn; he plays 4 B—N6.

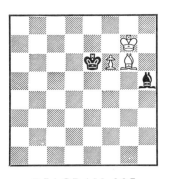

DIAGRAM 227

Position after 4 B—N6

There is no way out for Black. If he plays 5 . . . B×B, the White King recaptures and the final push of the Pawn cannot be stopped. If he tries to salvage the Bishop by moving off the diagonal White plays 6 P—B7 at once and the Bishop does not have time to find another square from which it can sweep the crucial point KB2; the Pawn will Queen on its next step.

This, of course, does not nearly exhaust the possibilities of end-game combinations. To go into the various other types—Pawn and Knight vs. Rook, two Knights vs. three Pawns, etc.—would require much more time and space than should be allotted in a book for beginners. As your game improves, as you come to handle your pieces with more assurance you may want to study these other endings. If so, you are referred to the list of further reading in Chapter 13 and the list of books on end game.

You aren't being short-changed, though. The vast majority of games you play will either end in the middle game or will turn into one of the end games we have described. The others are really quite rare, as you will learn through your own experience.

Before we leave the subject of end games, however, we will consider two more aspects: the blockade and stalemates.

Passed Pawns, as you know, grow in strength as they approach their goal and, when they reach their sixth rank, seem to exert tremendous pressure on the defenders. Obviously, then, it's a good idea for the defender to keep them from reaching the sixth rank (and, of course, the eighth). And one way to do this is to set up a blockade.

DIAGRAM 228

Here, for example, Black has blockaded, with his Rook, the White Pawn. This is the primitive situation, so to speak: one Pawn, one piece blockading it. White's hand is forced; he must play 1 K—Q4 to protect his one remaining hope. Black will then play 1 . . . K-Q3 and a temporary impasse will have been reached. In this situation, though, the opposition is just too much for the Pawn; he will eventually fall, for White, by a series of checks from the flank, will force the King to abandon his foot soldier.

Now, however, let us examine a somewhat more complex situation.

DIAGRAM 229

Here the two White pieces, instead of trying to block the Pawn, are simply "keeping it under observation"; if it moves, it can be captured. What is the result?

White, in effect, immobilizes two pieces—his only two pieces—by chaining them to the job of watching the Pawn. He cannot remove one of the guards without upsetting the whole structure. (Suppose, for example, he played B—B1; Black could then play P—Q5 with complete safety because the Pawn could not be captured—and the Pawn would be that much closer to its goal.)

If White keeps the set-up intact with, say, 1 B—R1, Black can still play 1 . . . P—Q5, sacrificing the Pawn for an open file for his Rook and an open diagonal for his Bishop. The dead Pawn breathes life into the Black pieces.

White's best bet is to blockade the Pawn at once with N—Q4. This not only fixes the Pawn, but it also gives the Knight a central square from which to exert his strength. And remember, too, that the blockading piece is, in effect, protected not only by his own men, but by the enemy Pawn as well; the Pawn shuts off the file and forestalls a frontal attack on the blockading piece.

Sometimes the blockade can be broken by forcing a change in blockading pieces.

DIAGRAM 230

Materially, Black is ahead, but positionally he is weak. His Bishop at this point serves only one function—to blockade the Rook Pawn. The White King cannot approach the blockader to attack it without losing valuable time. If, however, the Rook instead of the Bishop, were doing the blockading, the King could move at once to N7 and force the issue. So—

1	R—Q8ch	R—N1
2	R×B	R×R
3	K—N7	R—Q1
4	P—R8/Q	R×Q
5	K×R	

White now has a won end game. By the process described earlier in this chapter he will force the Black King to give up his Pawn and the White Pawn will go on to Queen.

Stalemate

Stalemate is only chess-talk for a draw, though of a particular kind. Both players may agree to a draw when it becomes obvious (or seems to be obvious) that neither one is going to get the upper hand. This is not stalemate. It is only an armistice.

Stalemate comes about when the player whose turn it is to move cannot do so, having no legal moves at his disposal. The player who is far behind and sees no chance for victory would do well to look for a way to bring about a stalemate. Better half a point than none at all.

The example that follows shows how carelessness can bring about stalemate.

DIAGRAM 231

It is Black's move. Everything has gone his way so far—obviously. And it is evident, too, that he has played according to Hoyle. His King escorted the advanced Knight Pawn on the road to glory; the Rook lent his support from the rear; the Bishop kept the enemy King at a distance. White, left with nothing more than a blockaded Pawn, has nothing to look forward to—unless Black, at the last moment, throws away the fruits of his labor.

If Black plays 1 . . . P–N8/Q the game is a draw. It then is White's turn to move and what can he move? Nothing. The Pawn is stuck and the King cannot legally budge. He is not in check and therefore the game is stalemate.

This is one case in which a Pawn must be under-promoted; he must become, not a Queen, but a Knight. The final move of the game would then be:

1 . . .   **P–N8/N mate**

Here is a fascinating example of how a beleaguered player can turn a loss into a draw. This is the end of a game, played in the Rostov-on-Don Championship tournament in 1959. Bebchuk had the White pieces, Zubikov the Black. The position after Black's 12th move (12 . . . Q×RP) was as follows:

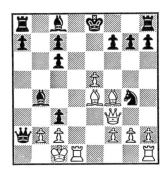

DIAGRAM 232

The first thing that strikes the eye is that, if Black had the move, he could mate at once, with Q–R8. It's also apparent that Black has an edge in material (be-

ing a minor piece and a Pawn to the good, although the tripled Pawns on the Queen Bishop file are vulnerable). But White, though in a shaky situation, manages to turn a loss into a draw by capitalizing on the exposed position of Black's uncastled King.

The game went on:

| 13 | B×Pch | K–B1 |
| 14 | R–Q8ch | . . . |

White, of course, cannot ease up for a moment; Black still threatens mate on the move.

14	. . .	K–K2
15	B–N5ch	P–B3
16	P×Pch	P×P
17	R–K1ch	B–K3

(Black cannot play K–B2 for this would be followed by 18 B–Q5ch and Black would lose his Queen; he cannot play K×R either, for this would allow a forced mate in three moves.)

| 18 | R–Q7ch | K–B1 |

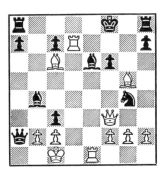

DIAGRAM 233

Position after 18 . . . K–B1

19	B–R6ch	N×B
20	Q×Pch	N–B2
21	R×Nch	B×R
22	Q×Rch	B–N1
23	Q–B6ch	B–B2
24	Q–R8ch	B–N1
25	Q–B6ch	drawn

This is stalemate by perpetual check. White can keep shifting his Queen back and forth, giving check now at R8, now at B6; Black can keep shifting the Bishop to block the check. White, of course, cannot make a move without check because Black continues, all this while, to threaten mate with one move. Black, on the other hand, cannot try for a win with Q—B2 (in anticipation of Q×Qch, B×Q; B×R, P×Pch, which would give Black a winning material advantage) because White could then play Q—R6ch, Q—N2; Q—B4ch, which would give White a Bishop and a Rook.

Both sides had to use caution and the most cautious moves available led to perpetual check and stalemate.

You saw another example of forcing a draw, in the end game between Alekhine and Reti earlier in the chapter. Thus, you see, it is possible at times to turn a loss into a draw by bringing about a stalemate. Notice the words "at times"; there are, like it or not, situations in which you will have to lose. The best you can do under those circumstances is resign with dignity (it is only the eccentric genius, like Nimzovich, who can get away with a resignation in which the loser leaps up on the table, knocking the chessboard and pieces in all directions, and shouts "Why must I lose to this idiot?").

Chapter Seven

THE MIDDLE GAME

No Holds Barred

THOUGH IT MAY SOUND painfully obvious, the middle game differs sharply from the other two parts of a chess game in this respect: it has no firm beginning and no definite ending. The opening, of course, starts with the first move; the ending, just as much of course, ends with checkmate, with the resignation of one player or with a draw.

But where does the middle game start? And where does it end?

It starts where the opening ends and it ends where the end game begins. And where is that? Well, we may be able to establish some vague kinds of criteria. We can say with a fair degree of certainty, for example, that once most of the pieces have been developed the opening is over. But has the middle game begun yet? If both sides are still maneuvering for, say, advantage in the center, then some chess analysts would say the game is still in the opening stage; others would hold that the middle game has begun.

And where does it end? Again, we can say it has ended when most of the pieces have been exchanged. But if one side has a Queen and Bishop and five Pawns and the other has two Rooks, a Bishop and six Pawns, is this still middle game? Or has the end game begun? Again, opinions would differ.

Chess, after all—and despite what some of its more vigorous proponents say—is not a science. Exactitude is not the hallmark of chess analysis; the human element plays too big a part for this to be the case.

Many times (most of the time in the games of rank amateurs and grandmasters) the game ends in the middle game, without the end game's ever having been reached. This happens with amateurs because one side or the other—or both—fails to see what is happening; one of the players says "check!" and—to his and his opponent's complete surprise—they find it is not only check, but checkmate, too. With grandmasters the game frequently ends in the middle game because, quite the contrary, both sides can see well ahead; a minute advantage accrues to one of the players, both sides see it and the side that has permitted this advantage to come about feels (and rightly, too) the weakness will only grow worse and worse. He resigns.

The great majority of players—those who fall between the extremes of rank amateur and grandmaster—refuse to resign when a weakness develops. They figure (and rightly, too—again) there is always a chance their opponent may blunder and that things will reverse themselves. They fight on to the bitter end game.

And to all players (except fanatical specialists) the middle game is the best part of chess. Here the preparations end and the battles begin. Here is the clash of forces; here is the chance for dynamic combinations, brilliant sacrifices, powerful attacks. Even the player who is defensive by inclination enjoys the middle game most of all; here he has the opportunity of finding the right defense and reducing to nothing all his opponent's onslaughts. There is certainly a great pleasure to be derived from conducting a well-organized defense.

For the attacking player the middle game is the meat and potatoes of chess—the rest is appetizer and coffee.

For the positional player—the player who relies on quiet, consolidating moves and long-range strategy—the middle game is his chance par excellence to improve his position, tempt his opponent into weakening himself, and then to infiltrate and destroy.

No matter how you slice it, then, the middle game is the most appealing part of a chess contest. The end game, for many, is too logical, too strict, too mechanical; the opening, for many, is too routine, too cut and dried. But the middle game is the breeding ground of surprises—delightful ones for the victor, unnerving ones for the loser. It is the great challenge.

There is another great attraction of the middle game, and this is an attraction it should not really have: it is the undiscovered country. The openings can be taken from "the book"; there is no mystery about them. The end-game positions and rules also can come right out of the book.

But there is no "book" of middle games. The player is strictly on his own, playing in uncharted territory.

This does not mean, however, that there are no guides; on the contrary, there are sound principles to steer around the shoals and reefs. They are not as clear and as well formulated as opening or end-game principles, but they are available nonetheless.

It is the purpose of this chapter to lay down those guiding principles.

The literature of chess is studded with books whose titles run like this: "Great Combinations," "One Hundred Brilliant Games," "A Treasury of Winning Sacrifices." The games contained in these collections are full of fire and dash, slashing attacks and intricate combinations. Most of these winning attacks come in the middle game, and therein lies a clue; if some sort of criteria can be established by which to recognize potential combinations . . .

Combinations, after all, don't just happen; they are made. And it is not surprising that the same players— Marshall, Spielmann, Lasker, Alekhine, to name some of the more famous—came up with "unexpected" or "brilliant" combinations time after time. They were not miracle workers; they simply knew where they were going in the middle game. They created the circumstances that made their sacrificial combinations possible.

These players were able to evaluate a position accurately; they were intimately acquainted with principles.

Basic to those principles are the three elements of any chess position: force, space and time. And since they are so basic, let's examine those elements in some detail.

Force

The element of force is self-evident. If one side has three Pawns to the other side's two, that first side has an advantage in force. And force is the most active of the three elements.

Earlier, you learned that the Queen is the most powerful piece on the board; that the Rook is next in order of power, and so on. But what makes the Queen so strong?

Her speed!

Because she can move along files, ranks or diagonals she can get from any point to any other point (provided there is no obstruction) faster than any other piece; she doesn't have to zig-zag or hop around. If she is on the Queen's wing and her help is needed at the other side of the board, she can get there in a hurry.

Force, then, can be considered as the sum of all the pieces, taking into account their individual and collective speed. (Do not, however, confuse speed with mobility; a piece, such as a Queen, can be capable of great speed, but if its movement is restricted its mobility is nil.)

Other things being equal, an advantage in force, if great enough, should insure victory.

But other things, in chess, are rarely, if ever, equal.

Space

One of the things that keeps "other things" from being equal is the element of space. This is a more subtle factor than force, but it is just as important. It may be —and in fact often is—even more important than force. A player with a marked superiority in force will still lose if he commands no space and his opponent dominates the board. In the following position, for example, Black—though ahead in force—is behind in space and, as a result, is in no position to take advantage of that material superiority.

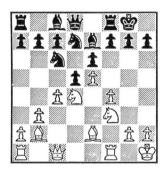

DIAGRAM 234

Black is a Pawn ahead. A plus. But he is confined (and confined is the perfect word) to his own four ranks. White, on the other hand, commands not only his own share of the board, but part of Black's as well. His advanced King Pawn is planted firmly in Black's territory and is well protected. Black cannot play 1 . . . P—B3 because of 2 N×P, forking Queen and Rook.

This is an exaggerated example. Space does not actually have to be occupied to be controlled. Pieces— and even pawns—can control space remotely. As in the following position.

DIAGRAM 235

This position arises from a variation of the Ruy Lopez. White, you see, occupies only one square in enemy territory, the characteristic Bishop at QN5. The Bishop is there only temporarily; for the moment, we can disregard it in figuring White's spatial advantage.

The White King Pawn, though still on its own side of the "frontier," has a strong say in what goes on in Black's camp. It controls the squares Q5 and KB5. The Queen, too, exerts a powerful influence. Now, from a simple mechanical point of view, we can deduce White's advantage. His advanced Pawn and pieces control or sweep a total of 14 points in Black's territory (Black's QR2, QR3, QN3, QB3, QB4, Q1, Q2, Q3, Q4, K4, KB3, KB4, KN2 and KR1). Black's pieces control only three points in White's territory (QN4, QR3 and KR4).

The situation is not as bad as it looks for Black—though it is bad enough—because it is his move.

Here is a position that is less one-sided:

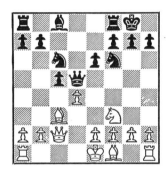

DIAGRAM 236

This position arises in a variation of the Nimzovich-Indian Defense. Examining it from the point of view of force we find that White has a minute advantage—the two Bishops against Black's Knight and Bishop. Now from the point of view of space, where does the advantage, if any, lie?

White pieces strike at (remember, the White pieces "see" through Black pieces, but not through their own) seven Black points (QR4, QB4, K4, KB4, KN3, KN4, and KR2). Black pieces strike at thirteen White squares, almost twice as many. The proportion—or disproportion—is not nearly as bad as in the previous example. In addition, White has the move.

Time

The third element—and the most intangible of the three—is time. Force can be seen and counted. Space, too, can be counted. What about time, though? Can it be mathematically pinned down?

To a certain extent, yes. It is possible to "count tempos." Take the following position, which arose in a game between Capablanca and H. Steiner in Los Angeles in 1933.

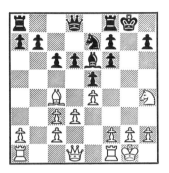

DIAGRAM 237

To count the tempos for White: his Pawn at K4 is one; the Pawn at Q3, two; the Bishop at B4, three; the Knight at R4, five (it required two moves to get the Knight there); castling, six, and the obvious capture at QB3, seven. Black's total is arrived at this way: The Pawn at K4, one; the Pawn at Q3, two; the Pawn at QB3, three; the Bishop at K3, four; the Knight at K2, six (two moves to get there), and the capture at KB3, seven.

The tempi are even.

But this is deceptive. There is no way to tell from the position how many moves were lost by either side; how many times, for example, the White King Bishop had to move to get where it is, or the Black Knight. Captured pieces, of course, carry their tempi with them when they disappear. At best, then, this counting of tempi can only be approximate. And at worst it can be completely misleading, as it is in this example (White has a strong game because of the fractured Pawn position in front of the Black King).

The mere number of moves is misleading, too, because moves must also be reckoned from the point of view of their timing. A move that is good at one point may be bad at another; a series of moves, if inverted in time, may take on a completely different character. Chess, after all, is not played one move at a time, any more than a book is read a word at a time. A well-conducted game is played in sequences of moves.

The Law of Relativity

The three elements, obviously, are not distinct things; they have a vital bearing on each other and the player who tries to ignore one element while concentrating on another will find this out soon enough. An advantage in time can and should be converted ultimately into an advantage in space and from there into an advantage in force (sometimes the middle step can be eliminated and a time advantage can be converted directly into material superiority).

Why convert? Because time alone rarely is sufficient to force victory. Space, properly exploited, can be used to do the job, but it's a ticklish business. Force, on the other hand, is overwhelming. Who, having nothing but a Pawn, would go on fighting if faced with a Rook and Queen?

If you will think back a page or two you will recall that it was said the power of a piece depended upon its speed. And what is speed but an expression of time? Force, then, can be expressed in terms of time. It can also be expressed in terms of space. A Queen commands more space than a Bishop; ergo, she is more powerful; ergo again, she has greater force.

Frequently, an advantage in one element is accompanied by a disadvantage in another. Gambits, for example, are openings in which one side gives up material (force) for a superior development (time and space). The objective you should strive for is a balancing of the elements; to concentrate on one at the expense of the other is to invite defeat.

If, however, you have a powerful advantage in, say, time, you should (some theorists—Steinitz, among others—insisted that "should" was too mild a word; that the player with the powerful advantage was under a moral obligation; that the word is "must") act to convert that advantage into a stable one. In other words, the player with the better position should attack.

You must judge carefully, though. A minimal advantage in one of the more unstable elements (time and space) calls for a cautious procedure; if you rush headlong into an attack it may, and probably will, backfire. Such a minimal advantage demands a slow consolidation of position. A minimal advantage in the more stable element (force), such as a plus of one Pawn, also demands slow and cautious play.

But a strong advantage in time should be converted as quickly as possible into the more stable advantage of space. And a strong advantage in force (say, an extra Rook) calls for a powerful attack at once.

The player who has an advantage in all three elements must play vigorously; if he plays timidly, trying to conserve his advantage instead of using it aggressively, he may find the advantage petering out.

A position—any position—can be analyzed mechanically from the point of view of the three elements. That is, the tempi can be deduced, the space computed and the forces compared. Take, for example, the following:

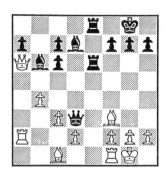

DIAGRAM 238

Force is equal. Tempi? White has eight visible tempi to Black's nine, not too great a disadvantage. Space? Black controls, actually or potentially, 20 squares in White's territory; White controls 17 in Black's. Again, not too great a disadvantage for White.

The position came about with White's 17th move, Q—R6. This was intended to stop the threat of . . . Q×Rch, which would be followed by K×R and then . . . R—K8 mate. What actually followed, after 17 Q—R6, was 17 . . . Q×B.

White has no choice, he must capture the Queen. He cannot afford to play a piece down, especially since he already is behind in time and space. Besides, if he tries anything else, Black can follow through with 18 . . . Q×BPch; 19 R×Q, R—K8 mate.

The sacrifice of the Queen breaks up White's Pawn position in front of the castled King. The game (no point in being coy; Black was the great Paul Morphy, White was Paulsen) continued:

18	P×Q	R—N3ch
19	K—R1	B—R6
20	R—Q1	B—N7ch
21	K—N1	B×Pdis ch
22	K—B1	. . .

Notice that White has no say in what is happening; all his moves are forced.

22	. . .	B—N7ch
23	K—N1	B—R6dis ch
24	K—R1	B×P
25	Q—B1	. . .

White again has little choice; any other move would lead to mate at once; this move prolongs the agony a trifle.

25	. . .	B×Q
26	R×B	. . .

Force is almost even now, but White is woefully behind in space and time. And that is just the arithmetical disadvantage. Positionally, he is through. His Kingside Pawns are gone—except for the inadequate little King Rook Pawn—his pieces have little scope and his King is in stalemate position.

26	. . .	R—K7
27	R—R1	R—R3
28	P—Q4	. . .

A last-ditch attempt to free himself. It doesn't work.

28	. . .	B—K6

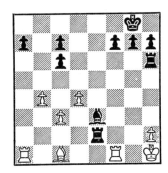

DIAGRAM 239

Position after 28 . . . B—K6

White resigned here. He can do nothing to stop the mate. For example: 29 B×B, R/R3×Pch; 30 K—N1, R/K7—N7 mate.

What happened in this game? How did Black, with only a minimal advantage in the three elements, bring about such a quick victory?

To begin with, the advantage in time was greater than our computation indicated; we did not take into account the fact that it was Black's move. Having the move is always an advantage (unless you are in zugzwang, of course).

Then, Black converted his slight advantage into a new and more powerful imbalance: an inferiority in force (the sacrifice of the Queen) for an overwhelming superiority in space and time. This superiority in the unstable elements manifested itself as a positional advantage.

And therein lies a point to remember: the over-all balance of the three elements must be looked at in light of the general position. When—as in this case—the castled King's Pawn protection is destroyed and

heavy pieces (here, the Rooks) are in a position to bear down upon that weakened King, the defending side must almost inevitably go on losing tempo after tempo to fend off mate. This piling up of tempi (look at all the forced moves White had to make above) results, eventually, in converting the time-advantage into a space advantage. And, as we noted earlier, a space advantage, properly handled, can lead to mate; it need not go through the intermediate stage of being converted to a material advantage. Black, in the example above, could have mated his opponent even if he had been a piece down (as he would have been had White played 29 B×B) because his spatial superiority was too great for White to overcome.

Other points to remember in evaluating a position are:

1. Are the forces coordinated and cooperating with each other or are they only in each other's way?
2. Are the moves on which you base the tempo-count valid moves or do they contribute nothing to the solidity or effectiveness of the position (the move P—KR3, for example, unless specifically warranted by a threat, is a useless move; nevertheless it must be counted in adding up the tempi)?
3. Is a loss in one element—the sacrifice of a Pawn, for example—compensated?
4. If one side has Pawns or pieces posted in enemy territory, are those Pawns or pieces firmly planted? Or are they weak and only targets for attack. Can the side with the outpost pieces keep the supply lines open to support them, or will they have to give up tempi by retreating?
5. Are there tactical possibilities that can affect the plan?

This last point needs more discussion. With the very first moves of a game each side makes plans. Of course, at the outset no definite plan can be formulated. But as the game progresses possibilities present themselves. An idea takes shape: the possibility of a King-side attack, for example, or a chance for a thrust in the center.

Suppose White has noticed a weakness in Black's defenses and has laid a plan to exploit that weakness. Now suppose further that Black makes a move that permits White, at the cost of abandoning his plan, to gain in time, space or material. White must decide whether the gain is worth it. Should he abandon his plan, which calls, say, for a Queen-side attack, to seek an advantage on the King's wing? Is Black baiting a trap? Has he overlooked something?

White must take into account, before making this

decision, the effect upon his chances. Will the shift weaken his position? Will he be able, after this diversion, to re-establish a plan, a strategy? Or will he have to flounder around before being able to coordinate his forces again?

Here is an example of what we mean:

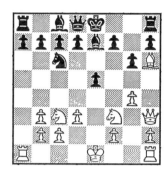

DIAGRAM 240

This position was brought about with White's 11th move (the game was between Alekhine and Levitski; the eighth in a match played at St. Petersburg in March, 1913). White's strategy calls for a King-side attack. He plans to play B—N7, which will force Black's hand. Black will play R—N1 and White will follow through with Q×P, giving him a powerful wedge on Black's crucial second rank.

Black sought at this point a tactical diversion. He played

| 11 . . . | **P—B4** |

White, however, figured—and quite correctly—that he was in no position to abandon his original plan. Had he played P×P, Black would have gone on with 12 . . . P—Q3 and then 13 . . . B×P. This would have forced White to give up his attack and concentrate on the action in the center. White's forces would have become uncoordinated.

The game continued as follows:

| 12 | **B—N7** | **P×P** |
| 13 | **Q—R6** | **B—B1** |

Black feels he has better chances this way. After 13 . . . P×N; 14 B×R he has a lost game.

| 14 | **B×B** | **R×B** |
| 15 | **N—KN5** | |

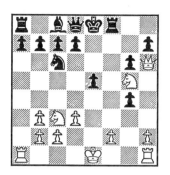

DIAGRAM 241
Position after 15 N—KN5

White, having elected to ignore the tactical diversion, has got his King-side attack rolling. He has, as you see, sacrificed two Pawns (a disadvantage in force) for a superior position and a going attack (advantages in time and space). What actually happened in the rest of the game was that Black, trying to get out of his difficulties, launched a counter-attack in the center. But White's better position (his time-space advantage) gave him the flexibility to meet and overcome that attack. The original plan, calling for an attack on the King from the King's flank, had to be (or rather, could be and was) abandoned to cope with the tactical situation that arose in the center. But White came out of it with coordinated forces and went on to win.

To play without a plan is anarchy; it gets you nowhere and quite quickly at that. But to form a plan and then adhere to it come what may is just as bad; it gets you into trouble. If chess were solitaire it would be feasible to set your sights on one object and pursue it relentlessly. But chess is a clash of minds; your plan must adapt itself to your opponent's ideas as well as to your own. It must be flexible and pliant.

Pawn Play

One of the keys to success in the middle game (as, indeed, in the opening and end game) is your handling of Pawns. You must bear in mind at all times that a Pawn move is forever; you cannot retreat a Pawn from its position—you can only push it ahead. This special power (or lack of power) in Pawns makes them unique, and their handling, of necessity, must be keyed to this condition.

In their initial position, lined up along the second rank, the Pawns present a solid and almost impregnable front. Indeed, if the Pawns were lined up along any rank they would present a formidable kind of Maginot Line (a poor simile; the Maginot Line, though an effective defense, was, we know, not utilized properly. This should not happen in your handling of the Pawns). Once they have moved forward, though, they leave "holes" in the defense. To attack a solid line of Pawns the enemy must maneuver along the files, vertically; to attack Pawns that are staggered or out of touch with each other, he can attack horizontally, vertically, diagonally—any which way.

The "hole" left by the moving of a Pawn is also called a weak square, a somewhat more polite term and, in consequence, preferred by some writers. Whatever you want to call them, here they are:

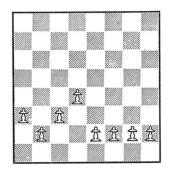

DIAGRAM 242

The Pawn structure here invites trouble in the form of enemy occupation of the holes, or weak squares. In this case the white squares on the Queen's wing are weak. If any enemy piece occupies one of those white squares, White will not be able to dislodge it by Pawn attacks; he will have to bring pieces to bear on the invader. If Black, for example, had a Bishop at his K3 and a Queen at KB2, he could play B—QR7 and feel quite safe in doing so. He would thus occupy the weak square and White would have no Pawn with which to try to pry the Bishop loose. (Knights, it should be said right here, are the pieces par excellence for occupying weak squares. They are particularly troublesome when they can post themselves in a hole and get Pawn protection too.)

The axiom might be put this way: When Pawns are placed on white squares, the black squares are weak; when they are placed on black squares, the white squares are weak.

This does not mean a Pawn should never be advanced; you could hardly expect to play chess without pushing a Pawn or two now and then. What it does mean is that you ought to have a mighty good reason for advancing a Pawn. To do so just because it is the first thing you think of, or the first hunk of wood you lay your hands is not the kind of play that will win prizes. You must have an objective in mind—even if it be a vagueish kind of strategic objective—to justify a Pawn move.

A common error, not only with beginners, but—oddly enough—with more advanced players, too, is the pushing of the King Rook Pawn to KR3 for no reason other than that they are worried by the possibility of a pin. Look at the following position:

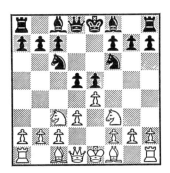

DIAGRAM 243

This game is still in its early infancy. There are no heavy threats hanging anywhere and, therefore, no need to take precautions. Yet how many players, in this and similar positions, play P—KR3 (as Black) or P—QR3 (as White). The Pawn move is a weakening one, creating a semi-hole at KN3 or QN3.

Even worse than this is the playing of P—KN3 when there is no intention of fianchettoing or of posting the King at KN2. What results is this:

DIAGRAM 244

And there is a weak square at KR3. That square can never be given Pawn protection. A piece will always have to be on guard; should that piece be needed elsewhere, it will not be available—it will be glued to its post.

Don't, at this point—or any point—jump to the conclusion that you should never play P—KR3 or P—QR3 or P—KN3; there are times when such a move may be necessary to prevent something worse than the weakening of a square. The point is that the move should not be made without a valid reason.

In the normal course of a game it is almost impossible to keep a position free of holes. The trick is to create as few as possible, to permit them to be created only at the least susceptible moments, to keep your Pawn formation flexible enough to compensate for the holes, and to keep your pieces mobile enough to defend against invasions via such holes.

Even the greatest chess players, be it said, have failed to follow these principles. Here, for example, is a position from a game between Emanuel Lasker and José Capablanca at St. Petersburg in 1914:

DIAGRAM 245

There is, as you see, a glaring hole at Black's K3. White proceeds to occupy it, playing 11 N—K6.

The Knight is unassailable. Here is the position twenty moves later.

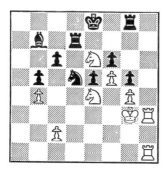

DIAGRAM 246

A lot of maneuvering has taken place, some Pawn exchanges have been made—but the Knight is still in his domineering spot. Now, he moves again—to another hole! The game proceeded as follows:

1	N/K6—B5	B—B1
2	N×R	B×N
3	R—R7	R—B1
4	R—R1	K—Q1
5	R—R8ch	B—B1
6	N—B5	resigns

The Knight, having occupied a hole, remained unmoved for twenty moves. Then, when it did move, it went to another hole and, from there, forced Black to lose the exchange. Then, as you see from move 6 given above, the remaining Knight jumped into a hole and

forced Black's hand again, this time leaving him no choice but to resign. There was no defense against the threat of N—N7ch or, worse yet, N—K6ch.

Though Capablanca lost this game he was well aware of the dangers of creating holes. In fact, his book *Chess Fundamentals* devotes a chapter to "The Influence of a Hole," and in it Capablanca uses as an illustration a game between Janowski and Kupchick at the Havana International Masters Tournament of 1913. The hole to which Capablanca refers is at Black's K4 in the following position:

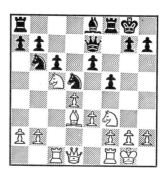

DIAGRAM 247

Black unthinkingly created the hole when, earlier, he played P—KB4 to dislodge a White Knight at White's K4. The Knight was dislodged, all right, but only went on to greater things. What followed from this position was:

1	N—K5	. . .

Occupying the hole

1	. . .	R—N1
2	R—K1	R—B3
3	Q—B3	R—R3

Black is about to make a demonstration ("demonstration"—this is chess-talk for a feint) on the King side.

4	Q—N3	R—B1
5	P—B3	R—B2
6	P—QR3	K—R1
7	P—R3	P—N4

Here comes the demonstration. White, however, is flexible enough to fend off any threats. Remember, too, that Black is here disobeying a fundamental premise: he is attacking on a flank without having effective control of the center. The answer to that is, we know, a counter-thrust in the center. Which is just what White does.

| 8 | P—K4 | P—B5 |
| 9 | Q—B2 | N—K6 |

Now it is Black who occupies a hole; but Black, lacking White's mobility and control in the center, is in no position to utilize such occupation. As we now see.

| 10 | R×N | P×R |
| 11 | Q×P | N—B1 |

DIAGRAM 248

Position after 11 . . . N—B1

White exchanges a Rook for a Knight and Pawn and emerges with a powerful position. Black, on the other hand, is generally cramped and has little prospect of freeing his game without seriously compromising it. The game continued:

12	N—N4	R—N3
13	P—K5	R—N2
14	B—B4	B—B2

White calls the tune; Black dances.

| 15 | N—B6 | . . . |

Right into the hole. Unlike White, Black cannot afford to exchange here. The Knight stays where it is, threatening all sorts of incursions.

15	. . .	N—N3
16	N/B5—K4	P—KR3
17	P—KR4	N—Q4
18	Q—Q2	R—N3
19	P×P	Q—B1

Not 19 . . . P×P; for this would be followed by 20 K—B2 and Black would be able to do nothing about the threat of R—KR1ch.

| 20 | P—B4 | N—K2 |

Black loses more and more space; White expands in proportion.

| 21 | P—KN4 | P×P |
| 22 | P×P | resigns |

DIAGRAM 249

Final Position (after 22 PxP)

The Black King is almost without a move. Black can do nothing to stop the coming mate. If he plays B—N1 (to be able to interpose against a check), White simply follows through with 23 Q—R2ch, K—N2 (forced); 24 B×P and if then 24 . . . B×B; 25 Q—R7mate.

The advance of Pawns creates not only weak squares, but weak Pawns, as well.

DIAGRAM 250

Here, for example, the advance of the Queen Rook and Queen Bishop Pawns has created a weakness—a hole—at QN3. It has also left the Queen Knight Pawn without the protection of its fellow Pawns. The Queen Knight Pawn is "backward" and, as such, is vulnerable to attack.

Ideally, we have already noted, a line of Pawns is strongest when each member of the line is in a position to protect those adjacent to it. In the position above the weak Queen Knight Pawn can be made strong by the move P—QN4. This, however, would leave the Queen Rook Pawn backward. (A general principle is discernible here: almost any move you make—with rare exceptions—will have its advantages and its disadvantages. And this is especially true of Pawn moves.)

A backward Pawn frequently becomes the target of an attack, and its defense may be crucial. It would be quite impossible to count the number of games that have been lost because of backward Pawns. The owner of the backward Pawn tries to get out of his difficulties by pushing it forward, if possible; if this can't be done safely, he tries to defend it, if he can do so without compromising his position; and if this can't be done he may try to exchange the bad Pawn. Sometimes the best thing to do with a backward Pawn is give it away; trying to defend it or strengthen it or exchange it may only lead to a deteriorating position.

An isolated Pawn is a special case. Sometimes it is weak, sometimes strong. If it is a passed Pawn, of course, it is potentially powerful, and the fewer pieces on the board the greater its power. But in the middle game, when the board is full of men and threats, an isolated Pawn is more likely than not to become a weakness rather than an asset. It is, in effect, a backward Pawn no matter where it is, because it is deprived of Pawn protection.

In the following example, Alekhine shows how to take advantage of an isolated Pawn. His opponent, playing White, was Potemkin; the game was played at a tournament in St. Petersburg in 1912. This was the position after White's 8th move:

DIAGRAM 251

White's Queen Pawn already is backward, though not irreparably so. White will try to remedy this weakness, only to create a greater one.

The game continued as follows:

| 8 | . . . | O—O |
| 9 | P—Q4 | . . . |

The Queen Pawn is no longer backward; but White did not consider this reply:

| 9 | . . . | P×P |
| 10 | P×P | . . . |

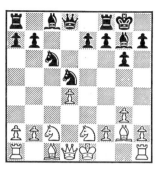

DIAGRAM 252
Position after 10 P×P

Now the white Queen Pawn is isolated; though not formally backward, it is functionally so. It has no way of getting Pawn protection.

Black now puts pressure on the weak Pawn.

| 10 | . . . | B—N5 |

Pinning one of the weak Pawn's defenders.

| 11 | P—B3 | . . . |

White dislodges the Bishop, but

| 11 | . . . | B—B4 |

the threat is renewed. Black could win the weak Pawn now with . . . B×N; Q×B, N×P.

12	N—K3	Q—R4ch
13	K—B2	N/Q4—N5
14	N×B	Q×N

Of course not P×N, breaking up the King-side Pawn.

| 15 | P—N4 | N—Q6ch |
| 16 | K—N3 | N×QP |

The weak Pawn falls and the rest—despite the capture of the Black Queen—is academic.

DIAGRAM 253
Position after 16 . . . N×QP

The game continued:

17	P×Q	N×Pch

If 18 K—N4, P—R4ch; 19 K—R3, N—B7 mate. Or 18 K—N4, P—R4ch; 19 K—N5, B—R3 mate. Or 18 K—R3, N—B7 mate.

The game pivoted around the rise and fall of White's Queen Pawn. That old saw about "for want of a nail . . . etc.," can be applied easily to chess, in which case it would go something like this: "For want of protection, a Pawn was lost; for want of a Pawn, the center was lost; for want of the center, the position was lost; for want of position, the game was lost."

Since the Pawns cannot remain on their original squares, a way must be found to push them with the least amount of weakening. In abstract, there is such a way, and its end-result is the Pawn chain.

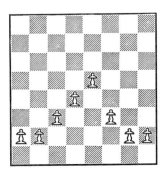

DIAGRAM 254

The line of Pawns that begins on QN2 and ends at K5 is a solidly forged Pawn chain. It can be used to support pieces, to hamper the enemy and provide protection.

Because the Pawn at the top is linked to the one behind it, and that one in turn to the one behind *it*, and so on, a Pawn chain, to be effectively broken, must be attacked at its base. The owner of the chain, of course, will concentrate his defensive maneuvers around the base of the chain.

Despite its strength, however, a Pawn chain does create weaknesses (again: few advantages in chess are unaccompanied by disadvantages). The White squares on the Queen's Wing in the diagram above, for example, are weakened as a result of the forming of the Pawn chain. It ought to be remembered, too, that a Pawn chain is strongest when its base is close to the second rank; the further the base gets from that rank the more vulnerable to attack it becomes.

A great deal of the maneuvering that goes on in the middle game is concerned with Pawn chains. One side seeks to break through with an attack against the base of the chain; the other tries to defend.

In a game between Alekhine and Nimzovich in 1930, Alekhine took the precaution of establishing a healthy Pawn chain. The game opened like this:

1	P—K4	P—K3
2	P—Q4	P—Q4
3	N—QB3	. . .

(Nimzovich, were the roles reversed, would probably have played 3 P—K5, for he was a great believer in this move. To quote from his book *My System:* ". . . 3 P—K5 above all things checks the movement of the Black Pawns, and therefore implies a blockade. But we know that Pawns, especially those in the center, are consumed by an enormous desire for expansion, i.e., to press forward, and we have consequently inflicted on the enemy a not inconsiderable hurt. Moreover, thanks to P—K5 there are now two theatres of war on the board, of which the one is Black's K wing and the other the center.")

3	. . .	B—N5
4	P—K5	. . .

Alekhine inflicts "a not inconsiderable hurt" on his opponent.

4	. . .	P—QB4

This attacks the base of the short Pawn chain at White's Q4 and K5.

5	B—Q2	N—K2
6	N—N5	B×Bch
7	Q×B	O—O

And now White welds his Pawn chain firmly.

8	P—QB3	

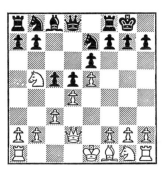

DIAGRAM 255

Position after 8 P—QB3

White went on to use his Pawn chain as a springboard for a powerful Queen-side attack. Nimzovich lost in 31 moves.

Lest you conclude that, having established a Pawn chain, you are thenceforth immune from attack, we present the following example. This is from a game between Pillsbury, a talented American whose promising chess career was cut short by his early death, and Emanuel Lasker, played in Nuremberg in 1896. The position after 20 moves was:

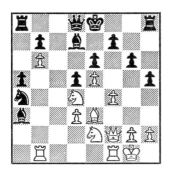

DIAGRAM 256

Black has established a double Pawn chain running from KB3 to KR4 and Q4. White now played 21 P—B5, forcing the break-up of the chain. Black, it is true, had the better Pawn formation. But a Pawn formation, despite its importance, is not everything. It must serve as the basis for maneuvers by the pieces; it must fit in with the general scheme. Here Lasker has neglected too many factors. His Knight and King Bishop are misplaced (actually the Bishop is mobile enough to get back where it belongs quickly; but the Knight is out of the picture) and he has left his King exposed in the center of the board. It is only a sort of logical justice that White should disrupt the Pawn chain and then go on to victory. The game continued:

21	. . .	NP×P
22	N—B4	P—R5

A precaution to prevent the penetration of the White Queen to the weak square N2.

23	R—R1	B—K2
24	R×N	. . .

White, having a solid attack in the works, can afford to lose the exchange and thereby deflect the Bishop.

24	. . .	B×R
25	N/Q4×KP	P×N
26	N×KP	B—Q2
27	N×Q	R×N

DIAGRAM 257

Position after 27 . . . RxN

Black's weaknesses are showing. Most of his Pawns are isolated. They do not, with the exception of the Queen Rook Pawn, even have the compensation of being passed Pawns. And Black's general lack of mobility—his pieces being tied down to the defense of Pawns—gives him a mild case of cramps. In addition, he cannot really afford more exchanges.

He resigned on the 50th move.

Strong players have always recognized the value of the Pawn chain—the power of the screen it throws up, a screen behind which the pieces can safely maneuver for position. Here, for example, is how the great British master McDonnell used a Pawn chain to outmaneuver his French rival LaBourdonnais in their famous match of 1834. The game opened:

1	P—K4	P—QB4
2	P—KB4	. . .

White's second move is no longer considered a valid reply to 1 . . . P—QB4 (this is the Sicilian Defense, about which more in the next chapter)

2	. . .	P—K3
3	N—KB3	P—Q4
4	P—K5	. . .

This Pawn will become the spearhead of the White Pawn chain.

4	. . .	N—QB3
5	P—B3	. . .

Preparing to make the final move in the forging of the chain.

5	. . .	P—B3
6	N—R3	N—R3
7	N—B2	. . .

The Knight is now posted on a square from which it can support the coming thrust P—Q4.

| 7 | ... | B—K2 |
| 8 | P—Q4 | ... |

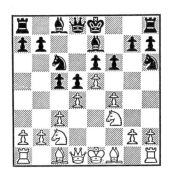

DIAGRAM 258

Position after 8 P—Q4

The game continued as follows:

| 8 | ... | O—O |
| 9 | B—Q3 | P—B5 |

Now Black, too, has set up a Pawn chain, in opposition to White's. This vis-a-vis of Pawn chains is a very common formation.

| 10 | B—K2 | B—Q2 |
| 11 | O—O | P—QN4 |

Black now undertakes a plan to break up White's Pawn chain by attacking its base. (Nimzovich correctly pointed out that the base of the White Pawn chain in such a position is not the Queen Knight Pawn, but the Queen Bishop Pawn, because the Queen Knight Pawn has no Black counterpart obstructing it, as do the other members of the chain.)

| 12 | N—K3 | P—R4 |

An inaccuracy, unless Black had in mind not only a breaking-up of the White Pawn Chain, but a breakthrough on the Queen's wing as well. In view of White's flexibility, though, such a plan would seem to be ill-advised. The move, then, can only be construed as imprecise.

| 13 | K—R1 | P×P |

Another shift. Black seems to be trying to play both sides of the board at once.

| 14 | BP×P | ... |

White maintains his chain intact.

14	...	N—B4
15	P—KN4	N×N
16	B×N	B—K1

Black here plans to take advantage of the weakening of White's King-side Pawns.

| 17 | Q—Q2 | B—N3 |
| 18 | N—N5 | ... |

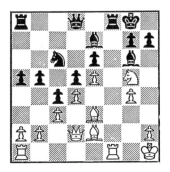

DIAGRAM 259

Position after 18 N—N5

Notice how White, under the shield of his Pawn chain, has wide flexibility in the maneuvering of his pieces. Notice, too, that the apex of the Pawn chain hinders his opponent.

| 18 | ... | B×N |
| 19 | B×B | Q—Q2 |

White moves farther and farther into enemy territory, cutting Black's available resources. All this is made possible by the Pawn chain, which cuts the board in two, immobilizes the center and hampers Black.

| 20 | P—KR4 | ... |

White continues with his plan of attacking the castled Black King.

| 20 | ... | P—N5 |

And Black tries a diversion on the Queen's wing, attacking—too late—the base of the White Pawn chain.

| 21 | K—R2 | P×P |
| 22 | P×P | P—R5 |

The chain is still intact, and from its (real) original base, the Pawn at QB3. If this Pawn could be attacked, Black might have a better chance.

23   **P—R5**   . . .

But White does not give Black a chance to attack the base; he presses his King-side attack.

23   . . .   **B—K5**
24   **P—R6**

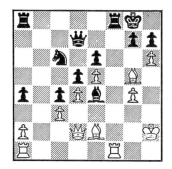

DIAGRAM 260
Position after 24 P—R6

The beginning of the end. The Pawn at R6 is the edge of a powerful wedge that will pry open the castled King's position. White won some 15 moves later.

The subject of Pawn play—how the Pawns can be used to carry out assaults, how they can assist in offensive and dcfensive maneuvers, how they can be set up to put a "bind" on the enemy, how they can determine the course of the coming end game—all these considerations and many others are rightfully in the province of the middle game. We will go into some of these aspects later in the chapter; but we will, because of lack of space, be unable to treat all the elements of Pawn play.

If you want to go further into such studies you would do well to read, after you have mastered this book, one of the more advanced works. Nimzovich's *My System* has some excellent chapters on Pawn play; this is for the advanced player. There is also a book by Hans Kmoch called *Pawn Power in Chess* that will give you some important insights into this aspect of chess. Perhaps the best treatment for the player who is just emerging from the beginner stage (though it is just as useful for the advanced player) is found in Reuben Fine's wonderful *The Middle Game in Chess,* which, at this time, is unfortunately out of print. It's worth hunting for, though.

Meanwhile, there are other general principles of the middle game that we haven't touched yet. For example—

Open Files

In the chapter on end games, as well as so far in this chapter, you have come across the warning that doubled Pawns are weak and should be avoided. True enough. But consider the following position:

DIAGRAM 261

It is White's move. If he thinks "One should never, no never permit one's Pawns to become doubled" he will miss his big chance. Because, by playing 1 P×P (thereby doubling his Pawns on the King Rook file) he will open the King Knight file for his Rook/N1. Black, of course, will be unable to reply 1 . . . P×P because his King Knight Pawn is pinned. But even if Black's King were at R1 and he played 1 . . . P×P, White would stand to gain. By permitting the doubling of the Pawns he creates a lane of attack for his Rook. Thus the play might run:

1   **P×P**   **Q—B2**
2   **R/R2—N2**   **N—K3**
3   **Q—N3**

Black will be unable to find adequate defenses to the mating threats facing him on the King Knight file (and on the King Rook file if White pushes the more advanced Rook Pawn).

The moral is another variation of an old theme: you can afford to create a weakness in one direction if, at the same time, you create an even greater strength in another.

The strength in this case was the half-open file. Half open? I thought—you say—that it was open? Well, let's take another look at open files:

DIAGRAM 262

Here White has no Pawn on his Queen Bishop file. For him, that file is open. But there is a Black Pawn on the file. Therefore, for Black it is closed. In addition, if White had a Rook at QB1, he could penetrate, at this point, only as far as his QB6 with it, by playing 1 R×P. The file, then, is half-open.

Black, for his part, has a half-open King Rook file. Same reasons.

If no Pawns at all obstruct a file, that file is open. As, for example, the Queen file in this position:

DIAGRAM 263

The Queen file here is wide open. The first side to capture the file (with R-Q1, for example) 'will have a telling advantage.

What is so important about capturing an open file? The open file is in chess what a line of supply is in war. But it is more. Not only can supplies be moved along that corridor, but troops and reinforcements can be moved. The open file is the path along which the invasion of enemy territory will move.

The ideal piece with which to secure the open file is the Rook. The Bishop, naturally, is of little use, since its power runs along diagonals. The Knight is not much better. The Queen is good, but she is vulnerable to attack. But the Rook—ah, the Rook seems to have been invented specifically to occupy and control files.

The Rook can turn an otherwise closed file into an open or semi-open file by making the appropriate zig-

zag move. In the following position, for example, the White Rook at KN3 controls a half-open file even though that file still has a White Pawn on it.

DIAGRAM 264

The point is that the Rook's view is unobstructed; his own Pawn is behind him.

A Rook posted on an open file represents a strong direct threat. Even more, though, it represents a potential invasion. That's because the Rook on the open file is in a position to penetrate to its sixth, seventh, or eighth rank. From those advanced ranks its power fans out not only along the file but along the rank as well, threatening captures and even checkmate.

Look at this position, for example:

DIAGRAM 265

The diagrammed position, of course, is not possible; it is only a demonstration. Notice that the Rook threatens:

(a) the capture of the Bishop
(b) mate at K8 (prevented only by the Bishop)
(c) the capture of the Bishop Pawn
(d) the capture of the Queen Knight Pawn (via a skewer)

To prevent mate the Bishop must remain on the diagonal K1–QR5. It cannot do this and, at the same time, protect both threatened Pawns. One of the Pawns must fall.

Thus the Rook on the seventh, attacking everything on the defender's second rank, is a dangerous invader.

Even without penetrating to the seventh rank, though, the Rook on an open file is dangerous. For that reason, the struggle for control of an open file is often a violent one.

Only the disappearance of a Pawn can open a file (unless, as mentioned earlier, the Rook gets in front of its own Pawns by zig-zagging; but this is time-consuming). In the following example Black gains control of the King Bishop file:

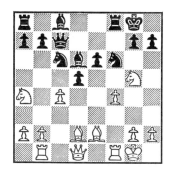

DIAGRAM 266

In this position (reached with White's 15th move in a game between Schallop and Tarrasch in 1889) the King Bishop file is still in dispute. White and Black both have Rooks posted there, but the situation is very much in a state of flux. The game continued this way:

| 15 | . . . | P–KR3 |
| 16 | P–QB5 | . . . |

A tactical error that, as you will see, permits Black to gain control of the King Bishop file.

| 16 | . . . | P×N |
| 17 | P×B | . . . |

Compounding the error.

17	. . .	Q×P
18	P×P	N–K5
19	R×Rch	. . .

White disregards a fundamental rule: when a file is in dispute, let your opponent make the first capture. Then, when you recapture, you will be in possession of the file.

| 19 | . . . | Q×R |

And Black seizes the file.

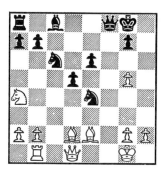

DIAGRAM 267

Position after 19 . . . QxR

As for that fundamental rule, here, in its essence, is how it works:

DIAGRAM 268

The one open file—the King file—is in dispute. Each side occupies it with a Rook and each side's R/K1 is protected by a R/QR1. It would be a mistake to capture the opposing Rook. For if 1 R×Rch, R×R and the position then would be:

DIAGRAM 269

Position after 1 RxRch, RxR

The recapturing side now has possession of the open file. It also has the initiative.

The following example is taken from a game played between Steinitz and Vasquez in Havana in 1888. White demonstrates the sometimes not-too-gentle art of forcing open a file. The position after Black's 10th move was this:

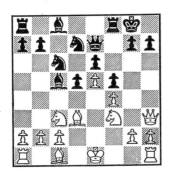

DIAGRAM 270

The game continued as follows:

11   P–KN4   . . .

This move pries open the file whether Black likes it or not—and he certainly did not like it. Black can't reply 11 . . . P×P because White would follow this with 12 Q×Pch, K–B2; 13 B–N6 mate. Perhaps such a quick end would have been, after all, more to his liking than what actually happened.

11   . . .   P–KN3
12   P×P   KP×P

The file is now open for White. However, because of the Black Bishop at B4 he cannot immediately occupy the file with his Rook. The game continued:

13   N×P   Q–N2
14   B–Q2   P–QN4

Black tries a little ruse. He tempts White to play N–B7, which supposedly gives White a chance to capture the troublesome Bishop. White, however, has his own scheme, and refuses to be diverted.

15   B–B3   B–N2
16   P–K6   . . .

Unmasking a double attack and, at the same time, pushing a Pawn further into enemy territory.

16   . . .   N–B3

Black protects the Queen and saves the Knight. But to no avail.

17   N×Nch   R×N
18   O–O–O   B–K6ch

Useless.

19   K–N1   B×P
20   B×BP   . . .

If Black plays 20 . . . P×B White will follow through with KR–N1, pinning and winning the Queen. If he plays 20 . . . R×B, White can come out ahead with B×Q, K×B; R–Q7ch (winning the Bishop on the next move).

20   . . .   Q–B1

So Black takes the precaution of getting his Queen out of its dangerous spot.

21   KR–N1   . . .

Now at last White occupies the open file with his Rook.

DIAGRAM 271
Position after 21 KR–N1

And what can Black do? Play 21 . . . R×B? Hardly. For then 22 R×Pch, P×R; 23 Q–R8 mate.

21   . . .   P–N5
22   B/B5×P   resigns

Mate is threatened all over the place.

Doubled rooks are more than twice as dangerous as one Rook. They support each other for all sorts of excursions and incursions. For that reason, once you have occupied a file it is a good idea to double your Rooks on that file. For example:

DIAGRAM 272

Here White has posted a Rook in the heart of enemy territory and has backed it up with the second Rook. Mate is threatened on every side. Should Black, for instance, try to protect the Queen Knight Pawn with QR—N1, White simply plays N—Q7, winning the exchange. If Black tries KR—QN1, then P—KR4 and, since the Knight must move, Black's King Bishop Pawn must fall. If Black tries P—N3, White plays R—B7 and Black must lose the Queen Bishop Pawn.

Earlier in this chapter (page 89) we quoted a Paulsen-Morphy game to illustrate the principles of balance (or imbalance) in the factors of force, space and time. That same game, looked at from another point of view, serves as an excellent example of the power of doubled Rooks. We start this time with the position after White's 16th move.

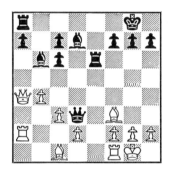

DIAGRAM 273

Now Morphy played 16 . . . QR—K1, doubling his Rooks on the wide open King file. The immediate threat is . . . Q×Rch, followed (after K×Q) by R—K8 mate. White therefore played Q—R6 and the position is shown in diagram 238 on page 89.

The power of the doubled Rooks is immense. As you know, Morphy now played Q×B, sacrificing his Queen and winning. However, he could have played Q×Rch. And whether Paulsen replied K×Q or Q×Q victory would have followed. For example:

17	. . .	Q×Rch
18	K×Q	R—K8 mate

17	. . .	Q×Rch
18	Q×Q	R—K8
19	P—R3	. . .

(not 19 Q×R, R×Q mate)

19	. . .	R×Q
20	K×R	

And, with two strongly posted Bishops and a Rook on an open file, mate would have been a simple matter of technique. Morphy, being a true Romantic, of course chose the more spectacular way. But the point

is still that the doubled Rooks on the open file made the sacrifice possible.

You will find, as you play more and more chess, that threats are powerful weapons in and of themselves; the threats don't actually have to be carried out —they can create weaknesses just by being there, just by their potential. Here, for example, is how the threat of destruction on the seventh rank by a Rook brings about a favorable end game.

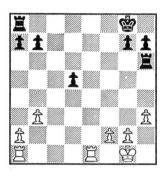

DIAGRAM 274

This was the position after Black's 26th move in a game played between Tarrasch and Taubenhaus in Ostend in 1905. Tarrasch now played 27 R—K7.

Taubenhaus, seeing the futility of trying to defend, tries instead to steer for a favorable end game. He played 27 . . . R—KB1. What followed was:

28	R×NP	R—B2
29	R—N8ch	R—B1
30	R×Rch	K×R

And Black cannot hope to win the end game. His isolated Queen Pawn is weak and—in addition—White has extra Pawns on both wings.

The threats brought by the invasion of the Rook on the seventh rank forced Black's hand and resulted in (for him) a lost end game.

To wind up our all-too-brief discussion of open files and the invasion by Rooks, here is a game between Alekhine and Euwe, played at their 1935 match. The opening was what is called a French Defense (1 P—K4, P—K3; 2 P—Q4, P—Q4).

The position after Black's 19th move was:

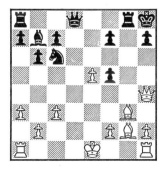

DIAGRAM 275

Black, with 19 . . . R—KN1, has just taken possession of the open file. The threat is . . . Q×Q; B×Q, R×B. White, however, has a trick or two. For instance:

| 20 | B—B3 | Q—Q6 |

A telling invasion of White's home territory. With a strongly posted Rook, a Queen in the heart of the enemy's territory and a great deal of mobility, Black should, by all rights, have an easy time of it; it looks like a shoo-in. But instead of pressing home his advantage, he fritters it away, which only serves as further proof of the principle that he who has the advantage should make immediate and effective use of it.

| 21 | B—K2 | Q—K5 |

Foo! Black beats an ignominious retreat when he should have played vigorously with, for instance, 21 . . . Q—B7.

| 22 | Q×Q | P×Q |

By permitting White to steer for the end game Black throws away his chances.

| 23 | B—R4 | . . . |

Threatening B—B6ch, which would prove to be the end of Black.

| 23 | . . . | P—KR3 |

Black, now playing strictly on the defensive, gives his King an escape hatch to prevent the loss of the exchange.

| 24 | O—O—O | . . . |

Better late than never, and better now for vigorous play.

24	. . .	QR—K1
25	B—B6ch	K—R2
26	P—KB4	P×P e.p.
27	B×P	N—R4
28	R×B	N×B
29	R—Q7	. . .

DIAGRAM 276

Position after 29 R—Q7

White's plan is right. Having seized the initiative he proceeds to exploit it to the fullest, by invading the seventh rank.

Threats: R×NP and R×BPch.

29	. . .	N—B4
30	R×Pch	K—N3
31	R×P	. . .

Both threats carried out.

31	. . .	N—Q6ch
32	K—N1	K—B4
33	R—Q1	

Black resigned eight moves later.

Once more, as we come to the end of a discussion, we apologize for cutting it short. And once more, we offer the suggestion that you look into the subject further after you get through with this book for beginners. You'll find a lot of meaty material on open files in such books as *My System* and Tarrasch's *The Game of Chess.*

King Safety

We did not mention this factor before because, no matter what the situation on the board, no matter how well posted one side's pieces may be, no matter what rank he occupies—if his King is endangered he has to look to that before all else.

In analyzing a position fully, then, the factor of King safety must be taken into account. It is the deus ex machina of chess. When all seems hopeless for White, for example, but Black leaves his King in an exposed position, the game can reverse itself quickly and dramatically.

If the King is uncastled the attacker should aim to force him out into 'the open, then bring all available pieces to bear against him. If he is castled, the attacker may first have to strip away his defenses. And remember, even if you have to part with everything but a Pawn, if the end result is checkmate your sacrifices will have been worth it.

How do you know when to attack the King? There are some general guides that can be used. When, for example, you have more material available for attack than your opponent has for defense your attack should succeed (note the word "should"; if your opponent can get a breather and find a tactical finesse you may find yourself on the defensive).

And there are general guides for the conduct of the attack, too. First, clear the field for action—that is, get direct access to the enemy King by opening files or diagonals. Then, array your forces for a mass attack. Then, strike home.

That is all very well, you may say, but how does a player go about doing these things?

Here is an example:

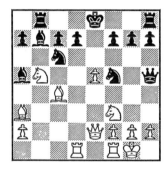

DIAGRAM 277

This was the position after Black's 15th move in a game between Kolisch and Anderssen played in Paris in 1860. Before showing the continuation, let's analyze the position.

Force: Black is a Pawn ahead.

Space: White stands somewhat better, principally because of the Rook on the half-open Queen file. In addition, his Bishops look right into Black's home grounds. In actual count, White's Pawns and pieces observe 14 enemy points. Black's pieces observe 14 enemy points too. Despite the mathematical equality, though, White is better off in space; his pieces are functioning; Black's are passive.

Time: White has eleven visible tempi, not counting "vanished" tempi, that is, pawns that have left the board. Black has nine visible tempi.

King Safety: Any questions? White is snugly castled. Black stands as exposed as a stripper on the runway.

Total: Black's slight edge in material is offset by his backwardness in space and time. His King is in danger.

Conclusion: White should launch a direct attack on the King.

And this is just what White did. He began by clearing the field—opening lines to the King—with a sacrifice.

| 16 | R×P | K×R |

Now he starts moving in on the exposed King.

| 17 | P−K6ch | K−B1 |

(Not 17 . . . P×P; 18 Q×Pch, K−Q1; 19 R−Q1ch, N/B3−Q5; 20 N/N5×N, N×N; 21 R×Nch, B−Q4; 22 R×Bch, Q×R; 23 Q×Qch, K any move; 24 Q×B and Black is finished.)

| 18 | P×P | B−R1 |

Black tries for counterplay by bringing his Queen Rook into the game.

| 19 | N×Pch | |

Another sacrifice, this time to hobble the wandering King.

| 20 | . . . | N×N |
| 21 | Q−K6ch | |

The closing-in.

22	. . .	K−Q1
23	R−Q1ch	N−Q3
24	R×Nch	. . .

And still another sacrifice. White sees that Black cannot possibly mobilize his disrupted forces in time to get them to the defense of the beleaguered King. He can afford to throw whatever he has into the attack.

| 24 | . . . | P×R |
| 25 | Q×Pch | |

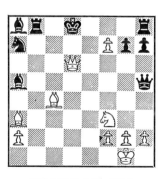

DIAGRAM 278

Position after 25 QxPch

Analyzing the elements now, we see that White is two Rooks down and three Pawns ahead, a minus equivalent to about a Rook and two Pawns. In space, however, he dominates the board. Time? Time can't really be calculated, but we can see that Black (in theory, anyhow) has a strong attack available to him. If he could possibly play . . . R—N8ch White would be hard pressed. But time is on White's side; Black must attend to his King's safety first.

26	. . .	K—B1
27	B—K6ch	K—N2
28	B—Q5ch	Q×B

Black must give up his Queen. Any move by the King (and he has only one move—to B1) would lead to mate in short order.

It ought to be mentioned here that, when conducting an attack against the King, exchanges ordinarily are to be avoided, especially when the attack involves sacrifices. This is only common sense; if we give up two Rooks and the attack falls apart because we permit the defender to exchange pieces, we stand in a bad way. Tactical finesses, however, more than compensate in this case.

29	Q×Qch	K—R3
30	Q—B4ch	K—N2
31	Q—K4ch	N—B3
32	N—K5	. . .

White can take this "time out" here because the Black King blocks the Rook's path.

32	. . .	K—R3
33	Q—B4ch	K—R2
34	B—B5ch	R—N3
35	B×Rch	. . .

The end of Black's one last, weak hope.

35	. . .	B×B
36	N×Nch	B×N
37	Q×B	resigns

White gave up everything but his Queen and, by forcing Black's hand, turned spatial and temporal advantages into a material advantage.

Here is an example of an attack against the castled King. The attacker was Alekhine, the defender Tarrasch; the game was played in 1925 in Baden-Baden. The position after White's 22nd move was this:

DIAGRAM 279

What is the analysis?
Force: White is a Pawn ahead.
Space: White observes 13 Black squares; Black observes 21 White squares.
Time: White has 12 visible tempi, Black has 11 visible tempi.
King Safety: Roughly equal. Both Kings are castled, both have slightly weakened Pawn positions.

But—the big "but"—it is Black's move. And coupled with his advantage in space, this proves too much for White. Alekhine played:

| 22 | . . . | B×P |

Step No. 1. Black opens lines to the King, at the same time stripping the King of his defenses.

| 23 | P×B | . . . |

White's reply was not the best. He could have put up a better fight with 23 Q—Q2.

| 23 | . . . | Q×N |
| 24 | R×Rch | R×R |

White tries to take the wind out of Black's sails by exchanges. In this case, though, Black's natural reply serves only to increase the pressure on the open file.

| 25 | B—B1 | . . . |

Trying to bring troops to defend the King in his weakened condition.

| 25 | . . . | R—K4 |

Black maneuvers his Rook around for a direct assault by way of the open King Knight file.

| 26 | P—B4 | R—N4ch |
| 27 | K—R2 | . . . |

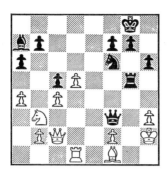

DIAGRAM 280
Position after 27 K—R2

Black can now afford a second sacrifice, again to denude the King of his defenses and make him more easily accessible.

27	. . .	N—N5ch
28	P×N	R×NP
29	B—R3	R—R5
30	resigns	

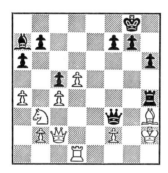

DIAGRAM 281
Position after 29 . . . R—R5

There is no defense against the coming . . . Q×B. If White tries K—N1, Black plays . . . Q×B and White cannot stop . . . Q—R8 mate.

General Principles

We can now summarize some general principles for the conduct of the middle game.

¶ The three basic elements to be considered in evaluating a position are force, space and time. The first is more stable than the other two.

¶ Gains in one or two of the elements usually, though not invariably, are accompanied by losses in the remaining elements. The over-all balance is what gives the position (and hence the game) its potential.

¶ An advantage in one element can be converted into an advantage into one or both of the others. Advantages in space and time, being of temporary nature, should be converted, where possible, into an advantage in the more stable element, force.

¶ A minimal advantage in any of the elements demands cautious—but not timid—play. Plunging headlong into an attack with only a minimal advantage can lead to a reversal of positions. However, a sizable advantage in force calls for an attack. And sizable advantages in space or time call for action to convert the space or time into advantages in material.

¶ Time works for the weaker side when there is an advantage in space. Unless the stronger side makes use of his advantage it will dissipate itself.

¶ Pawns are the best protection for pieces and for their fellow Pawns. Posted next to each other they constitute an almost impregnable barrier. They must be moved only when there is good reason for moving them.

¶ A Pawn move leaves weak squares in its wake. These squares can be occupied by the enemy, and the invading pieces, if both Pawns on files adjacent to the weak square have been moved forward, cannot be dislodged by Pawns.

¶ A Pawn left behind by pawns on both sides of him is backward. He is a natural target for attacks and the square in front of him is a natural one for occupation by enemy pieces.

¶ One way of minimizing the weakening effects of Pawn moves is to forge Pawn chains where one link can defend the next. The closer the base of the chain is to its side's second rank, the stronger the chain.

¶ Pawn chains should be undermined at the base.

¶ Pieces posted in "holes," though they constitute threats to the enemy, are of little value if they cannot be supported. This support should be by Pawns, though pieces will do. And, like other advantages, they are only as good as their permanency. If the lines to the outpost pieces cannot be maintained (to bring up reinforcements) the outpost pieces will become targets and will lose tempi by being forced to retreat.

¶ Sometimes doubled Pawns, which cannot support each other, should be created if, in so doing, lines are opened. This is especially true when the opened line is a file that can be occupied by a Rook.

¶ A Rook on an open or semi-open file constitutes a threat of invasion. If the Rook reaches the seventh or eighth rank he threatens to capture Pawns and pieces that remain there and, with the help of other pieces or Pawns, he threatens mating attacks.

¶ When possible, double Rooks on an open or semi-open file. They protect and support each other and more than double their individual power.

¶ All other factors become void when the King is endangered. A side can have material, spatial and temporal superiority and still lose in short order if its King can be assaulted and overcome.

¶ In conducting an attack against the King the first thing to do is to clear the lines, to establish a direct route between the attacking forces and the defending King. Sometimes a sacrifice accomplishes this.

¶ The attacking side should, if possible, avoid exchanges, on the theory that if the attack peters out and the attacker has weakened his forces or his position in conducting the attack, the roles will become reversed. The defender, conversely, should try to take the wind out of the attacker's sails by forcing exchanges, particularly of such heavy pieces as Queens and Rooks.

¶ The attacker must try to strip the defending King of his defenses. If sacrifices are needed they should be made. These must be calculated precisely, though, for if he gives away his Queen and finds he cannot bring the attack to a successful finish he might as well quit.

There is one little gimmick that may not have been too apparent from some of the examples and that has not been discussed. That is the bypassing of the middle game.

If one side has an advantage of, say, an extra Pawn on each wing, then that side may try to dispense with the middle game and bring on the end game, which would be easily won. This is done by forcing exchanges. The vice versa, of course, is that when one side has such a permanent disadvantage he should try at all costs to avoid bringing on the end game; his best chances lie in complicating the middle game.

There are other general principles for the middle game, but some of these—the blockade, overprotection and the use of the long diagonal, for example—require a solid understanding of the more fundamental axioms. There are dozens of books available for the study of these more advanced principles. Meanwhile, mull over what you have learned so far. In fact,

STOP!

right now and give yourself:

Self-Testing Quiz No. 14

(a) *In the following position, if White were to move, what is a good move? Give a reason, in terms of general principles, for each move you select.*

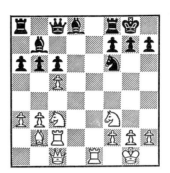

DIAGRAM 282

(b) *Analyze the following position from the point of view of force, space, time and King safety.*

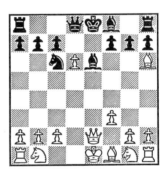

DIAGRAM 283

(c) *What move can Black make in the position above to regain a piece? What would the force-space-time-King safety picture be after that Black move?*

(d) *What are good moves for White in the following position? On what principles?*

DIAGRAM 284

(e) *What are Black's weak points in the following position? What are White's weak points? Which side has the better game?*

DIAGRAM 285

(f) If, in the position above, White plays Q—R5 and Black follows with R/K2—B2, can White force a win with a sacrifice? (these positions are from a game Schlechter-Marshall played in 1905)

If you did well on the quiz you can go on now to:

Smothered Mate

You know from your reading on end games that certain minimum forces are required to bring about mate. In the middle game, however, the forces required may be considerably less because the defending King may be so hemmed in by his own men that a single Pawn can administer the coup de grace. For example:

DIAGRAM 286

If it is White's move here he can mate with 1 P—B7. This is called a smothered mate, the King being smothered by his own men. The position shown above is an unlikely one. But smothered mate is not unlikely, and the "classical" smothered mate is the following.

DIAGRAM 287

The play runs this way:

1	Q—B4ch	K—R1

(Not 1 . . . K—B1, for then 2 Q—B7 mate.)

2	N—B7ch	K—N1
3	N—R6 dbl ch	K—R1

(Again not 3 . . . K—B1, for then 4 Q—B7 mate.)

4	Q—N8ch	R×Q
5	N—B7 **mate**	

DIAGRAM 288

Position after 5 N—B7 mate

Smothered mate can and sometimes does happen in the middle game. It is probably the neatest trick to be found there, and the player who forces smothered mate, like the golfer who breaks par, the bowler who hits 300 and the fisherman who lands the one that usually gets away, rarely stops talking about his feat. If it can be forced in the castled King's corner the rest of the board doesn't matter. The losing side may have a Queen, a Rook, two Bishops, two Knights and a battery of Pawns ready to leap on the attacker's King; if mate comes, what good will all that do him? The pay-off in chess is checkmate and many chess nuts will tell you it isn't how you play that counts, it's whether you win.

Here is an example of something close to a smothered mate. Though the Black King is not actually done in by his own men's occupying all flight squares, they do help him to lose in very convincing fashion. And, since true smothered mate rarely occurs in master games, this one is all the more remarkable. Tchigorin handled the White pieces, Schiffers the Black; the game was played in 1880. This was the position after Black's 23rd move:

DIAGRAM 289

White played 24 Q×Nch and what followed was:

24	. . .	R×Q
25	R×Rch	K—N1

Other moves are not much better. Try 25 . . . R—B2, for example, and you will see that White can still mate in three.

26	B—B4ch	R—B2

No alternative here.

27	R—K8ch	K—N2

Again, because of the pin on the Rook, there is no alternative.

28	N—K6 mate	

DIAGRAM 290
Position after 28 N—K6 mate

Mate on the Eighth Rank

Just as smothered mate is rare, so mate on the eighth rank is common. It becomes possible when the guard on that eighth rank is insufficient and the King has no escape route. Here is the essence of such a mate:

DIAGRAM 291

The play is 1 . . . R—Q8ch; 2 N—K1, R×N mate.

The mate on the eighth rank is not always so simple; often the operation is a complex one, many moves deep. But before going into these complex types, here is a sample of a situation that illustrates how the threat of mate (even when mate can be avoided) can equalize or reverse the balance of power.

DIAGRAM 292

White, at first glance, does not seem to have much at his disposal. If he plays 1 R—K8ch Black can reply 1 . . . R×R or 1 . . . B×R and still come out a piece ahead because the Black Queen can be brought quickly to the defense. But 1 Q×B works.

If Black replies 1 . . . R×Q, then 2 R—K8 next move is mate. That threat must be parried, and the time (one move) required to parry the threat is all White needs to coordinate himself. Meanwhile, Black has lost his material advantage—the Bishop—and must stay on the defensive.

You will often find in chess books such things as: "Black must play 27 . . . R×B in order to stop * * *" and there follows a string of moves, perhaps twelve in all, which ends with Black's being checkmated. Then you notice that if Black does make the suggested move—that is, 27 . . . R×B, in this instance—it turns out to be mate in three moves.

Why, you may properly ask, should Black do one thing to avoid mate in 12 when by so doing he gets mated in three or four?

Good question, and the answer is that this is an old

chess book convention, one of those hoary traditions that probably never made sense to begin with, make still less sense now and yet are still carried on. We have tried to avoid these inanities. But, since you have read this far in this book, you are undoubtedly already a chess bug and will go on to buy other books. So be prepared; don't let the conventions throw you.

The example that follows is a spectacular one and has frequently been quoted. You'll see why.

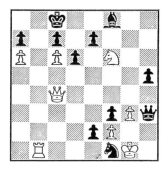

DIAGRAM 293

Black has a mate in one by Q—R7 or Q—N7. But, fortunately for White, it is not Black's move, and White saves the game with a couple of remarkable sacrifices. The play (White is Anderssen, the unofficial world champion who lost so gracefully to Paul Morphy) was as follows:

1   Q—K6ch   . . .

White gives up his Queen first.

1   . . .   Q×Q
2   N—Q7   . . .

And now the Knight. Black must capture it because R—N8 would be mate.

2   . . .   Q×N

Black figures that after 3 P×Q, K×P he will still have two pieces against a Rook as well as an overwhelming seven Pawns against three. But he does not figure on this turn of events.

3   R—N8ch   K×R

The capture of the Rook is forced.

4   P×Q

Now the capture of the Queen is decisive. No matter what move Black makes (try them all—go ahead)

White follows with 5 P—Q8/Q and it's mate on the eighth rank.

Mate with Rook and Bishop

Another fairly common middle-game mate, and one that might be considered a first-cousin to mate on the eighth rank, is the mate with Rook and Bishop. Probably the most famous example of this mate occurred in a game played in a box at the Paris Opera House during a performance of the Barber of Seville. The White pieces were handled by Paul Morphy, then on his celebrated tour of Europe; the Black pieces were handled, in consultation, by two prominent amateurs, the Duke of Brunswick and Count Isouard. The two noblemen took the trouble of arranging the board so that Morphy faced the back of the box. This piqued Morphy somewhat, as he wanted to see the opera. Perhaps this spurred him on to polish off the two amateurs in such short order.

The noblemen used Philidor's Opening (about which more in the next chapter), which is not such a good opening at best and which, against Morphy, is chessboard suicide. Here, in its entirety, is the game:

1   P—K4   P—K4
2   N—KB3   P—Q3

Black's second move is characteristic of Philidor's Opening; it can lead to a constricted position and lack of mobility.

3   P—Q4   B—N5

A better move would be 3 . . . N—Q2 or 3 . . . N—B3 or even 3 . . . P×P

4   P×P   B×N
5   Q×B   P×P
6   B—QB4   . . .

Without further ado White already threatens mate. He is developing rapidly and effectively while Black diddles away.

6   . . .   N—KB3
7   Q—QN3   Q—K2
8   N—QB3   P—QB3
9   B—KN5   . . .

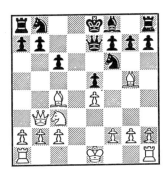

DIAGRAM 294

Position after 9 B—KN5

This game never really gets much beyond the opening. Just as it starts to enter the middle game stage . . . but we're jumping ahead.

| 9 | . . . | P—QN4 |

A tactical error that gives White a chance to force a win by starting with a sacrifice.

10	N×NP	P×N
11	B×NPch	QN—Q2
12	O—O—O	. . .

DIAGRAM 295

Position after 12 O—O—O

White castles Queen-side, bringing his Queen Rook into play at once on the open Queen file. This capture and control of the open file is decisive. In conjunction with the two Bishops it proves Black's rapid undoing.

| 12 | . . . | R—Q1 |
| 13 | R×N | . . . |

White now sacrifices the exchange.

| 13 | . . . | R×R |
| 14 | R—Q1 | . . . |

But he is still in control of the open file; the White Queen Rook is pinned.

| 14 | . . . | Q—K3 |
| 15 | B×Rch | N×B |

DIAGRAM 296

Position after 15 . . . NxB

And now the final sacrifice and the most spectacular. But it is well founded because it removes the block to mate at Q8.

| 16 | Q—N8ch | N×Q |
| 17 | R—Q8 mate | |

DIAGRAM 297

Position after 17 R—Q8 mate

This is, as you see, a mate on the eighth rank, made possible by the Bishop at KN5. Here are other, not quite so brilliant, examples of the mate with Rook and Bishop.

The position shown below occurred in a game between Bhend, from the Swiss team, and Lokvenz, of the Austrian, at the Chess Olympiade in Amsterdam in 1954.

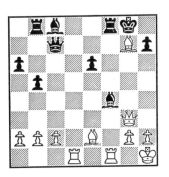

DIAGRAM 298

There is, you might say, a family resemblance between this position and the one after Black's 15th move in the Opera Box game. White has control of the open files with his Rooks; White Bishops are poised to aid the Rooks. Notice that if there were no Black Bishop on the King Bishop file White could mate at once with R×R.

The play was as follows:

1	B—R6 dis ch	K—R1
2	R×B	R×R
3	Q×R	Q×Q
4	R—Q8ch	. . .

And Black can only interpose to stave off mate for a moment.

| 4 | . . . | Q—B1 |
| 5 | R×Q mate | |

DIAGRAM 299

Position after 5 RxQ mate

The mate with Rook and Bishop, aside from occurring on the eighth rank, shares other characteristics with the "pure" mate on the eighth rank (that is, the mate with Rook alone or with Queen). For one thing, the loser's eighth rank is insufficiently guarded. In both Rook-and-Bishop examples given the King was denied the protection of a Rook because one of his own pieces —in both cases a Bishop—masked that potential defender's power. For another, the attacker is in control of an open file. And third, the defending King is generally without mobility.

Here is our final example of a Rook-and-Bishop mate; it is from a game between two formidable grandmasters, Reti and Tartakower, played in Vienna in 1910. Grandmasters don't usually let themselves fall into mating traps. But Tartakower did. And grandmaster games usually run at least thirty or more moves (except when a "grandmaster draw" is agreed to after, say, 10 moves, which isn't very sporting). But this game lasted only 11 moves, something of a phenomenon for chess on this level. The position after White's eighth move (O—O—O) was this:

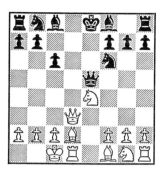

DIAGRAM 300

Position after 8 O—O—O

For some reason Tartakower failed to see the possibilities of the position, so he played:

| 8 | . . . | N×N |

Which was followed by

9	Q—Q8ch	K×Q (forced)
10	B—N5 dbl ch	K—K1
11	R—Q8 mate	

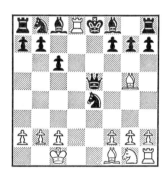

DIAGRAM 301

Position after 11 R—Q8 mate

Once more the pattern emerges: the attacker in control of the open file; the defending King without mobility; the defender's eighth rank insufficiently guarded. And—something we haven't specifically mentioned before—the defender's Queen off on a square where it can play no role in the defense.

Sacrificing to Conquer

Before going on to discussions of attacks against specific points, let's take a more detailed look at an offensive device (in the sense of an attack, not in the sense of something repulsive) that has cropped up again and again: the sacrifice.

In the very beginning, when he has just barely learned the moves, a chess player does not even contemplate sacrifices. Give up a piece? Why, I'd be crazy! Throw away my Queen? Waddayou—outa your mind? To the very beginner, material is everything, positional superiority nothing; it doesn't even exist as a factor.

As he learns more, however, and reads collections of master games, he sees that sacrifices frequently lead to brilliant victories. So he reverses his field and starts throwing his pieces away—on pure speculation. He "feels" a mating attack is in the air so he tosses a Rook into the pot. Then he throws in a Bishop. Then his Queen. Then he resigns.

A mating attack, it is true, is worth everything you have; all you need is the material to bring about mate. But the attack must be calculated to a nicety. If it peters out and you have given up all your pieces, where are you?

Sacrifices can be classified, roughly, into three types.

Clearance sacrifices. These are designed to clear the lines for further attack, to open files or diagonals, to bring more pieces into play.

Deflecting sacrifices. These are designed to get an enemy piece out of play. You have seen these, as well as clearance sacrifices, in the sections on mate on the eighth rank and mate with Rook and Bishop.

Stripping sacrifices. These are designed to strip the defending King of his protection, usually his Pawn protection.

In the attack on the point KR7 or the point KR8 (probably the weakest points in a castled King's position) these sacrifices are used quite frequently. Here is what might be called a model position:

DIAGRAM 302

The play would run as follows:

1	B×Pch	. . .

A stripping sacrifice, depriving the Black King of his Pawn protection.

1	. . .	K×B
2	N−N5ch	K−N1
3	Q−R5	

And it is mate next move.

If Black plays 2 . . . K−N3 instead of 2 . . . K−N1 he can hold out a trifle longer. For example:

2	. . .	K−N3
3	Q−N4	P−B4
4	Q−R4	N−Q4

To try for freedom.

5	P−K4	. . .

Giving the Knight the added protection of the Bishop. Now Black cannot play . . . Q×N

5	. . .	N−B3
6	P−K5	. . .

Black now must give up a Knight.

6	. . .	N×P
7	P×N	B−K2

To free the King Rook.

8	P×N	B×P
9	Q−R7 mate	

If Black plays 8 . . . R−R1 instead of 8 . . . B×P, White can follow with N−B7 and emerge from the complications with more material, a far more secure position and a vast superiority in mobility.

If, in the "model position" shown, the White King Pawn had been at K5 instead of K3, the ending would have been much quicker. The play would then proceed this way:

1	B×Pch	K×B
2	N−N5ch	K−N3
3	Q−N4	P−B4
4	Q−R3	any
5	Q−R7 mate	

Attack on KR7 and KR8

The attack on KR7 or KR8 frequently involves action along the King Rook file, by Rooks or Queen. As in the following example.

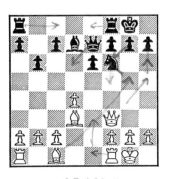

DIAGRAM 303

The position is from a game between Tarrasch and Mieses, played in a match in Berlin in 1916. The play was as follows:

1	B—KN5	QR—B1

Black aims for a Queen-side field of action. He would do better to strengthen his King side because the point KR7 (Black's KR2) is defended only by the King and Knight, and White, with a great deal of mobility, can bring pressure to bear on that point.

2	KR—K1	KR—K1

Black fails to see what is going on. His play is too passive. He ought to dislodge the Queen Bishop with . . . P—KR3.

3	Q—R3	Q—Q3

Unpinning the Knight. But too late.

4	B×N	. . .

Now, with the only defender gone and with his King's Pawn protection about to fall apart, Black is through.

4	. . .	P×B
5	Q—R6	. . .

White's last move is doubly strong: not only does it bring the Queen up for the kill, but it also prevents the escape of the King by way of . . . K—B1. It also clears the route for the Rook.

5	. . .	P—KB4

Black tries to stave off the finale by closing the long diagonal to the White Bishop.

6	R—K3	. . .

Bringing the Rook around in a zig-zag move. In effect, White will create an open file despite the presence of his own Pawns.

6	. . .	Q×P

This is a futile attempt to protect the point KN2 which, when the White Rook moves to Knight file, will be an Achilles' heel.

7	P—QB3	. . .

This forces the Black Queen off the protective diagonal. Mate at KN2 can't be stopped. Black resigned.

Notice how Tarrasch, in attacking the point KR7, forced a decisive weakening of the castled King's position that permitted him to shift the attack to the newly weakened point KN2.

The technique used by Tarrasch—of switching from an attack on one weak point to an attack on another—is a common one, especially when the weak points are tied together. Naturally, you would expect the weak point KR7 to be closely linked to KN7 and KB7, and such, indeed, is the case. In this next example the attack on the castled King never really seems to focus on any one of those weak points; the defender has all he can do to shift his forces to fend off one attack, when the next one gets moving. The White pieces were handled by Alekhine, the Black by Tartakower; the game was played in 1927.

The position after Black's 13th move was:

DIAGRAM 304

White's pieces are poised for a King-side attack. Having castled Queen-side, he is also ready to bring his King-side Pawns into the battle. The play was as follows:

14	N—R6ch	. . .

A double-edged sacrifice. Not only does it start stripping the King of his Pawn protection, but it clears the diagonal for the King Bishop.

(A good point to remember: in attacks on the castled King one of the best offensive pieces is the King Bishop which, as you know, is often sacrificed at KR7 to bait the mating trap. The King Bishop is particularly potent when supported by a Knight posted on the fifth or sixth rank.)

Black cannot decline the sacrifice. If he plays 14 . . . K—R1 White follows with 15 N×Pch, winning the Queen. If he plays 14 . . . K—B1 it is mate at once by 15 Q×KBP.

14	. . .	P×N
15	B×Pch	. . .

A second sacrifice, again denuding the King of his Pawns. In addition, it deflects the King Knight from his effective position. The sacrifice—like all properly calculated sacrifices—cannot be declined. 15 . . . K—B1 leads to 16 B×P mate. 15 . . . K×B leads to Q×Pch. Other moves all mean trouble. Actually, Black's only reasonable move here was 15 . . . resigns. But he did the best he could.

15	. . .	N×B
16	Q—N4ch	K—R1
17	R×Q	R×R
18	Q—K4	N—QB3
19	Q×N	. . .

White is gathering the harvest now.

19	. . .	B—KB1
20	N—B5	B—B5
21	B×RP	B—Q4
22	Q—B7	QR—B1

Black can do little more than stall for time.

23	Q—B4	R—B3
24	B×B	. . .

White exchanges here not only to save tempi (the Bishop at R6 would have been a problem to defend, and would have consumed time) but also to disconnect the Black Rooks.

24	. . .	R×B
25	Q—K5ch	N—B3
26	N—Q6	resigns

DIAGRAM 305
Position after 26 N—Q6

Look at the miserable Black King! Not a Pawn around to cover his nakedness. He looks—if you will pardon this brief lapse into the all-too-common chessbook failing of making people out of chess pieces—kind of forlorn moping there in the corner.

Oh, the position, yes. Black has no way to save the Knight. And with the fall of the Knight, what has he left? So he quit.

The attacks shown so far have been made on the castled King when his three Pawns (at his KB2, KN2 and KR2) were unmoved. The attack takes a somewhat different form when one or more of these Pawns have been moved. Usually the Pawn that has been moved is the Rook Pawn.

Here is a "typical" position in which a sacrifice leads to mate:

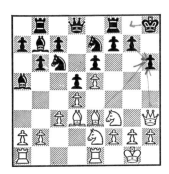

DIAGRAM 306

The play is as follows:

1	B×P	P×B

If Black plays 1 . . . K—N1, 2 B×P is decisive.

2	Q×Pch	K—N1
3	Q—R7 mate	

The King Knight is the "natural" defender of the point KR2. When the Knight is not at his post (KB3) the attack is easy. When he is there, sacrifices may have to be made to get the attack moving. Here is an example from a Steinitz-Lasker game (Nuremberg, 1896). The position after White's 23rd move was:

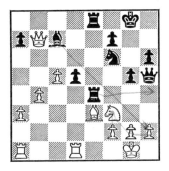

DIAGRAM 307

The White Pawns in front of the King are unmoved and the Knight is at his post. But a sacrifice leads to a quick finish. The play was:

23	. . .	B×Pch
24	N×B	R—R5
25	P—B3	. . .

(Tartakower and duMont have pointed out that mate follows after 25 Q—B7 as follows: 25 . . . N—N5; 26 Q—Q7, R×N; 27 Q×Rch, K—R2; 28 P—N3, R×P; 29 B×R, Q—R7ch; 30 K—B1, Q×B mate.)

25	. . .	R×N
26	Q—B7	R—R8ch
27	K—B2	Q—R5ch
28	Q—N3	Q×Qch
29	K×Q	R×R
30	R×R	R×B

And Black, a piece to the good and with the attack still being felt, wins easily.

You have seen the pieces in action. Now let's take a more detailed look at the way Pawns can get into the act. If one of the defending King's Pawns has been moved, the attacker simply blockades that Pawn, then attacks it. By so doing the attacker can force open one of the vital files that bear down on the castled King.

Thus, in this position,

DIAGRAM 308

the attacker plays 1 P—N5 (blockading the Black King Knight Pawn), then follows through with P—R5 or P—B5 (depending upon which file—the Rook or Bishop—he wants to open. This, in turn, depends upon the placement of Rooks or Queen).

In this position

DIAGRAM 309

White can force open a file with 1 P—B5 followed by P—N5. And in this position

DIAGRAM 310

White can force a file with P—R5 followed by P—N5.

The technique is the same if the whole position is shifted downwards, provided, of course, that relationships remain the same. Thus, in the following position, White can force open a file with 1 P—N4 followed by P—R4 or P—B4.

DIAGRAM 311

The advance of the Pawns, if the attacker's King were behind them, could be dangerous to him. Usually, then, a Pawn storm is preceded by castling on the opposite wing. In addition (and this has been said before), an attack on a flank should never be started unless the attacker has control of the center. If control is impossible, the center should be frozen—locked—to prevent counter-action there.

Here is an example of what we mean.

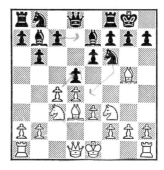

DIAGRAM 312

This position came about with Black's 7th move in a game played in 1900 between Pillsbury and Marco.

The situation here is still quite fluid in the center. Pillsbury, envisioning a King-side attack, decides to close the center. He played 8 P×P.

If Black had replied 8 . . . N×P the center would have remained fluid, and the ensuing complications might have worked out better for Marco. But Black played 8 . . . P×P, going along with White's plan to lock the center.

White followed through with 9 N—K5. This serves a triple purpose: it consolidates White's control of the center, gives him a strongly posted Knight to assist in the coming King's-wing attack, and it clears the route for his Queen.

The play continued as follows:

9 . . .   QN—Q2

Black continues with a normal development. This move, characteristic of the so-called Orthodox Defense to the Queen's Gambit Declined, tends to restore some of the tension in the center, especially in view of Black's fianchettoed Queen Bishop. White goes ahead nevertheless with his plans for a King-side attack (the center, if not frozen solid, is still stable enough to permit this action).

10 P—B4   P—B4

Black's 10th move, normally a sign that he has freed himself and equalized, is pointless here. Black is trying for a Queen-side skirmish when he should be attending to the King's wing.

11 O—O   . . .

Unusual, to say the least. (A King-side attack, as we noted, usually is preceded by castling long, to insure the safety of the King. White, however, seeing the Queen-side demonstration coming, prudently decides to castle away from it and to take his chances when the big Pawn-push comes.)

11 . . .   P—B5

On with the Queen-side push. Tsk tsk! Black is blithely unaware of the dangers on the other flank.

12 B—B2   P—QR3
13 Q—B3   . . .

White begins to mobilize his troops for the attack, shifting them to the scene of the coming action.

13 . . .   P—N4

DIAGRAM 313
Position after 13 . . . P—N4

Appearances are deceiving. Black seems to have the better position; his Pawn chain seems to be solid, his King seems to be secure, he has mobility and a potential Queen-side onslaught in the works. White, on the other hand, seems to have unduly loosened his Pawn structure (his King Pawn, at the moment, is backward and creates a "hole" at K4). But many factors involved in analyzing a chess position are hidden. Which is why the outcome of a game, deduced from any given position, is no more precise than the prediction of weather from any given set of meteorological conditions. Not everything can be taken into account. Besides, Marco played one thing obviously badly: he neglected to remember that Pillsbury was, by nature, an attacking player, and a successful one at that.

14 Q—R3   . . .

With this move White forces a weakening of the castled King's Pawn position. The defending Knight at KB3 can be captured and the assault on Black's KR2 then becomes overwhelming. For example: N×N; Q×N; B×N, B×B and mate follows quickly.

14 . . .   P—N3

This stops the immediate threat of mate at KR2, but irreparably weakens the Pawn position.

15 P—B5   . . .

Pillsbury starts to pry open files.

15 . . .   P—N5
16 P×P   . . .

Black has no time now to carry through his Queen-side assault. He must keep his attention riveted to the King's wing.

16 . . .   RP×P
17 Q—R4   . . .

White focuses on Black's KB3 (notice the flexibility of the attack and the interdependence of the squares in front of the castled King; the attack shifts now here, now there, and as one square gets protection, another weakens).

| 17 | ... | P×N |

Black still trying for counterplay on the other flank.

| 18 | N×N | ... |

The end of one of the defenders of Black's KB3—the double end—because not only is the Knight eliminated, but the defending Queen now is forced away. A beautiful diversionary tactic.

18	...	Q×N
19	R×N	P—R4
20	QR—KB1	...

Doubling Rooks.

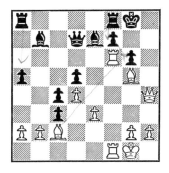

DIAGRAM 314

Position after 20 QR—KB1

The picture has changed completely, and White's advantages are now glaringly obvious.

| 20 | ... | R—R3 |

Trying to bolster the weak KB3. But too late. Here comes the culminating combination.

| 21 | B×P | P×B |

White now has his Rooks doubled on a wide open file and the defending King is all but stripped of protection.

22	R×Rch	B×R
23	R×Bch	K×R
24	Q—R8ch	...

And now the other open file is used.

| 24 | ... | K—B2 |
| 25 | Q—R7ch | resigns |

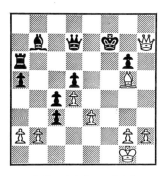

DIAGRAM 315

Position after 25 Q—R7ch

Black cannot save his Queen. If he plays 25 . . . K—K3, 26 Q×P is mate. If he plays 25 . . . K—K1, 26 Q—N8 is mate. Besides which, White, after 22 . . . B×R, had announced mate in six anyway, as follows:

23	R×Bch	K×R
24	Q—R8ch	K—B2
25	Q—R7ch	K—B1
26	Q×Q	any (say, P×P)
27	B—R6ch	K—N1 (forced)
28	Q—N7 mate	

Attack on KB7

You have seen, in the previous section, how an attack against KR7 or KR8 can also involve an attack against KB7 or KN7. So let's get one thing straight right now: there is no such thing as a pure attack against just one fixed point. There are, to be sure, certain techniques for maneuvering against specific points—but they are not fixed points. An attack, a good attack, should be a fairly flexible thing, capable of being shifted as the situation changes.

Why, then, have we isolated KR7 and KR8 and, now KB7, as objectives?

KR7 and KR8 you already know; KR7 is protected, after castling, only by the King and the Knight at KB6 it is weak. KR8, too, is vulnerable.

KB7 is vulnerable, before castling, because it is protected *only* by the King. It is, in fact, the weakest point on the entire board. After castling it can be given added protection, but usually at the cost of a cramped position.

Therefore: attack it.

The attack against this weak point is often carried

120

out by the Queen with the support of a minor piece, usually the King Bishop or a Knight. And the signal for the attack is all too frequently the advance of the defender's King Bishop Pawn, which opens up the diagonal KN1—QR7. Even without that weakening advance (let's not be dogmatic; the advance of the King Bishop Pawn is sometimes the signal for an attack by the side doing the advancing) attacks against KB7 are possible. And our first example (thank you again, Mr. Morphy) demonstrates that:

DIAGRAM 316

This position came about with Black's 13th move (Black being Von der Lasa; the game was played in Berlin in 1839). As you can see, quite a few exchanges have already taken place. Still, both sides have just completed their development and the game is just entering the middle stage. The play continued:

| 14 | QR—Q1 | B×P |

White sacrifices the Pawn for the sake of a more effective mobilization of his forces.

| 15 | P—QN3 | B—B3 |
| 16 | P—B4 | . . . |

And here is that "sometimes" case where the move P—KB4 means the start of an attack on KB7 by the side that has moved the KBP. Morphy, by pushing that Pawn, forces open the King Bishop file.

| 16 | . . . | QR—Q1 |

Counter-action in the center.

| 17 | P×P | . . . |

The file is open.

| 17 | . . . | Q×P |
| 18 | R—B5 | . . . |

Morphy wastes no time in posting his Rook effectively. The centrally stationed Black Queen must retreat, losing time.

COLLIER GUIDE TO CHESS

| 18 | . . . | Q—Q3 |

Black keeps his Queen mobile. His strategy is correct; he works in the center, keeping White occupied there to ward off an attack on the wing. His tactics, however, are faulty.

| 19 | P—K5 | . . . |

A Pawn fork. Simple, but so effective. Black has only one decent move.

| 19 | . . . | Q—B4ch |

He uses the diagonal opened by the advance of the King Bishop Pawn to check and wriggle out of the fork.

| 20 | K—R1 | N—K5 |

Black now hopes to deflate White's attack by exchanges. White cooperates, but it doesn't work out the way Black had hoped.

| 21 | N×N | R×Rch |
| 22 | Q×R | B×N |

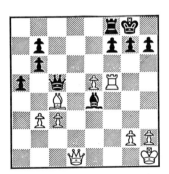

DIAGRAM 317
Position after 22 . . . B×N

The stage is set for a sacrificial assault on KB7.

| 23 | R×P | R×R |
| 24 | Q—Q8ch | . . . |

The insufficiently guarded eighth rank, plus a pinned Rook.

24	. . .	Q—KB1
25	B×Rch	K×B
26	P—K6ch	resigns

Black can play only 26 . . . K—N1, after which P—K7 is decisive. Notice how effectively Morphy uses tactical devices such as the pin, and strategic devices such as Pawn advances combined with assaults on weak squares.

The next example is a sort of double exercise. Both sides launch assaults on their respective KB7's. White whips up a fancy combination, only to find he hadn't figured it precisely enough; he neglected to take into account all the possible replies. The game was played in Warsaw in 1844; White was Hoffmann, Black von Petroff. The position after White's 6th move was this:

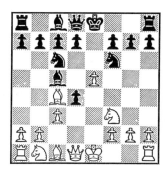

DIAGRAM 318

White has played off the beaten track. As a result, the middle game actually begins here, although neither side has completed his development. This is frequently the case when one of the players goes off on a strange tangent; complications come quickly and the opening stage never really has a chance to fully develop.

The play was:

| 6 . . . | N—K5 |

Having been prematurely attacked, Black responds by counter-attacking, the focus of his intentions being his KB7 (White's KB2, guarded only by the King).

| 7 B—Q5 | . . . |

And still White pursues his odd path.

| 7 . . . | N×KBP |

White must recapture, giving up his right to castle and sending his King off on a journey from which it will never return.

8	K×N	P×P dis ch
9	K—N3	P×P
10	B×P	. . .

Black has three Pawns for his Knight, plus more security than White.

| 10 . . . | N—K2 |

And now it is White's turn to assail KB7.

| 11 N—N5 | . . . |

This maneuver—posting a Knight at KN5—is one of the commonest you will find. As you see, it attacks KB7; if a Queen or Bishop supports the attack it can be devastating. Here, a Bishop does lend support— temporarily.

| 11 . . . | N×B |

And there goes the support.

| 12 N×BP | . . . |

DIAGRAM 319

Position after 12 NxBP

Nevertheless, White continues. He figures on 12 . . . K×N; 13 Q×Nch, K—K1 (but not 14 Q×B because of 14 . . . Q—N4ch; 15 K—B2, R—B1ch, etc). What he didn't figure on was

| 12 . . . | O—O |

One of those moves that really deserve the adjective "brilliant." He gives up his Queen for control of the open King Bishop file.

| 13 N×Q | B—B7ch |

And here goes the wandering King.

| 14 | K—R3 | P—Q3 dis ch |
| 15 | P—K6 | N—B5ch |

That open file can be murder.

| 16 | K—N4 | N×KP |

Black threatens mate in two with . . . R—B5ch and . . . R—R5

| 17 | P—N3 | . . . |

To cut off the Bishop's supporting role.

| 17 | . . . | N×N dis ch |

Oh, this is too gruesome to watch!

| 18 | K–R4 | R–B5ch |

The Pawn is pinned and the Rook is quite safe.

| 19 | K–N5 | . . . |

Unpinning the Pawn.

19	. . .	N–K3ch
20	K–R5	P–N3ch
21	K–R6	R–R5ch
22	P×R	B–K6 mate

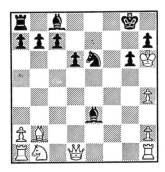

DIAGRAM 320

Position after 22 B—K6 mate

The attack on KB7 sometimes turns into a mate on the eighth rank, as in this example:

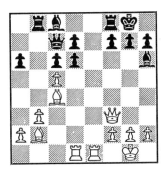

DIAGRAM 321

Here the play would be as follows:

| 1 | Q×Pch | R×Q |
| 2 | R–K8 mate | |

Aside from demonstrating the techniques of attacking certain points, you ought to have learned from the sections on attack some basic pointers about defense. For instance:

Don't expose your King unnecessarily by (a) loosening the Pawn position in front of the castled King, or (b) letting the King's "natural" guard, the Knight at KB3, go wandering off somewhere.

Don't let the line of communications between your pieces become weak. In other words, don't let your pieces get out of contact with each other. A piece stationed somewhere on the Queen's wing, if needed in a hurry to defend the King, ought to be able to get where it's needed quickly.

To see how well you learned these and other lessons, try out:

Self-Testing Quiz No. 15

(a) *The following position is one that occurs with frequency in an opening known as the French Defense. If it were White's move, what move would be good and why?*

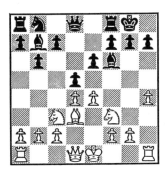

DIAGRAM 322

(b) *If you figured that one correctly, and Black replies . . . B–K2, how could you, as White, now launch an attack that, at the least, nets you a clear Pawn and, at the most, brings about mate?*

(c) *What move should Black* not *make in the following position?*

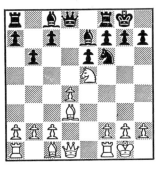

DIAGRAM 323

(d) *In the following position White threatens what?*

DIAGRAM 324

(e) How would you, as Black, counter White's threat in (d) if it were your turn to move?

(f) In the following position Black, though uncastled, has a tremendous advantage. He has, in fact, several—but what is the most telling one? And how could you, as Black, turn that advantage into victory? (Hint: a sacrifice of a major piece is involved.)

DIAGRAM 325

Common Errors and How to Exploit Them

Just what are common errors? Good question. Well, almost any error you can think of is reasonably common. Such as playing P—KR3 when it's not needed; such as advancing a Knight when it's needed for protection; such as making premature attacks; such as underestimating the strength of an attack.

Errors such as leaving a piece en prise—that is, leaving a piece in a position to be captured with no recompense—these are not really errors. They are gross blunders and we won't even bother to consider them.

But some errors crop up with more frequency than others. And these we will consider—briefly, to be sure—but consider nonetheless. Such as how to capture a straying Bishop.

The Bishop is the easiest piece to imprison. The typical position would be something like this:

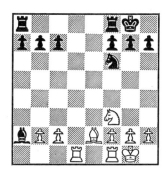

DIAGRAM 326

The play would be 1 P—QN3 followed by 2 R—R1. The move of the Knight Pawn imprisons the Bishop; the Rook captures it.

Before moving a Bishop make sure no such imprisonment and subsequent capture is possible. It can happen even on an almost-full board.

As is often the case, the threat of something—rather than the actual carrying out of the threat—can be enough to turn an advantage. Take, for example, this position, which could reasonably be expected to occur in any of several variations of what is called the Queen's Pawn Opening:

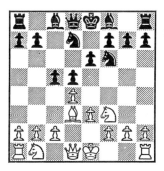

DIAGRAM 327

It is White's move. He must play 1 P—B3 if he wants to keep his King Bishop on the aggressive diagonal QN1—KR7. If he neglects 1 P—B3 (playing, say 1 O—O or 1 N—Q2 or, worse yet, 1 N—B3), Black follows with 1 . . . P—B5, threatening to capture the Bishop unless it gets off that diagonal. White must then retreat the Bishop to K2 or B1, losing a tempo, and Black can then seize the initiative with . . . N—K5.

Here is another example, one that could occur in, say, a Ruy Lopez or a Giuoco Piano. Black played his Queen Bishop to KN5 and White, after moving his Queen to break the pin, played P—KB3. Black played the Bishop to his KR4. White followed with P—KN4 and Black again retreated the Bishop, to his KN3. Now White closes the trap.

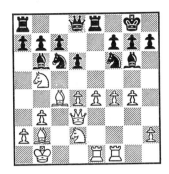

DIAGRAM 328

White plays 1 P—B5 and the Black Bishop is lost. Somewhere along the line, before the chase began, preferably, Black should have played (the lesser of several evils) P—KR3 or P—KB3 to give his Bishop an escape hatch.

Again we warn you: Bishops are easy prey to such traps.

Even more disastrous than losing a Bishop is losing a Queen. And, surprising as it may seem, Queens do fall into traps, though not as easily as Bishops, being able to move more freely.

The Queen, you must remember, is the most valuable piece you have. She cannot be blithely exchanged for a minor piece or even for a Rook unless some strong advantage in time or space results from the exchange. "Strong" is not a strong enough word; let's make that "unless a winning advantage results."

Here is an example in which a chess master lets his Queen fall into a trap. The game was played in 1911; White was Nimzovich, Black Leonhardt. The position after White's 28th move was this:

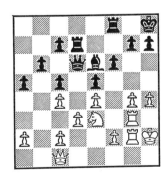

DIAGRAM 329

White has a glaring hole at his Q4, But it is only a temporary hole because (and here is one of those situations where a doubled Pawn is an asset rather than a liability) he has the move P—QB3 in reserve. Black reasonably gives in to ambition and plays 28 . . . Q—Q5, occupying the hole. The play continued:

29 **N—Q5**   . . .

And the Black Queen is trapped. Black tries to make the best of a bad situation.

29 . . .   **R×N**

He rescues his Queen, all right, but the ransom is too high.

30 **P—QB3**   . . .

The reserve move.

30	. . .	**Q×QP**
31	**KP×R**	**Q×P/B5**
32	**P×B**	**Q×KP**
33	**Q—B2**	. . .

White won easily. He got a Rook and Bishop in exchange for a Knight and three Pawns. In addition, he was able to consolidate his aggressive position while Black made forced moves (loss of time) getting his Queen out of her difficulties. As for material, Black has (after White's 33rd move) eight Pawns to White's five; but two of those Pawns are doubled, giving White, in effect, a whole Rook for two Pawns. Not a bad swap.

Because of her great power, the Queen is often over-used by beginners. One of the ways in which she is over-used is to have her wander all over the board, giving pointless checks and making pointless Pawn captures (such pointless Pawn captures are called Pawn snatching and it is something to stay away from, as you will see). All too often these power-mad beginners end up by losing their Queen; or they save the Queen and lose the game. Here is an example from a game between two amateurs, one a rank beginner, the other an experienced player.

The position after White's 9th move was this:

DIAGRAM 330

We will not comment on the first nine moves. But it is obvious that Black has played in accordance with a rather odd set of rules. Now he follows through. The play continued:

9 . . .   **Q—Q4**

Bringing his Queen into play too soon. He should have played 9 . . . O—O or, consolidating, 9 . . .

B—Q2. We can only guess that he hoped to capture the King Pawn with this sorry move.

10	N—K4	N×P

Well, well—he did capture the King Pawn. But watch.

11	N×N	Q×N/K4

And now the Queen hunt is really on in earnest.

12	**B—B4**	**Q—Q4**
13	**B—B3**	. . .

Threatening N—B6ch or N—Q6ch and the capture of the wandering Queen.

13	. . .	**Q—B4**

Black, you will notice, does not have much choice. Almost any other move loses the Queen at once.

14	**B—Q6**	. . .

Black cannot play 14 . . . B×B, for this would be followed by 15 N×Bch and the Queen falls.

14	. . .	**B—N3**
15	**B—R5**	. . .

Again the harried Queen must retreat, leaving behind a big hole in the defense.

15	. . .	**Q—Q4**
16	**B×N**	**K×B**
17	**R×Pch**	. . .

And the rest is inevitable.

17	. . .	**Q×R**
18	**B×Q**	**K×B**
19	**Q—R5ch**	. . .

Black resigned shortly afterward. A fine example of how not to use your Queen.

Among the Pawn Snatchers

The most common way in which Queens get in trouble is by Pawn snatching. And the Pawn most commonly snatched is the Queen Knight Pawn. It happens in game after game among beginners. The Queen charges forward to grab the unprotected Queen Knight Pawn; then the Queen's owner finds out the "gain" was a mirage.

And even masters fall into the trap. As witness this game between two giants of the early part of this century, Tchigorin (White) and Tarrasch. The position after Black's 11th move was this:

DIAGRAM 331

The play continued:

12	**O—O**	**Q×P**

The Pawn-snatch.

13	**B—Q2**	**B×N**
14	**B×B**	**Q—N4**
15	**P×P**	**B—B5**
16	**Q—K3**	**N—N5**

Black tries his own brand of Queen-hunt.

17	**Q—N5**	**N×KP**
18	**N—Q4**	. . .

Black, possibly in a belligerent mood because his breakfast had been bad, runs around making idle threats. White uses time gained to coordinate and consolidate his position.

18	. . .	**P—B3**
19	**Q—N3**	**Q—R3**
20	**N—B5**	**N—N3**
21	**P—KR4**	. . .

The beginning of a King-side attack made possible by Black's time-consuming "threats" and Pawn-grabbing. We will now skip to the position after Black's move No. 40.

DIAGRAM 332

Position after Black's 40th move

The action, of course, has shifted to the King side because of White's invasion there. The play continued:

41	R–B2	Q–R4
42	R–B3	R–N5
43	R–KR3	R/B2–N2
44	N–N6ch	P×N
45	P×P	resigns

If Black had tried 43 . . . K–N1, White would have followed through with 44 N–B3 and Black's Queen would have fallen. He chose what he thought was a line with some counterplay, only to find that he not only had no counterplay, but also was about to be mated. The Queen, of course, is lost here. Too much adventure, and too ambitious a Queen. Poor play for a master.

Pawn snatching can be dangerous any time. Here is a sample of what it can lead to in the very opening stages of a game. The position shown below comes about in the Queen's Gambit when Black tries to get too many Pawns for his money. The opening moves are:

1	P–Q4	P–Q4
2	P–QB4	P×P
3	N–KB3	P–QB4
4	P–K3	P×P
5	B×P	P×P

This last move is the clincher. Black is trying to reap a harvest he has not properly sown.

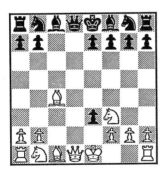

DIAGRAM 333
Position after 5 . . . PxP

Black probably expects 6 Q×Qch, K×Q. But White takes advantage of Black's Pawn-snatching with

6   B×Pch

And now, after . . . K×B, 7 Q×Q wins the Queen fair and square.

Where Is My Wandering Queen Tonight?

Closely related to Pawn-snatching is the evil of letting a piece wander around the board to make idle threats. The danger in both Pawn-snatching and wandering is twofold:

a) The wandering piece can be driven into a trap.

b) The King can be assaulted because the wandering piece is not around to help in the defense.

Here is an example from master play, the opponents being Charousek and Maroczy. The position after Black's 20th move was:

DIAGRAM 334

The White Queen has spent a good deal of time making pointless threats. Now she makes another one.

21   Q–R6   . . .

And Black efficiently refutes the move.

21   . . .   P–K4

The always-powerful thrust in the center.

22   P–R5   P–KN4

The Pawn advance is neatly counteracted.

23   B–N6   . . .

White, getting desperate, tries a trap. If Black plays 23 . . . P×B, 24 RP×P wins. But Black doesn't fall for the trap.

23	. . .	R–N2
24	P–B3	Q–N3

Troubles begin to close in on White.

25   P×NP   Q–Q1

This threatens to win the White Queen with . . B×P

26	B B2	B–QB1
27	resigns	

White's threatening position is hollow. Black, however, can now play . . . B×P, winning the White Queen.

And one more example, showing the effects of letting a Queen get out of play. The loser (Steinitz, playing White) went Pawn-fishing with his Queen. Too bad.

The position after Black's 22d move in this game (played in 1896) was:

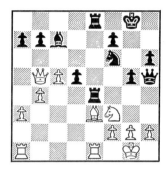

DIAGRAM 335

Now White gets a Pawn-snatching obsession.

| 23 | Q×P | . . . |

The Queen Knight Pawn, as usual. Black, however, has a nice refutation.

23	. . .	B×Pch
24	N×B	R—R5
25	P—B3	R×N
26	Q—B7	. . .

White now works feverishly to get his Queen back to where it can lend a hand. Because he let her wander, he wastes time doing so.

26	. . .	R—R8ch
27	K—B2	Q—R5ch
28	Q—N3	. . .

At last the Queen is back where she belongs. But it is too late.

28	. . .	Q×Qch
29	K×Q	R×R
30	R×R	R×B
31	resigns	

Black is a Knight up. The Black pieces were handled by Lasker. The moral of this example is: don't go grabbing Pawns way out in left field when your pieces belong at home defending the fort. (Pardon our mixed metaphor. No? All right, then let's make it: "don't go grabbing Pawns over on the flanks when your pieces belong back at headquarters.")

Winning Combinations

Now that you know what to look for, we'll present the grand finale—some fine examples of combinations taken from master play.

The first is from a game between Jackson and Noteboom played in 1930. The position after Black's 32d move was:

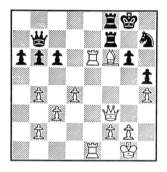

DIAGRAM 336

White now sacrifices (temporarily) his Queen in a play that breaks down Black's defenses.

33	B—K5	R×Q
34	R×Pch	K—B2
35	R—N7ch	K—K3

(If Black plays 35 . . . K—K1 White follows with 36 B—B7 dis ch and mate next move.)

| 36 | R×Q | . . . |

Regaining the Queen.

36	. . .	R/B6—B2
37	R×P	K—Q2
38	P—B3	N—B3
39	R×RP	resigns

And here is an example of a sacrifice that cuts the enemy's lines of communications, disrupting the effective cooperation of his forces. The players were Monticelli and Fine; the game was played in 1934. The position after White's 17th move was:

DIAGRAM 337

The play was:

| 17 | . . . | R—Q6 |

White's forces are effectively cut off from each other.

18	P×R	N×Bch
19	K—B2	B—QB4
20	Q—R3	N—Q5ch
21	K—B1	Q—N6
resigns		

If White plays 22 N—K3, Black plays . . . Q×QP, threatening mate in four different ways.

And an example by Alekhine, played against Asgeirsson in 1931.

DIAGRAM 338

The play was:

1	R×Nch	B×R
2	N—K4	Q—N5
3	N—Q6ch	K—B1
4	Q—B6ch	P×Q
5	R—B7	mate

It is, incidentally, the square KB7 that figures in this sprightly combination. Why not go back and re-read the section on attacking the point KB7?

Before ending this chapter, a few words about defense are in order. Actually, a separate chapter on defense is unnecessary; you have been learning all along how to defend; you need only reverse the procedures for attack to arrive at the procedures for defense. In other words:

(a) Where, as an attacker, you want to open lines, as a defender you want to keep them closed.

(b) Where, as an attacker, you seek to avoid exchanges, as a defender you try to bring them about.

(c) Where, as an attacker, you try to put a bind on the enemy, cramping his position, as a defender you seek to find space in which to maneuver.

When you find yourself in an uncomfortable position you should remember that offense is always the best defense. And if offense is impossible, remember to defend only against direct threats.

Go back over some of the games used as illustrations, especially those that illustrate combinations. Try to rearrange one or two pieces on the losing side in a way that will prevent the combination. Analyze each position to see where the weaknesses are and fix in your mind the results of such weaknesses. Then try not to let such weaknesses come about in your own positions.

Remember, too, that once a sound combination gets rolling there is usually little or nothing that can be done to prevent its reaching a successful conclusion. Oh, often enough mate can be staved off, but only at the cost of a Queen or a Rook or two—which is tantamount to resignation anyhow. The thing to do is to see to it that you don't get into a position in which such forceful combinations are possible.

For further reading on the middle game see the list of books at the end of Chapter 13.

Chapter Eight

THE OPENING

Building a Foundation

THOUGH IT has not been presented to you as such, you have already learned some of the basic elements of opening play. For the opening—despite all the elaborate and often bewilderingly complex systems that have been devised—is fundamentally nothing more than development. The more logical and efficient the development, the better the opening.

As was already pointed out (or was it harped upon?), the first dozen moves in a chess game are as vital to the structure of the game as a foundation is to the structure of a home. If the opening is slipshod the game will not stand; little weaknesses created in the opening develop into gaping holes.

At the risk of being repetitious, then, we will go over, quickly, some of the material presented in Chapter 4.

The essence of development is the quick and efficient mobilization of your forces. At first, your pieces are locked in behind your Pawns; you must move some Pawns to allow the pieces to get into action, to exert their powers. The fewer moves you make in developing, the more rapid your development will be—moving a piece more than once (unless it is to take advantage of your opponent's error) is time-consuming and destructive. A corollary is that the fewer Pawn moves you make the stronger your position will be.

Dr. Tarrasch, in fact, used to advise his pupils—in jest, of course—that the best way to win was never to make a Pawn move. The element of truth in that joke is obvious.

Knights have what could be called a natural tendency to develop to B3; from that position they easily defend the weak Rook Pawn and keep an eye on the center; they are also in a position to leap right into the center should the opportunity present itself.

Bishops are aggressively posted at B4 or N5; they can also be played to N2 (this is called the fianchetto position—from the Italian, meaning "from the flank"), but this requires the moving of the Knight Pawn and a consequent weakening of the Pawn structure.

In general, Knights are developed before Bishops. And, too, the Queen is generally not developed too early in the game, being rather sensitive to assaults by pieces of lesser value. Rooks get into the picture only when files are opened for them, or if they are rather laboriously developed by a zig-zag motion.

The object of development, aside from mobilizing your own forces, is to hamper the development of the enemy. A move that does both things at once is worth more than passing consideration.

White, having the first move, has, by birthright, so to speak, the initiative. It is his job to retain it, capitalize on it and convert it into victory. Black's prime job is to try to maintain a balance, not permitting White to increase his advantage; he will also try to seize the initiative should his opponent err.

So much for our brief recapitulation of the elements of opening play. Now let's look at them more closely.

Theory in Tension

In the Ninth Edition of *Modern Chess Openings,* which is frequently called the bible of opening play, more than fifty opening systems are listed, ranging from such well-known systems as the Ruy Lopez and the Sicilian Defense, to such esoterica as Bird's Opening and the Hromadka System. And under Sicilian Defense, for example, there are twenty-odd variations, each with a whole range of sub-variations and by-plays. Obviously no man can possibly commit to memory all the hundreds of variations. Yet, when master meets master over the board mistakes in the opening are rare, even when little-known (or even new) variations are tried. Why?

Because the masters know the why's and wherefore's of opening play. They know the theory behind the openings and, as a result, they never make bad moves (What, never? Well, hardly ever—after all, even a chess master is more or less human).

The same three factors that operate in the middle game operate in the opening: force, space and time. One can be changed into the other, too, just as in the middle game. A Pawn, for example, can be sacrificed for time (such a sacrifice in the opening is known as a gambit).

Early in the book you were told that a Bishop was worth about three and a half Pawns, that a Queen was worth about ten Pawns, and so on. By the same token, a Pawn can be evaluated in terms of time or space; it is worth approximately three tempi. Its value with respect to space cannot be fixed even as approximately as this—conditions must be measured carefully to say whether the sacrifice of a Pawn is worth a particular advantage in space.

In the opening, too, the Pawns are not all of equal value; a center Pawn is worth considerably more than a flank Pawn. Which, incidentally, gives rise to the general rule that it is better to capture toward the center than away from it. As for example:

DIAGRAM 339

White has just played B×N. Black should recapture with NP×B, capturing toward the center. Black will thus retain his King Pawn for a later advance (the NP capture also has the advantage of opening a file for the King Rook).

Considered in a vacuum—in that "all-other-things-being-equal" sense—the moves P—K4 and P—Q4, together, constitute an ideal. Together, they open diagonals for both Bishops and for the Queen, they control the squares QB5, Q5, K5 and KB5, they afford powerful protection for pieces that may be posted in enemy territory and they cramp the enemy game. In addition, they constitute at all times a threat to the enemy; they can, under the right circumstances, roll on, crushing enemy resistance.

In openings in which the first move is P—K4, then, White's big objective is P—Q4. When he opens with P—Q4, his objective will be P—K4. Even in the so-called irregular openings (other than 1 P—K4 or 1 P—Q4) the objective is essentially the same.

For Black, too, P—Q4 and P—K4 are the desiderata that determine his tactics.

In a well-played opening, however, it is not quite so easy to take control of the center. After 1 P—K4, the thrust P—Q4 must be carefully prepared; the stage

must be set. If it is not, well, consider the following:

| 1 | P—K4 | P—Q4 |

The thrust by Black, intended to undermine at once White's strong point in the center, fails, because of

| 2 | P×P | Q×P |
| 3 | N—B3 | |

and the Black Queen must retreat, losing time. Wait, you say, Black loses a tempo but gains a Pawn and is, according to the rule of thumb, ahead two tempos. But is he? Not at all; White, too, has captured a Pawn and the net loss to Black remains a tempo, and a vital one at that. White uses the time to increase his development. Coupled with his initial advantage of the move, it constitutes a tremendous bonus for White, an almost insurmountable bonus.

Suppose White tries the same thing:

| 1 | P—K4 | P—K4 |
| 2 | P—Q4 | . . . |

Here White seeks to undermine Black's strong point. It fails for the same reason.

| 2 | . . . | P×P |
| 3 | Q×P | N—QB3 |

And now it is White who must retreat, giving up his advantage of the move. The initiative shifts to Black.

There is, in addition to the loss of tempi, another disadvantage in this ill-prepared thrust. To understand it, we will have to examine once more this business of the ideal of the opening.

After 1 P—K4, White has a strong foothold in the center. Black must do something to weaken that foothold and, in abstract, the best he can do is to get rid of the White King Pawn—eliminate it from the picture. Without a White Pawn at White's K4, Black would be free to post a Pawn at his own Q4, thus achieving his first main objective.

What Black is aiming for is equality—the destruction of White's birthright of the move and the initiative. What White aims for is the prevention of such a move by Black and the strengthening of his initiative.

As long as the center remains contested there is tension there. White plants a Pawn in the center; Black does the same. White attacks Black's Pawn; Black defends it. White threatens a second thrust in the center; Black parries by preparing a defense to such a thrust.

This is known as maintaining the tension.

By playing 1 P—Q4 in reply to 1 P—K4 Black immediately relieves the tension and permits White to attend to matters other than the control of the center.

White, in playing P—Q4 after 1 P—K4, P—K4, does the same—he relieves the tension in the center and frees Black's hand.

It must be borne in mind, too, that the mere presence of a Pawn in the center is no guarantee in and of itself of sure success. The center Pawn must be free and mobile. If it is locked in it can threaten nothing; if it is free to move it constitutes an ever-present threat. The following Pawn structure, in games beginning with 1 P—K4, P—K4, is the ideal one from White's point of view.

DIAGRAM 340

White, you will notice, has eliminated Black's King Pawn. He also has a free and mobile Pawn in the center, as opposed to Black's somewhat restricted Pawn. White, too, has a firm defender ready for the posting of a piece at KB5 or Q5. In short, he is set to invade.

Any opening that leads to this Pawn structure, is favorable for White, provided that White follows through. If White, having established such a structure, fails to use it to attack, his advantage will dissipate itself (in the end game, for example, such a structure might, indeed be a liability for White, instead of an asset).

As for Black, as long as he can maintain a balance, a sort of symmetry, he has nothing to fear. White's only advantage remains the move.

In general, White tries to avoid exchanges in the opening, because such exchanges tend to free Black's game, opening lines for his men. White tries to maintain the tension or, if that proves impossible, to lock the center and keep it frozen, preferably with Black pieces cramped.

There are times, however, when exchanges become necessary. Such as:

1	P—K4	P—K4
2	N—KB3	N—QB3
3	P—Q4	P—Q4
4	P×QP	Q×P
5	N—QB3	B—QN5

DIAGRAM 341
Position after 5 . . . B—QN5

It can be said right off the bat that White's fourth move was a bad one and that Black's fourth was even worse. But the point at the moment is that both sides are building up the tension in the center. And Black, who is defending, does not want to give up his tempi.

After 6 B—Q2, the Black Queen is again threatened. Black could retreat her, but in so doing he would turn over to White the undisputed control of the center and would, in the process, lose a couple of tempi to boot.

In such a case, Black's best bet is to exchange (as it might well be under many other circumstances, since exchanges, as a rule, ease Black's game). So Black plays 6 . . . B×N. This would be followed by 7 B×B, P×P, N×P. The tension in the center has been relieved and both sides are now free to go about the business of furthering their development.

Here Black forced White to exchange and White had little say in the matter. No doubt it was brought on by White's ill-prepared fourth move; he should have prepared more carefully for P—Q4.

Suppose Black tries to maintain his King Pawn this way:

1	P—K4	P—K4
2	N—KB3	P—Q3

With his second move White threatened the Black King Pawn, and Black protected it with P—Q3. This system is known as the strong-point system: it consists of maintaining the King Pawn at all costs. Under some circumstances it is a desirable system. In this case, however, the strong-point idea fails because 2 . . . P—Q3 locks in the King Bishop and restricts Black's development; King-side castling will be difficult, if not impossible, and Black invites a cramping bind by White.

A more desirable system is the counter-attack. Here Black gives up his King Pawn but, at the same time, forces White to do the same or suffer a weakened position. An example of the counter-attacking system will be found in the next section in the so-called main line of the opening known as the Giuoco Piano.

Often the beginner, in playing the opening, realizes he has a number of adequate moves at his disposal but does not know how to decide which is best. One way to do so is to figure the tempi involved. Take the following situation, for example:

DIAGRAM 343

DIAGRAM 342

This position comes about through the first seven moves of a variation of Petroff's Defense, a well-known opening. The moves are:

| 1 | P–K4 | P–K4 |
| 2 | N–KB3 | N–KB3 |

(the idea for Black here is, instead of defense of his own King Pawn, a counter-attack against the White King Pawn)

| 3 | N×P | P–Q3 |

(Black cannot play N×P at once, for after 4 Q–K2 either the Knight falls or worse things—such as the loss of the Queen—will follow)

4	N–KB3	N×P
5	Q–K2	Q–K2
6	P–Q3	N–KB3
7	B–N5	. . .

If Black now plays 7 . . . Q×Qch he gives away a tempo and helps White to develop (White will follow with 8 B×Q). A far better move is 7 . . . B–K3; no tempi are lost, development proceeds and Black does not hand to White on a silver platter the right to get a big lead in development at no extra cost.

It is sometimes possible to surrender the center temporarily with a view to re-occupying it under better conditions later. As in the following situation:

A simple counting of tempi will show that White, somewhere in the first few moves, threw away a tempo. By all rights he should have the move in this situation; he doesn't, and Black takes advantage of it by playing 1 . . . P×P, which, at first glance, seems to be giving up the center. There follows:

| 2 | P×P | P–Q4 |
| 3 | P–K5 | N–K5 |

And Black reoccupies the center, this time with a piece and a Pawn. He has a strong position.

What we have presented so far in this chapter is really no more than a mere sketch of the general principles underlying opening play. But to present these principles in an abstract, ivory-tower sort of way is to neglect the practical applications of these principles. You must learn to see these principles at work, under what might be called battle conditions.

And this is what will be done in the sections that follow. Bear in mind, however, that you are not being asked to memorize by rote the various openings and variations. Rather, you are advised to study them with an eye to extracting from them the basic principles that make one variation better than another for White or for Black; that make one move good and another bad. And remember, too, that the game does not end with the opening.

If a variation gives one side an advantage in the middle game it does not necessarily follow that the game is won for that side. Unless the side with the advantage follows through in the middle game, pressing home the attack, it may find that the advantage has disappeared in the end game and that, indeed, the advantage has turned into a marked liability.

Some openings seem to have little effect on the end game; these tend to lead into vigorous and forceful play in the middle game. Other openings lead, in general, to a relaxed kind of middle game and then find their real expression in the end game. If, for example, an opening gives one side a King-side Pawn majority, that side will try to bring the end game on without any alteration in the Pawn structure.

Here, then, is a cross-section of openings:

King's Pawn Openings

Openings in which 1 P—K4 is answered by 1 . . . P—K4 are, as a rule, characterized by sharp and often violent play. They lead to open positions in which the pieces move freely, in which exchanges are made often and in which some action always seems to be going on. It has been said that this characterization of the King's Pawn openings as open games is erroneous; that all games, sooner or later—even those that begin with 1 P—Q4 — become open.

True enough. But the fact remains that, using master play as a criterion, games opening with the King's Pawn do tend to show more tactical maneuvering and less quiet, strategic backing and filling. Combinations seem to crop up more regularly—and with more spectacular results—in King's Pawn openings than in Queen's Pawn openings. But enough of this sophistry —you can judge for yourself after you have played a couple of dozen of each kind of game.

GIUOCO PIANO

The Giuoco Piano (from the Italian, meaning "quiet game"—as often as not a misnomer) is one of the oldest and still one of the commonest openings. It is characterized by the following moves:

1	P—K4	P—K4
2	N—KB3	N—QB3
3	B—B4	B—B4

DIAGRAM 344

Position after 3 . . . B—B4

So far the symmetry remains unbroken. White still has the advantage of the first move and nothing more; Black has maintained the balance, not acquiring complete equality, but not giving up anything either.

What is the point of White's third move and Black's reply?

With 3 B—B4 White at once prevents Black's playing P—Q4, the key liberating move. Black's reply is in

kind. From this point on there are several divergent lines of play.

White can elect to keep things relatively quiet with 4 N—B3, a natural developing move that, in addition, keeps another eye on Black's Q4. What usually follows is:

4	. . .	N—B3

Again, a quiet developing move.

5	P—Q3	P—Q3

Both sides are intent upon keeping the King Pawn in place and intact; both do so in unobtrusive ways.

6	B—K3	. . .

Further preparation for P—Q4.

6	. . .	B—N3

Black anticipates the coming thrust and prepares for it. In this case the judicious withdrawal of the Bishop before it becomes mandatory is not a loss of tempo.

7	Q—Q2	. . .

White now develops his Queen and prepares to castle Queen side.

7	. . .	B—K3

Black threatens an exchange that would undermine White's center; the White QP would be forced to recapture, permitting Black to take over in the center.

8	B—N3	. . .

Retreating the Bishop to a square from which, if it is captured, recapture would not involve the loss of the center.

8	. . .	Q—Q2
9	O—O—O	O—O—O

DIAGRAM 345

Position after 9 . . . O—O—O

The board is completely symmetrical. The game has, indeed, been a quiet—even a dull one. For that reason this variation is seldom adopted by White nowadays. There are other, more promising lines to follow. The best of them begin with 4 P—B3, which is preparatory to P—Q4, an attempt to capture the center.

In reply to 4 P—B3, 4 . . . P—Q3 fails. Black's attempt to maintain the King Pawn by means of a strong point can only result in loss of the center, with no recompense, or a cramping bind. His best reply to 4 P—B3 is the counter-attack with 4 . . . N—B3.

The play then runs, in the main line, as follows:

5	P—Q4	P×P
6	P×P	B—N5ch
7	N—B3	N×KP
8	O—O	. . .

White, in return for the Pawn he has sacrificed—and it is not a real gambit because the sacrifice is only a temporary one—has a lead in development and the prospects of a healthy attack.

(If Black, incidentally, declines to take the King Pawn he gets nothing but trouble. The line runs like this: 7 N—B3, P—Q4; 8 P×P N/KB3×P; 9 O—O, B×N; 10 P×B, B—K3; 11 R—K1, O—O; 12 N—KN5 and Black is subjected to a powerful King-side attack.)

Black's best chances in the main line begin with

8	. . .	B×N

The line then runs as follows:

9	P—Q5	. . .

(If White takes the Bishop at once with 9 P×B, Black can reply P—Q4 then and there, equalizing the game.)

9	. . .	N—K4
10	P×B	N×B
11	Q—Q4	P—KB4
12	Q×N/B4	P—Q3

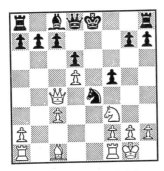

DIAGRAM 346

Position after 12 . . . P—Q3
in the main line

White has an excellent development but is a Pawn behind; Black, despite his lag, nevertheless has a firm position.

There are other more-or-less standard variations of the Giuoco Piano, one of the most popular being 9 . . . B—B3 (instead of 9 . . . N—K4). It runs this way:

10	R—K1	N—K2
11	R×N	P—Q3
12	B—N5	B×B
13	N×B	O—O
14	N×RP	B—B4

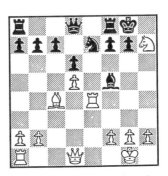

DIAGRAM 347

Position after 14 . . .
B—B4 in the variation
beginning 9 . . . B—B3

Chances are about equal at this point, though White has a strong King-side attack going. Still, with careful play Black can keep things on an even keel. The very fact that no one has a great advantage here is evidence of the soundness of this line for both sides. Still, with all the fireworks possible from such a position, "quiet game" is certainly a misleading name.

MAX LANGE ATTACK

The Max Lange attack is sometimes considered an off-shoot of the Giuoco Piano, sometimes of the Two Knights Defense (the Two Knights Defense is characterized by the moves 1 P—K4, P—K4; 2 N—KB3, N—QB3; 3 B—B4, N—B3). Strictly speaking, it is a variation of the Two Knights Defense rather than of the Giuoco Piano because Black's third move, N—B3, is not normal to the Giuoco Piano. The idea behind the development of the King Knight, rather than of the King Bishop, is that Black thus tries to blunt White's attack and to get a more secure position.

In the Max Lange White tries to take advantage of the exposed position of Black's King Bishop; Black, for his part, pins his hopes on a direct attack on the White King.

The normal line of the Max Lange runs as follows:

1	P—K4	P—K4
2	N—KB3	N—QB3
3	B—B4	N—B3
4	P—Q4	P×P
5	O—O	B—B4
6	P—K5	. . .

DIAGRAM 348

Position after 6 P—K5
in the Max Lange Attack

Notice that it is possible to start with a normal Giuoco Piano and arrive at this same position. This is called transposition—one opening becomes another—and is much more characteristic of Queen's Pawn openings than of King's Pawn. More about that later. If White tries to *transpose to* the Max Lange with 4 O—O, B—B4; 5 P—Q4, P×P; 6 P—K5, Black can get the upper hand with 5 . . . B×P; 6 N×B, N×N; 7 P—B4, P—Q3; 8 P×P, P×P; 9 B—N5, Q—K2.

After 6 P—K5 in the main line, the play generally moves this way:

6	. . .	N—KN5
7	R—K1	P—Q6
8	B×Pch	K—B1

(not K×B, which would be followed by N—KN5ch and a devastating attack)

9	Q×P	B×Pch
10	K—B1	B×R
11	Q—B5	N—B3
12	P×N	Q×P
13	Q×Q	P×Q

Black's King-side Pawn structure is shattered, but White isn't in such fine shape either. The game is about even. If Black, however, can head straight for the end game he can turn his Queen-side Pawn majority into an advantage. White will concentrate on pushing his united King-side Pawns and on breaking up Black's Queen-side Pawns.

There are many variations possible at several stages of the Max Lange, some favoring White, some Black. If the dashing character of the Max Lange and the general free-for-all it involves appeal to you, by all means cultivate it. You'll find a wealth of variations to play with in *Modern Chess Openings,* ninth edition.

RUY LOPEZ

The Ruy Lopez is one of the oldest known openings, but it remains—despite innovations, new systems, sup-posed refutations and improvements—one of the most popular openings in the repertoire. It crops up time and time again in master tournaments and still accounts for many White triumphs.

It is characterized by the following moves:

1	P—K4	P—K4
2	N—KB3	N—QB3
3	B—N5	. . .

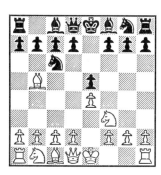

DIAGRAM 349

Position after 3 B—N5

The difference between the Lopez and the Giuoco Piano, notice, is only that here the King Bishop moves to QN5, instead of QB4, as in the G.P. Yet what a difference! Where the Giuoco Piano gave Black chance after chance to equalize, the Ruy Lopez is more likely to give him chance after chance to go wrong, and few chances to even the balance.

The basic idea is simple. With 2 N—KB3 White attacked the Black KP; with 3 B—N5 he continues that attack once removed—by attacking the KP's defender. The concept conforms to all the precepts of good chess: it develops a piece, it prepares for castling, it initiates a threat that must be parried.

Unlike the Giuoco Piano, the tension here is balanced on a pinpoint. A false step by Black and all is lost for him. Yet there are adequate defenses—and they must be set up.

Black's replies may be divided into two main types —those using 3 . . . P—QR3 and those that dispense with or postpone this move. In general, the latter systems are, at best, dull and barely adequate; they set up a reasonable defense and no more.

The systems using 3 . . . P—QR3, on the other hand, offer Black fair chances.

Here, too, is a case where the "natural" moves lead to a cramped game for Black and an excellent, almost an overpowering, one for White. Such moves might be:

3	. . .	P—Q3

Defending the KP a second time.

4	P—Q4	. . .

Attacking the KP a third time.

| 4 . . . | B—Q2 |

Unpinning the Knight.

| 5 | N—B3 | N—B3 |
| 6 | O—O | B—K2 |

Continuing development.

| 7 | R—K1 | . . . |

Preparing for the opening of the file.

| 7 . . . | P×P |

A more or less forced attempt to break the bind.

| 8 | N×P | O—O |
| 9 | B—B1 | . . . |

A judicious retreat that leaves White with a powerful Pawn center and Black with a cramped position. Notice that the Pawn formation is the "ideal" for White shown in diagram 340.

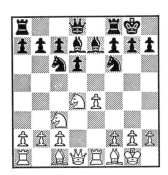

DIAGRAM 350

Position after 9 B—B1

It might be argued that Black, in the variation above, disregarded a fundamental principle—he shut in his Bishop with P—Q3.—and that this was the source of all his troubles. And we might just agree, except that here P—Q3 seems to have led to more problems than usual. Black's other source of discomfort is his failure to take vigorous action.

Black cannot pussyfoot against the Ruy Lopez; he must move with vigor and counter each thrust with—to borrow a phrase from the physics textbooks—an equal and opposite reaction.

One of the best lines for Black (best in that it gives Black a chance to break through and counter-attack if White is not careful) is the so-called main line of the Tarrasch Defense. It runs like this:

| 3 . . . | P—QR3 |

(Because this is the keystone to most of the really good defenses to the Ruy Lopez, we ought to examine this move more closely. What makes it so almost, well, indispensable? Without it, the Black Queen Knight is almost useless until deep into the middle game; it is glued to its post, depriving the King Pawn of true protection, immobilizing the Queen-side Pawns, playing almost no role except that of a statue and—it prevents Black's castling.

(Once P—QR3 is played the dead Knight takes on life. White has to leave the diagonal. He cannot play 4 B×N because this would be followed by 4 . . . QP×B; 5 N×P, Q—Q5! and Black regains his Pawn and has an excellent position to boot.)

| 4 | B—R4 | N—B3 |
| 5 | O—O | N×P |

Notice the similarity, at this point, to the Giuoco Piano; White temporarily gives up a Pawn and uses the time to castle.

| 6 | P—Q4 | P—QN4 |

Black deftly changes the subject, forcing White to shift his attention to the Bishop.

7	B—N3	P—Q4
8	P×P	B—K3
9	P—B3	. . .

White takes the precaution of preparing an escape route for the Bishop.

| 9 . . . | B—K2 |

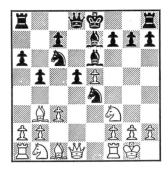

DIAGRAM 351

Position after 9 . . . B—K2

If you examine this position you will see that the chances are about 50-50; Black has been able to keep his Knight posted at K5, well within White's territory, and has developed with fair speed—no mean accomplishment.

In this same variation, Black has a choice, after 9 P—B3, of 9 . . . N—B4 or 9 . . . B—QB4. The first leads to some lively action in the center, the second to a lot of deft footwork on both sides of the board with quick exchanges of minor pieces and a reasonably even end game.

The Ruy Lopez, because of its age and its popularity, has been about as thoroughly investigated as any opening you care to think of. Almost any move you make—short of a real blunder—probably has been tried and analyzed at one time or another. The result is that the Ruy Lopez has literally hundreds of variations from which you can choose. Most of the more modern ones lead to lively play and seem designed to keep both players wide awake.

Here, for example, is the Nimzovich variation. The first few moves are repeated for clarity's sake:

1	P–K4	P–K4
2	N–KB3	N–QB3
3	B–N5	P–QR3
4	B–R4	N–B3
5	N–B3	P–QN4
6	B–N3	B–K2
7	O–O	P–Q3
8	P–QR4	B–N5

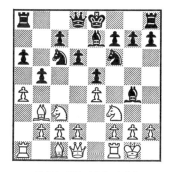

DIAGRAM 352

Position after 8 . . . B—N5

The tension in the center remains unbroken and White tries here for action on the Queen's wing. He intends to open a file for the Queen Rook and infiltrate that way. Black will try to counter this with a thrust in the center. Despite all the activity, however, this line proves to lead to nothing more than equality and the eventual outcome hangs heavily on middle game devices. (The opening of the file, incidentally, has the drawback of creating doubled Pawns for White, as well as, eventually, a weak and isolated passed Pawn. Whether White can or cannot use the passed Pawn as a lever to pry open the Queen's wing—or the center—depends on the tactical resources White can muster in the middle game.)

If Black should decide, against the better judgment of most players, to try the strong-point defense (3 . . . P–Q3), his only hope of coming out of it in good shape is to force as many exchanges as possible. The cramped position that results from 3 . . . P–Q3,

coupled with a big minus in the center, is sure to leave him with no counterplay.

But by exchanging, he takes the sting out of White's superior center and—even more important—clears the board so his remaining pieces have room in which to get around.

As for White, if he is faced with the strong-point system (known in the Ruy Lopez as the Steinitz Defense) his primary object is to avoid exchanges. He will also try—and this is an adjunct of his primary goal—to close the center.

There are several lines available in the Steinitz Defense. One of the principal ones runs this way:

1	P–K4	P–K4
2	N–KB3	N–QB3
3	B–N5	P–Q3
4	P–Q4	B–Q2
5	N–B3	N–B3
6	O–O	B–K2
7	R–K1	. . .

(White can also play 7 B×N, but the line given above prevents Black, temporarily, at least, from castling. For if 7 . . . O–O; 8 B×N, B×B; 9 P×P, P×P; 10 Q×Q, QR×Q; 11 N×P, B×P; 12 N×B, N×N; 13 N–Q3, P–KB4; 14 P–KB3, B–B4ch; 15 N×B, N×N; 16 B–N5, R–Q4; 17 B–K7, R–B2; 18 P–QB4.

DIAGRAM 353

Position after 18 P—QB4

(Black, as you see, winds up a piece to the bad. Ordinarily, all that exchanging ought to favor Black—but not at the cost of a piece. So 7 . . . O–O is out.)

7 . . .   **P×P**

With this move Black protects his investment. He is now ready and quite willing to do all the exchanging White may want. There follows:

8 N×P   **N×N**

So far so good for Black, who is rapidly equalizing.

9	Q×N	B×B
10	N×B	P—QR3
11	N—B3	O—O
12	B—N5	N—Q2

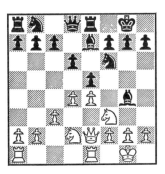

DIAGRAM 354

Position after 12 . . . N—Q2

White still has the better game, but it is far from a shoo-in. His Pawn formation is generally more fluid and he retains a more mobile center. But Black has succeeded in freeing his pieces and still holds a few aces.

You can see, even from the few variations presented here, that Black gets a better game more easily with 3 . . . P—QR3 than with 3 . . . P—Q3. The problem of the cramps doesn't arise with the former, as it inevitably must with the latter.

In general, it can be said that in most lines of the Ruy Lopez Black will find himself controlling less space than White. And this is White's cue to direct an attack against the Black King. Conversely, Black's best chances lie, as a rule, in a Queen-side attack and, with this in mind, he will try to maneuver so that a file on that flank is forced open.

We can derive from these asides some general rules that can be applied to most chess situations:

¶ Where one player is cramped, the other is in a position to—and indeed, must—launch an attack to take advantage of his extra space.

¶ The side that is cramped must endeavor, wherever possible, to exchange. This doesn't mean, of course, an uncontrolled free-for-all; it means, rather, an attempt to sweep off the board those pieces or Pawns, or both, that tend to keep the position locked. Black must not, in the process, allow an attack to get rolling.

So much, here, at least, for the Ruy Lopez.

Do you know the principles of opening play?

STOP

Self-Testing Quiz No. 16

(a) A game begins as follows: 1 P—K4, P—K3; 2 P—Q4. What are some logical continuations for Black?

(b) Set up an ideal ten-move development for White, disregarding Black.

(c) In the following position how can White, who has the move, cramp Black's position and make his development difficult?

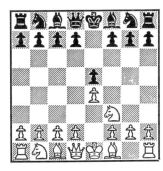

DIAGRAM 355

(d) If Black had the move in the position above, what should he play?

(e) Black, having the move in the following position, wants to prevent White's playing B—N5 (perhaps Black fears the Ruy Lopez). Therefore he plays 1 . . . P—QR3. Does this move work?

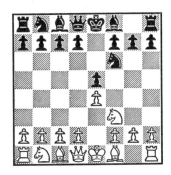

DIAGRAM 356

PETROFF'S DEFENSE

Petroff's Defense is characterized by the following moves:

1	P—K4	P—K4
2	N—KB3	N—KB3

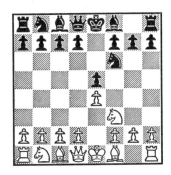

DIAGRAM 357

Position after 2 . . . N—KB3

The idea behind Black's second move is to counter-attack instead of defend. In this respect the opening is somewhat similar to to the Center-Counter Game for White (1 P—K4, P—K4; 2 P—Q4), in that the counter-attack is launched at once, with no elaborate preparation.

The Center-Counter Game, as you know, fails for White because of the resulting attack on his Queen. Does the same sort of thing await Black in the Petroff? The answer depends on how well Black carries out the theme. For example:

3 N×P   . . .

Here Black must break the symmetry. If he continues it with 3 . . . N×P, there follows 4 Q—K2 and —as pointed out earlier in this chapter—the Knight must remain where it is or lead to the capture of the Black Queen through discovered check. So Black plays

3 . . .   P—Q3

At this point White has only two good moves at his disposal, N—KB3 and N—B4. The more usual is N—B3, though in the Yugoslavian Championship Tournament of 1950, Fuderer, handling the White pieces, played N—B4 against Kostich and emerged from the opening with a somewhat better game. The continuation was: 4 N—B4, N×P; 5 N—B3, N×N; 6 NP×N, B—K2; 7 P—Q4, N—Q2; 8 B—Q3, N—N3; 9 N—K3. White's game is freer than Black's and his pieces are posted more effectively. About the only cause for complaint is White's doubled Pawns.

4 N—KB3   . . .

Now Black can safely play

4 . . .   N×P

So far White seems to have exchanged a tempo for a Pawn, not a bad idea, especially since the Pawn was Black's King Pawn. Now, however, it appears that Black gets back the Pawn and expresses a willingness to lose a tempo in the process. All even. White can play 5 P—Q3, force the Black Knight to lose time in retreating, and keep everything symmetrical.

The trouble with this is that it tends to keep things *too* well balanced. White wants to exploit his initiative and not just let it sit there. So he plays his best move, which is—as you might deduce from the general theory of openings—5 P—Q4.

Black, on the other hand, is willing to settle for full equality at the moment. So he counters by forcing the game back into a symmetrical position, with 5 . . . P—Q4. White continues his development, posting his King Bishop in a central position with 6 B—Q3.

DIAGRAM 358
Position after 6 B—Q3

Here Black must decide whether to try to maintain the symmetry or to seek to retain his hold in the center. If he plays 6 . . . B—Q3 an attack against the Queen Pawn may prove to be too great. Still, Black can try it in the hope that the sacrifice of the Pawn will give him a more aggressive position. Frank Marshall, for example, played 6 . . . B—Q3 against Alekhine at the St. Petersburg International Tournament of 1914. Though he lost the game it was not because of his sixth move but, rather, because of a faulty exchange later on.

In short, then, either 6 . . . B—Q3 or 6 . . . B—K2 are quite tenable for Black. So

6 . . .   B—Q3
7 O—O   O—O

Development—and the symmetry—continue.

At this point the range of choices for White broadens considerably. He can play 8 P—B4 in an effort to crack Black's center; 8 N—B3, with the same end in mind; N—Q2 with a view to forcing Black to exchange his powerfully posted Knight; R—K1 in an effort to build up pressure along the open King file, or even N—KN5 to feint on the King's flank and bring about Pawn weaknesses there.

Many of these lines have been quite throughly tested and analyzed; some have been neglected.

Let's look at the results of 8 P—B4. The main line runs this way:

8 . . .   B—KN5

(If Black tries B—K3, 9 N—B3 at once gives White much the stronger game.)

9	P×P	P—KB4
10	N—B3	N—Q2
11	P—KR3	B—R4

Black has no intention of giving up that pin without a struggle.

12	N×N	P×N
13	B×P	...

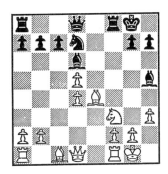

DIAGRAM 359
Position after 13 BxP

White is two Pawns up and has a solid position except for the slight weakness at KN3. Black, on the other hand, has a free game and plenty of play left. Whether his freedom is worth the two Pawns can be decided only by the subsequent maneuvering in the middle game. Against solid play by White the two-Pawn deficiency should prove too much. But (there are always buts in chess) Black should have no trouble regaining at least one of those Pawns, because of White's doubled Pawns. Black also has that half-open file for his King Rook.

ALEKHINE'S DEFENSE

This system, characterized by the move 1 . . . N—KB3, was really not originated by Alekhine, since an analysis of it appeared in Germany at least as far back as 1811. The name probably stems from Alekhine's use of the system to defeat Maroczy in the big 1924 New York Tournament.

The object of this rather strange-looking first move by Black is, theoretically at any rate, to tempt White into pushing forward his two center Pawns until they are out-of-touch with the rest of White's forces—until they become weak. Then Black launches a fierce attack against the shaky White center.

Before going into the pros and cons of this idea, it might be well to take a general look at openings in which Black does not immediately dispute the center with 1 . . . P—K4. As you might expect, Black's Pawn structure tends to be inferior; this is natural in view of the fact that Black voluntarily permits White to take over in the center.

It also has a strong effect on Black's objectives. Unlike openings in which 1 P—K4 is answered by 1 . . . P—K4, Black's goal here is not P—Q4, because this move only challenges the White King Pawn; Black must now do something to undermine White's Queen Pawn, as well. In the "normal" openings Black immediately opened up his game and equalized by playing P—Q4 (that is, when he could do so without ill-effect); here it won't work.

Now Black must try for the double freeing moves P—Q4 and P—K4, or P—Q4 and P—QB4 or again P—K4 and P—KB4.

This would seem to be just too much. If P—Q4 was a problem for Black in the "normal" openings, how can he be expected to play *two* freeing moves? Nevertheless, though the opening rubs theory the wrong way, in practice it works quite well.

The most usual response by White is 2 P—K5. Two other replies are more or less playable: 2 P—Q3 (which gives Black a chance to transpose into a variation of the Sicilian Defense—about which more later) and 2 N—QB3, which permits Black to equalize without any difficulty.

The move 2 P—K5 gives White time to develop while the Black Knight hops around looking for a safe spot to stay put. After the usual 2 . . . N—Q4, White continues the chase with 3 P—QB4, and the Knight moves on again, to N—3. White then completes his occupation of the center with 4 P—Q4.

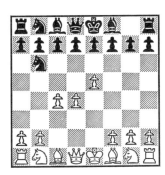

DIAGRAM 360
Position after 4 P—Q4

If, at this point, you were to call on abstract theory to help you in evaluating the position, you would be hard put to make a decision. White, it is true, occupies the center, apparently beyond challenge; but he has made nothing but Pawn moves, which theory says is unsound. He has opened lines for his pieces—a plus—but has let his Pawns wander without protection—a minus. Black, for his part, has moved his Knight not twice, but three times, and has succeeded in developing nothing else. He hasn't even bothered to move a center Pawn.

Well then, who's on first?

Black continues, usually, with 4 . . . P—Q3, the object being to get a foothold in the center, immobilize the White Pawns and start firing away at them.

White now has several lines to choose from. He can play 5 P—B4, which completes the occupation of the center and, theoretically, refutes Black's first move. He can try 5 P×P, which tends to simplify the situation. Or he can play 5 N—KB3 or 5 N—QB3, either of which is fairly solid, but slow-moving.

Because it is the most commonly adopted line—and because it shows clearly that the outcome of the game depends upon how well White can maintain that seemingly impregnable center—we'll look at the continuation 5 P—B4. In a game between Lasker and Tarrasch in 1923, the continuation was:

5	...	P×P
6	BP×P	N—B3
7	B—K3	B—B4

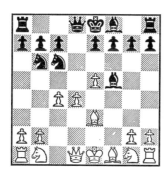

DIAGRAM 361

Position after 7 . . . B—B4

What happened? Black, for all his hopping around, seems to be ahead in development.

8	N—QB3	P—K3
9	N—B3	...

Not the best move. White should have played 9 B—K2, which would have taken the sting out of a possible 9 . . . B—KN5 by Black. However, since Black fails to take advantage of White's error, nothing is lost.

9	...	B—QN5
10	B—Q3	B—KN5

(Now this is a waste of time.)

11	B—K2	B×N
12	P×B	Q—R5ch
13	B—B2	Q—B5
14	KR—N1	...

DIAGRAM 362

Position after 14 KR—N1

Black, obviously, has failed to carry out his plan. The strategy was fine—lure the White Pawns forward, immobilize and weaken them, then destroy them. The tactics, however, were weak. Black's first big mistake was his time-wasting ninth move, followed by another time-waster on his tenth move. Subsequently, Black erred further, castling Queen side and neglecting to build up pressure in the center. He resigned after 47 moves.

Do not let Black's loss here force you to the conclusion that Alekhine's Defense is all wet; on the contrary, it has met with a good deal of success in tournament play, possibly because of the element of surprise that always seems to go with it. Here, for example, is the opening of a game played at the Hague in 1928, a game in which White resigned after 24 moves.

1	P—K4	N—KB3
2	P—K5	N—Q4
3	P—QB4	N—N3
4	P—Q4	P—Q3
5	P—B4	P×P
6	BP×P	N—B3
7	B—K3	B—B4
8	N—QB3	P—K3
9	B—K2	...

Here White plays correctly and, paradoxically, it does him no good because of subsequent blunders.

9	...	B—K2
10	N—B3	P—B3

The attack against the White center Pawns gets rolling. With this same move Black also starts to pry open the King Bishop file.

11	O—O	O—O
12	P×P	...

A mistake. White should have played Q—K1 in an effort to maintain his hold on K5.

12	...	B×P

DIAGRAM 363

Position after 12 . . . BxP

13	Q–Q2	Q–K2
14	QR–Q1	QR–Q1

Black builds up the pressure along the Queen file. A few moves later, having systematically undermined White's fast-waning strength in the center, Black launched an attack that brought a quick end to the game.

You can see, then, that the pros and cons of Alekhine's Defense are rather involved. The opening does ignore the standard principles of sound play—or does it? It all depends on the conduct of the middle game. This is one of those openings in which there seems to be a good deal of leeway in the beginning, but in which subsequent tactical developments play a powerful role.

Why not give Alekhine's Defense a whirl? You have nothing to lose but a game of chess.

SICILIAN DEFENSE

No question about it: the Sicilian Defense is the most popular opening for Black on the market. Why? Because its characteristic—its identifying—move, 1 . . . P–QB4, does more than merely accept the inevitable. It goes beyond a simple try for equality. It fights back at once.

Ideally, the Sicilian Defense gives Black the chance to counter-attack on the Queen's flank. And, normally, White will try to break through on the King's flank. The result is a slashing fight in which the side that gets there fustest with the mostest comes out on top.

White's usual plan, after the first several moves—in which he tends to grab somewhat more territory than Black—is to attack at once with his King-side Pawns, advancing the KNP and KBP as far as the sixth rank. If he castles long, which he frequently does, the Pawn-roller can move on without endangering the White King.

White may also try, if Black slips, to block the Queen Bishop file, usually with P–QB4. If this happens Black is finished, because his chances lie along that file, which he forces open early in the game and then proceeds to control with his heavy pieces.

Needless to say, one of Black's major objectives is P–Q4. And White, for his part, tries vigorously to prevent this liberating thrust by Black.

There are two main lines in the Sicilian. In one, Black plays his King Bishop to K2. This is known, in most variations, as the Scheveningen formation (the system was popularized at a tournament in Scheveningen, the Netherlands, in 1923). In the other, Black plays his King Bishop to KN2. This is the Dragon Variation (not played at a tournament in Dragon—wherever that may be— but named, possibly, for the curious shape of the Pawn formation that results).

There are quite literally hundreds of sub-variations within the two main lines, which is not surprising in view of the Sicilian's popularity. At almost every major tournament some innovation is tried; if it has any merit at all it finds its way into the standard repertoire. Naturally, we can consider only a few of these variations.

First, the Scheveningen.

The main line runs like this:

1	P–K4	P–QB4
2	N–KB3	P–K3
3	P–Q4	P×P
4	N×P	N–KB3
5	N–QB3	. . .

DIAGRAM 364

Position after 5N–QB3

Black's tactical objectives at this point are to finish his development, maneuver his Knight to QB5 and launch his Queen-side attack with Pawns. Part of the preparation for this attack, P–QR3, also serves a secondary purpose—preventing White's move B–QN5. Black also will start to mass his long-range pieces along the QB file. And, if White slips, he will play P–Q4, which will not only equalize, but also will give him a strong chance to undermine White along the Queen file as well as the Queen Bishop file.

White's principal objective—as in most variations of the Sicilian—is to build up a King-side attack while keeping an eye on the Queen Bishop file.

Black has two alternatives for his fifth move. He can play P–Q3, in preparation for B–K2, or B–N5 in preparation for counterplay along the Queen file. After 5 . . . P—Q3 the main line runs as follows:

6	B—K2	N—B3
7	O—O	P—QR3
8	K—R1	. . .

White's eighth move is designed to prevent a pin along the diagonal KN1—QR7. It also prepares the start of the King-side attack.

8	. . .	B—K2
9	P—B4	Q—B2
10	B—K3	O—O
11	Q—K1	B—Q2
12	R—Q1	P—QN4

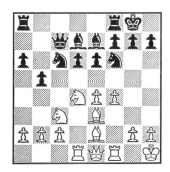

DIAGRAM 365

Position after 12 . . . P—QN4

As an alternative to 8 K—R1 White has N—N3; both accomplish the purpose of preventing the pin, which can become uncomfortable when Black builds up the pressure along the Queen Bishop file. Black also has an alternative—he can play 2 . . . N—QB3 instead of 2 . . . P—K3. The results are similar, and after 12 Q—N3, P—QN4, the diagram will be the same except for the White Queen's being at KN3.

Here is another line of the Scheveningen, incorporating some transpositions of moves and a number of alternatives:

1	P—K4	P—QB4
2	N—KB3	N—QB3
3	P—Q4	P×P
4	N×P	N—B3
5	N—QB3	P—Q3
6	B—K2	P—K3
7	O—O	P—QR3
8	B—K3	Q—B2
9	P—B4	B—Q2
10	Q—K1	N×N
11	B×N	B—B3
12	B—B3	B—K2
13	Q—N3	O—O
14	QR—Q1	KR—Q1

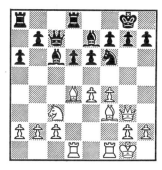

DIAGRAM 366

Position after 14 . . . KR—Q1

The game is fairly even. If Black tries P—Q4 White can reply P—K5, taking all the sting out of the Black thrust (as a rule, in the Sicilian, this reply by White to such a central thrust by Black usually neutralizes it).

Now let's see what happens if Black plays 5 . . . B—N5.

1	P—K4	P—QB4
2	N—KB3	P—K3
3	P—Q4	P×P
4	N×P	N—KB3
5	N—QB3	B—N5
6	B—Q3	N—B3

(or 6 . . . P—K4, followed by 7 . . . P—Q4)

7	N×N	NP×N

This closes the QB file, but opens the QN file in its stead.

8	O—O	O—O
9	P—K5	N—Q4

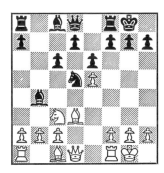

DIAGRAM 367

Position after 9 . . . N—Q4

The game is about even, despite the odd turn it has taken.

We turn now to the Dragon variation which, because it leads to livelier action and gives Black better control, has been gradually pushing the Scheveningen into the background. The Dragon is characterized by the fianchetto of the King Bishop. The advantage of this flank-posting of the King Bishop is that it gives that piece a long, sweeping control along the important (even the vital) diagonal KR1–QR8, which passes directly through the center.

Two main lines of the Dragon are distinguishable. One utilizes 2 . . . P–Q3, one 2 . . . N–QB3. Because there are more sub-variations of the latter main line, we'll look at that one first. The usual sequence of opening moves is:

1	P–K4	P–QB4
2	N–KB3	N–QB3
3	P–Q4	P×P
4	N×P	N–B3
5	N–QB3	P–Q3
6	B–K2	P–KN3
7	B–K3	B–N2

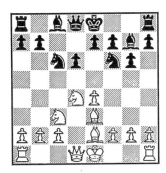

DIAGRAM 368
Position after 7 . . . B–N2

Notice that because of the Dragon Bishop, White's usual attempt to neutralize the center with P–K5 fails. This is one of the great advantages of this variation.

It is in this variation, too, that White has no alternative for move No. 7. If he plays O–O instead of B–K3, in hopes of launching his usual King-side attack, Black can follow through with N×P. And if White then replies N/B3×N, White wins the Knight at White's Q4. If White replies N/Q4×N, Black plays N×N and emerges with a better Pawn situation. As an alternative, White can, after playing 7 O–O, follow with 8 N–N3, getting the threatened Knight out of the way.

But back to the position in the preceding diagram. Several—a dozen, perhaps—variations have been tried at this point, including P–B4, N–Q5 and even P–K6. The best appears to be O–O.

8	O–O	O–O
9	N–N3	P–QR3

And Black begins his Queen-side assault.

10	P–QR4	. . .

White tries to prevent 10 . . . P–QN4. A better move is the more thematic B–B3, which protects the King Pawn so that White can play N–Q5. But this, in turn, must be preceded by P–B4.

10	. . .	B–K3

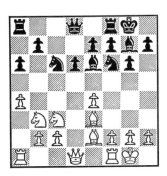

DIAGRAM 369
Position after 10 . . . B–K3

White's prospects are not good. His tenth move was ineffective and time-consuming, as well as anti-thematic. White's hopes lie on the King side and he is wrong, at this stage, to bother with his Queen side, which is not endangered yet.

Perhaps in this situation White's only real chance lies in forcing Black to exchange the powerful Dragon Bishop. He can try this with Q–B1 or Q–Q2 followed by B–R6. The Queen move, however, is likely to telegraph his intentions, and Black will take the precaution of playing R–K1. Then if White plays B–R6 Black simply plays B–R1, and the Dragon Bishop continues to operate along the same diagonal.

Here is an example of a way in which Black can go wrong in the Dragon variation:

1	P–K4	P–QB4
2	N–KB3	N–QB3
3	P–Q4	P×P
4	N×P	N–B3
5	N–QB3	P–Q3
6	B–K2	P–KN3
7	B–K3	B–N2
8	O–O	O–O
9	N–N3	B–K3
10	P–B4	. . .

This time the right move.

10	. . .	N–QR4

A different approach to the Queen-side attack.

11	P–B5	. . .

White, correctly disregarding the Queen-side demonstration, continues with his incursions against the Black King.

11	. . .	B—B5
12	N×N	B×B
13	Q×B	Q×N
14	P—KN4	. . .

On with the King-side assault.

| 14 | . . . | Q—N5 |
| 15 | P—N5 | N×P |

An error. 15 . . . N—Q2 accomplishes more and protects the point KB6, which is now too weak to stand.

| 16 | N—Q5 | |

DIAGRAM 370

Position after 16 N—Q5

Black has thrown away the game. He neglected the theme of the Dragon variation and failed to press the attack. Result: he left himself wide open for the incursions of the White King-side Pawns, backed by the White Rook at B1.

It has been said that the only trouble with the Ruy Lopez (the trouble for White, that is) is the Sicilian. By the same token, it can be said that (aside from poor handling, as in the game above) the only trouble with the Dragon variation is the Richter attack.

The Richter attack, characterized by the move 6 B—KN5, is designed to prevent the fianchetto of the Black King Bishop by threatening to double Black's King Bishop Pawns with 7 B×N. There are several quite playable variations, both for White and for Black, the most spectacular of which is one in which White castles Queen-side in preparation for an all-out Pawn assault on the Black King. It runs like this:

1	P—K4	P—QB4
2	N—KB3	N—QB3
3	P—Q4	P×P
4	N×P	N—B3
5	N—QB3	P—Q3
6	B—KN5	. . .

The characteristic move of the Richter attack.

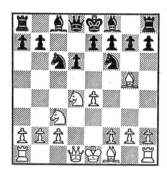

DIAGRAM 371

Position after 6 B—KN5

If Black now plays P—KN3 White can follow with B×N. Black will be forced to recapture with the King Pawn, thus effectively destroying his King-side Pawn defenses. White will then continue with his plan of castling long and storming the vulnerable Black King side with his Pawns.

| 6 | . . . | P—K3 |

Giving his Knight the protection of the Queen to prevent the doubling of the Pawns.

| 7 | Q—Q2 | . . . |

This attacking move was initiated by a player named Rauzer and, in conjunction with 6 B—KN5, is responsible for the name Richter-Rauzer attack in this line.

7	. . .	B—K2
8	O—O—O	N×N
9	Q×N	O—O
10	B—QB4	. . .

At this point the line breaks into a series of variations that begin with 10 P—B4; most of them permit Black to equalize without difficulty and one gives Black a decided advantage, which is why the Pawn move is generally avoided by White.

10	. . .	Q—R4
11	P—B4	P—KR3
12	B—R4	P—K4
13	P×P	P×P
14	Q—Q3	Q—B4

DIAGRAM 372

Position after 14 . . . Q—B4

The position is approximately even; the Richter-Rauzer attack, although it prevented the use of the Dragon formation, failed to do much more. Specifically, it failed to prevent Black from equalizing.

Though the Richter-Rauzer attack has a bark that is worse than its bite, efforts have nonetheless been made to forestall it. The most common is the substitution of 2 . . . P—Q3 for 2 . . . N—QB3. Of the half-dozen or more variations based on this idea, most lead to a rather even game. Here is one of those variations:

1	P—K4	P—QB4
2	N—KB3	P—Q3
3	P—Q4	P×P
4	N×P	N—KB3
5	N—QB3	P—KN3
6	B—K2	B—N2
7	B—K3	O—O
8	P—B4	P—QR3
9	B—B3	Q—B2
10	N—Q5	N×N
11	P×N	P—QN4

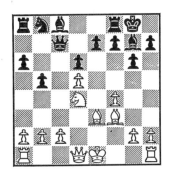

DIAGRAM 373

Position after 11 . . . P—QN4

An even game and one that leads essentially to much the same position as the "old" Dragon with 2 . . . N—QB3. As we noted, the Dragon variation played with 2 . . . P—Q3 tends to lead to drawish games. Here is an eighteen-move game played in 1936 between Alekhine and Botwinnik:

1	P—K4	P—QB4
2	N—KB3	P—Q3
3	P—Q4	P×P
4	N×P	N—KB3
5	N—QB3	P—KN3
6	B—K2	B—N2
7	B—K3	. . .

So far the same moves as in the variation quoted above. Now Black shifts.

7	. . .	N—B3
8	N—N3	. . .

To avoid the possible loss of Knight or Pawn or a compromising position in the center. Although the Knight is not as well posted at N3 as at Q4, nevertheless the move tends to consolidate White's position.

8	. . .	B—K3

Black develops prudently, with an eye toward eventual control of his QB5 and its occupation by a Knight.

9	P—B4	O—O
10	P—N4	. . .

The beginnng of what White hopes will be a decisive King-side assault.

10	. . .	P—Q4

Decisive. And an excellent illustration of the rule that an attack on a wing is best met by a counter-attack in the center.

11	P—B5	B—B1

A judicious and effective retreat.

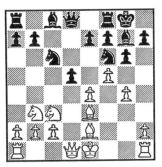

DIAGRAM 374

Position after 11 . . . B—B1

12	KP×P	N—N5
13	P—Q6	Q×P

The correct way to get rid of the dangerous Pawn. If Black had played 13 . . . KP×P White would have pushed on with his Knight and Bishop Pawns, penetrating right into the King's castled position. With the Queen on guard, however, the Pawn storm would blow itself out.

14	B—B5	Q—B5
15	R—KB1	Q×RP
16	B×N	. . .

Black disregards his loss of the Knight. More—he sacrifices a second piece to (a) end all threats of a King-side Pawn attack, and (b) destroy White's King-side Pawn defenses, which remain vital because of the exposed position of the White King.

16	. . .	N×P

White cannot refuse the sacrifice. If he does, Black can gobble up the White Pawns, exchange Queens and bring about an end game that would be impossible for White to win.

17	B×N	Q—N6ch
18	R—B2	Q—N8ch

Draw by perpetual check

DIAGRAM 375

Position after 18 . . . Q—N8ch

Summarizing now what we know about the Sicilian, we can say:

(a) It is a fighting line for Black, one in which White must stay on the alert every step of the way.

(b) Black's strategy calls for the control and occupation of the Queen Bishop file and, through that file, an attack on the Queen's wing. Tactically, he aims to post a Knight at QB5 and to push his Queen-side Pawns into enemy territory.

(c) White's strategy is based on control of the Queen file and an attack along the King's flank. Tactically he aims to post a Knight in the center and then to push his King-side Pawns, backing them up, if possible, with heavy pieces.

(d) One of the strongest lines is the Dragon, in which Black posts his King Bishop at KN2 to keep White from taking over the center.

(e) White can try to prevent the Dragon formation by using the Richter-Rauzer attack, characterized by 6 B—KN5. This prevents Black's playing P—KN3 by threatening to double his King Bishop Pawns and to wreck his King-side defenses.

(f) Black can seek to forestall the Richter-Rauzer by playing 2 . . . P—Q3 instead of 2 . . . N—QB3, but this tends to make the game drawish in character.

There are variations of the Sicilian in which these strategic and tactical considerations play no part. Most are highly positional, quiet games in which the center is locked. They tend to lead to draws. Here is an example of a closed Sicilian:

1	P—K4	P—QB4
2	N—QB3	. . .

White, as you see, takes the initiative in changing from a standard to a closed Sicilian. With 2 N—KB3 the normal variations result.

2	. . .	N—QB3
3	P—KN3	P—KN3

Both sides will fianchetto the King Bishop.

4	B—N2	B—N2
5	P—Q3	P—Q3

Several variants are open to Black instead of the symmetrical 5 . . . P—Q3. He can, for example, play 5 P—N3 for a double fianchetto; or R—N1, with a view to opening the Queen Knight file (instead of the normal Queen Bishop file). Others are unfavorable and are usually avoided.

6	B—K3	P—K3
7	P—B4	KN—K2
8	N—B3	N—Q5

Black is reversing roles with White here, seeking control of the center instead of operating on the flanks.

9	O—O	O—O
10	R—N1	Q—R4

DIAGRAM 376

Position after 10 . . . Q—R4

With their last moves both White and Black crystallize their intentions—White to seek an attack along the Queen Knight file, Black to try for counterplay in the center. The position is just about even.

This, then, ends our admittedly brief look at the Sicilian Defense. You are hereby urged to do some looking on your own, to experiment with it and learn its ins and outs. It will pay you well.

Queen's Pawn Openings

The openings that begin with 1 P—Q4 are, so-to-speak, mirror images of the King's Pawn openings. Where White and Black, in the King's Pawn openings, sought to play P—Q4 (usually after careful preparation), they now aim for P—K4. The object, of course, is the same: occupation and control of the center.

You will find that the Queen's Pawn openings present a peculiar problem to Black—the disposition of his Queen Bishop. In the King's Pawn openings, though his King Bishop sometimes was a thorn in Black's side, the Queen Bishop is almost always a thorn in the Queen's Pawn openings. Somehow, Black's Queen Bishop seems to get stuck, or to get itself wedged in somewhere where it is more a liability than an asset. And this is a clue to one of the keys to success for Black in these openings:

If Black can get his Queen Bishop out and effectively placed he is more than half-way along the road to equalizing.

For White, a central object will be the attack on Black's Queen Pawn. This time, however, that center Pawn is defended right from the start. The attack, therefore, will have to rely on Pawn power, rather than on pieces. And from this we derive a prime tactical goal for White:

He must strive to play P—QB4.

Sometimes this move is made early in the game, without elaborate preparation. Sometimes complex maneuvering precedes the move. The character of the game depends upon which of these two systems is adopted by White.

QUEEN'S GAMBIT

The Queen's Gambit is not really a gambit—that is, the Pawn is not surrendered more-or-less permanently for some compensating advantage. (The real gambits will be considered in the next section.) It is characterized by these moves:

1	P—Q4	P—Q4
2	P—QB4	. . .

If Black elects to take the Pawn (Queen's Gambit Accepted, known familiarly as QGA) he cannot ex-

pect to hold his material advantage long; if he tries to do so he will find himself either intolerably cramped or, ultimately, a piece behind. To maintain a good position and a material balance Black must give back the Pawn quickly.

By accepting the Pawn, Black aims to free his Queen Bishop at the cost of surrendering the center—temporarily, he hopes. There is a further disadvantage for Black in accepting the Pawn: he falls behind in development almost at once and lays himself open to a King-side attack.

The main line, of which there are many variations, runs this way:

2	. . .	P×P
3	N—KB3	N—KB3
4	P—K3	P—K3

Both sides are maneuvering for an immediate advantage. It is a case of who will be able to play P—K4 first (without, of course, compromising himself by doing it).

5	B×P	. . .

White regains the lost Pawn. Black, of course, must not try to maintain that initial advantage. Such efforts would boomerang quickly.

5	. . .	P—B4
6	O—O	P—QR3
7	Q—K2	N—B3

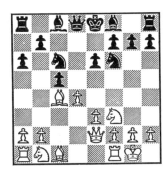

DIAGRAM 377

Position after 7 . . . N—B3

The older principal variation continued with 8 R—Q1, but it was unsatisfactory for White because it enabled Black to equalize easily. For example: 8 . . . P—QN4; 9 B—N3, P—B5; 10 B—B2, N—QN5; 11 N—B3, N×B; 12 Q×N, B—N2; 13 P—Q5 (normally a devastating thrust, but . . .), Q—B2; 14 P—K4, P—K4.

DIAGRAM 378

Position after 14 . . . P—K4 in the old variation

And Black has a free game, a good Queen-side threat percolating and an effective center. Notice, too, that the Queen Bishop, ordinarily a problem child, has been effectively developed at QN2.

For these reasons White rarely plays 8 R—Q1. A better variation of the main line begins with 8 N—B3. Thus, when Black advances his King-side Pawns and then plays his N to QN5, White can move his King Bishop to QN1, avoiding the exchange of pieces. This, in turn, permits White to play P—K4, with an overwhelming center.

When White adopts 8 N—B3, therefore, Black shifts too. The variation runs this way:

8	N—B3	P—QN4
9	B—N3	P—B5
10	B—B2	B—N2

10 . . . N—QN5 would accomplish nothing now.

11	P—QR4	P—N5
12	N—K4	N—QR4
13	N×Nch	P×N
14	P—K4	Q—B2
15	B—K3	B—Q3
16	QR—B1	R—KN1

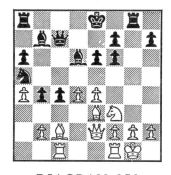

DIAGRAM 379

Position after 16 . . . R—KN1

White has a somewhat freer game and a better hold on the center. Black, for compensation, has threats in

reserve plus an imminent threat along the open King Knight file.

In general, the QGA is a tricky opening and leads to highly positional play. Careful consideration of every move is in order, but probably would not be enough; both sides have to be thoroughly acquainted with the various bylines and detours that have been investigated. It is a good idea for the beginner to avoid the QGA and to concentrate on the QGD, which—as you might easily guess—is the Queen's Gambit Declined.

QUEEN'S GAMBIT DECLINED

In the QGD Black can pursue one of several ideas:
    (a) Fight to maintain a Pawn in the center.
    (b) Counter-attack.
    (c) Permit White to set up a strong Pawn center, then seek to undermine it.

Black's alternatives, you'll notice, are similar to those he had in the King's Pawn openings. Similar advantages and drawbacks go with them. Fighting to maintain the Pawn, for example, can lead to a cramped position; counter-attacking can lead to a delicate balance of power in which Black must walk on eggs; permitting White to set up a Pawn center can (as in Alekhine's defense) boomerang if not handled properly.

The strong-point system, in which Black tries to maintain his center Pawn, is exemplified by the so-called Orthodox defense. This is characterized by the move 2 . . . P—K3.

In this (as, for that matter, in all games beginning with 1 P—Q4) Black must try to liberate himself with either P—K4 or P—QB4. Because neither of these moves can safely be made until the maneuvering has gone on for some time, Black's game tends to be cramped for quite a while.

In most cases Black emerges with a Queen-side Pawn majority, and his hopes usually are pinned on action on that wing. White, who comes through with a firmer center, bases his play on a King-side attack (axiom: where no counter-action in the center is possible, an attack against the King himself is called for). In some variations, however, White can use his minority Pawn structure to force a weakening of Black's Queen-side Pawns and a concomitant lessening of Black's mobility.

But these are generalizations. Getting down to particulars, here is one variation of the Orthodox defense.

1	P—Q4	P—Q4
2	P—QB4	P—K3

The cramps begin. Black shuts in his Queen Bishop.

3	N—QB3	N—KB3
4	B—N5	B—K2
5	P—K3	O—O
6	N—B3	QN—Q2
7	Q—B2	P—B3

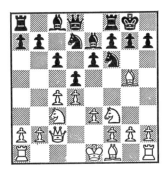

DIAGRAM 380

Position after 7 . . . P—B3

8	R—Q1	R—K1
9	P—QR3	P×P
10	B×P	N—Q4
11	B×B	Q×B
12	O—O	N×N
13	Q×N	P—QN3
14	N—K5	B—N2

Black tries to solve the problem of his Queen Bishop by a fianchetto.

15	P—B4	N×N

Notice that, just as in the cramped position of the King's Pawn openings, Black looks for every opportunity to exchange and thus loosen the position.

16	BP×N	P—QB4

The magic liberating move. Black, by forcing exchanges, has made this move possible. With it comes complete equality.

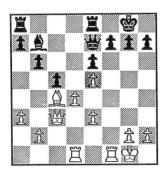

DIAGRAM 381

Position after 16 . . . P—QB4

Here is a variation that branches off at the seventh move, where White plays R—B1 instead of Q—B2. It runs this way:

7	R—B1	P—B3

(Suppose that at this point Black decides to make a break for it, and plays 7 . . . P—B4, instead. He might run into this: 8 BP×P, KP×P; 9 P×P, N×P; 10

B×N, B×B; N×P and White has liquidated Black's center, has occupied Q5, controls an open file and has six Pawns to Black's five. Which proves that, however desirable the freeing move P—QB4 may be, it can't be made unless the conditions are right.)

8	B—Q3	P×P
9	B×P	N—Q4
10	B×B	Q×B
11	O—O	N×N
12	R×N	P—K4

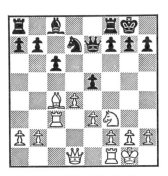

DIAGRAM 382

Position after 12 . . . P—K4

The Queen Bishop, with this move, becomes mobile, freeing Black's game. Chances are now approximately even. White, however, can counter the liberating move with an aggressive thrust—P—Q5. (A rather flexible rule that has not been mentioned yet is this: When Black plays P—K4 in a Queen's Pawn opening, White can negate, or almost negate, the effects of that move with P—Q5—provided, of course, that P—Q5 does not produce compromising side effects for White. Conversely, in King Pawn openings, when Black plays the liberating move P—Q4, White can try P—K5.)

White can improve the above variation by trying 11 N—K4 instead of 11 O—O. This tends to avoid exchanges which, as you know, generally favor Black. This variation might run like this:

11	N—K4	N/Q4—B3
12	N—N3	Q—N5ch
13	Q—Q2	Q×Qch
14	K×Q	R—Q1
15	P—K4	. . .

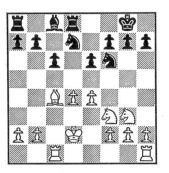

DIAGRAM 383

Position after 15 P—K4

The exchange of Queens, which usually favors Black and takes the teeth out of White's attacking prospects, has done Black little good here. White's center Pawns are poised to move on at the slightest provocation. Black, on the other hand, is not yet in a position to free himself with P—K4. And, despite appearances, White's King is quite safe; he can castle "artificially"—that is, by playing K—B2—N1—or he can keep the King where it is, or even play it to Q3 to bolster the momentum of the Pawns.

Nevertheless, the exchanges have given Black a freer game than he would have had without them, and the —perhaps temporary—pin of the White QP can be exploited with vigorous play. All in all, it can be said that neither side has a decisive advantage.

We will consider two more principal variations before leaving the Queen's Gambit Declined—the Cambridge Springs Variation and Lasker's Defense.

The Cambridge Springs Variation is characterized by the move 6 . . . Q—R4. The main line runs this way:

1	P—Q4	P—Q4
2	P—QB4	P—K3
3	N—QB3	N—KB3
4	B—N5	QN—Q2

Instead of the more usual 4 . . . B—K2.

| 5 | P—K3 | . . . |

(A trap is possible here if White mistakenly plays 5 P×P. There follows 5 . . . P×P; 6 N×P, N×N; 7 B×Q, B—N5ch and White winds up a piece behind.)

| 5 | . . . | P—B3 |
| 6 | N—B3 | Q—R4 |

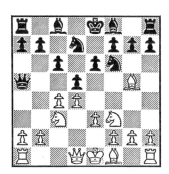

DIAGRAM 384

Position after 6 . . . Q—R4

Black's plan is to take advantage of the absence of White's Queen Bishop from the Queen side by putting pressure on the Queen Bishop file. White's replies, which are almost forced, give Black a chance to improve his position in the center and free his game.

The number of continuations from 6 . . . Q—R4 are almost as numerous as the master tournaments in which this variation has been played. We will examine only one of these.

| 7 | N—Q2 | . . . |

White swings the Knight over to bolster the Queen's wing.

| 7 | . . . | B—N5 |

Black responds by shifting another piece to the attack.

| 8 | Q—B2 | 0—0 |
| 9 | B—R4 | P—B4 |

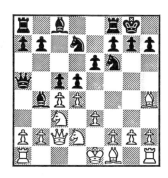

DIAGRAM 385

Position after 9 . . . P—B4

Black will now have little trouble bringing about complete equality.

In an effort to avoid the Cambridge Springs Variation White tries to exchange Pawns before the seventh move. This, however, leads into the so-called Exchange variation, which gives Black just as good a chance.

Lasker's Defense is based on the proposition that all chess pieces are created equal and that White, in the Queen's Gambit Declined has no inalienable right to hem in the Black pieces, cut down their mobility and, in effect, force Black to play on without them. Black, therefore, goes about freeing his game by forcing White to exchange. If, for example, Black can force White to trade his (White's) active and mobile Queen Bishop for Black's almost-useless Queen Bishop, Black will gain and White will lose. (Of course this can't be done on a direct swap, because the Bishops in question operate on different colors. But there may be indirect ways to bring this about.)

The key move in Lasker's defense is 7 . . . N—K5. And, although it is not absolutely necessary, it is, shall we say, prudent, to precede it with 6 . . . P—KR3, to avoid compromises on Black's first rank.

Here, then, is one of the several variations of Lasker's Defense:

1	P–Q4	P–Q4
2	P–QB4	P–K3
3	N–QB3	N–KB3
4	B–N5	B–K2
5	N–B3	0–0
6	P–K3	P–KR3

This move serves several functions. Aside from giving the Black King an escape hatch, it also pushes White into some sort of commitment: maintain the pin or don't. If White now plays B×N he gives Black the advantage of the two Bishops. If he retreats to R4 he announces he has no intention of doing this or, for that matter, of handing out exchanges for nothing. If he retreats to B4 Black can reply 7 . . . P–B4 with a satisfactory game.

       7 B–R4   **N–K5**

The key move. Like it or not, White must allow an exchange which, as we have said too many times already, takes the thumb-screws off Black's cramped position.

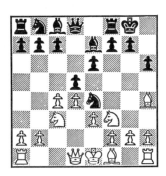

DIAGRAM 386

Position after 7 . . . N–K5

       8 B×B   **Q×B**

If White tries to avoid the exchange he only gives Black a chance to improve his game. For example: 8 B–N3, N×N; P×N, P–QB4 and Black (as in some of the previous variations) can solve his problem-child's difficulties with B–N2. If 8 N×N, P×N; 9 B×B, Q×B; 10 N–Q2 and Black can now play the liberating move 10 . . . P–K4.

After 8 . . . Q×B White has three "normal" continuations: 9 P×P, 9 Q–B2 or 9 R–B1. All three lead inevitably to further exchanges. We will pick for our examination—

       9 P×P   **N×N**

(Naturally not 9 . . . P×P. For this would be followed by 10 N×P with the loss of a Pawn, the loss of time and the loss of another liberating exchange.)

       10 P×N   . . .

And now the Pawn capture is possible.

       10 . . .   **P×P**

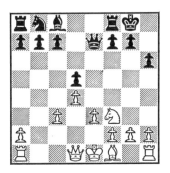

DIAGRAM 387

Position after 10 . . . P×P

Notice that:

(a) White does not have the same powerful center he had in other variations.

(b) White does not have a lead in development.

(c) Black has managed to force White to part with his powerful Queen Bishop.

(d) Black's problem child, his Queen Bishop, has no more problems.

From this point on the struggle is an equal one, Black no longer being handicapped by a cramped game. Lasker's strategy, carried out with tactical acumen, has paid off.

COLLE AND STONEWALL SYSTEMS

Queen's Pawn Games is the technical name for all Queen's Pawn openings except the QGD, QGA and the so-called Indian systems (about which a bit later). We will look at only two of these systems—the Colle System and, closely related to it, the Stonewall System.

The Colle System is, in effect, a Queen's Gambit Declined with colors reversed—that is, with White doing the defending and seeking P–K4 or P–QB4 to liberate his game. Why, then, does White adopt this system? Because, obviously, he is defending with an extra move at his disposal. If something like Lasker's Defense could equalize, what could it do with a free move thrown in? In adopting this approach White voluntarily shuts himself in with 3 P–K3, but he relies on the power of that free move to make this no more than temporary. Strategically, he aims for a King-side attack aided, if necessary, by a Pawn-roller.

Tactically, White plans a thrust in the center preceded by QN–Q2 to back up that thrust. If Black accepts an exchange in the center, White's closed-in Bishop finds itself freed. White's only remaining problem may be an isolated Queen Pawn. If he can get his attack into high gear quickly enough the Pawn problem will take care of itself.

As for Black, his best chances for equality lie in a relatively simple tactical device—the quick development of his Queen Bishop (made possible here by White's opening surrender of the center) and the solidification of his center.

With these ends in mind, then, a typical line becomes:

1	P—Q4	P—Q4
2	N—KB3	N—KB3
3	P—K3	. . .

The voluntary imprisonment of the Queen Bishop.

3	. . .	P—B4

No problem here because White has not monopolized the center.

4	QN—Q2	QN—Q2
5	P—B3	. . .

Notice how the Black and White roles seem to be completely reversed.

5	. . .	P—KN3
6	B—Q3	B—N2
7	O—O	O—O

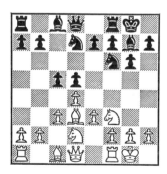

DIAGRAM 388

Position after 7 . . . O—O

8	P—QN4	P×NP
9	P×P	N—K1
10	B—N2	N—Q3
11	Q—N3	N—N3
12	P—QR4	B—B4

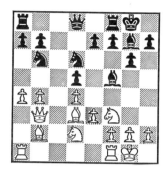

DIAGRAM 389

Position after 12 . . . B—B4

Having developed his Queen Bishop, Black's problems are now solved; there is complete equality in the position.

Black could have developed the Queen Bishop much earlier—on his third move—with an equally easy game. That line runs this way:

1	P—Q4	P—Q4
2	N—KB3	N—KB3
3	P—K3	B—B4
4	B—Q3	P—K3
5	B×B	P×B

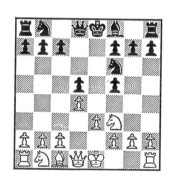

DIAGRAM 390

Position after 5 . . . P×B

Both sides soon will castle and Black will play N—K5, securing a powerful outpost in the center, which equalizes nicely.

One of the things that makes it just about impossible to learn the openings by rote is that new ones—new variations, sometimes entirely new systems—roll out of chess tournaments and matches like Fords out of Dearborn. And this production is a direct result of the hunt for improvements.

If Black devises a variation that takes all the sting out of some heretofore favorable system for White, White will, almost inevitably, come up with a countervariation, in due time, of course.

Obviously the search for improvements is a self-perpetuating process (or, in less formal and not-quite-such-polite terms, a vicious circle).

In his search for improvements in the Colle System, White came up with the Stonewall System, so called because (it was thought at first) the Pawn-piece barrier set up by White was impregnable. It is characterized by the following moves:

1	P—Q4	P—Q4
2	P—K3	N—KB3
3	B—Q3	P—B4
4	P—QB3	
5	P—KB4	
6	N—B3	

The Black moves have been omitted to make White's set-up stand out more clearly. And, before going into the pros and cons, let's look at the reasoning behind White's self-incarcerations.

White intends to launch, as early as possible, an assault directly against Black's castled King. The spearhead of that assault is to be the Bishop now at Q3, which aims at the more-or-less vulnerable Black KR2. White intends to back up the Bishop with the Queen and, if possible, with the King Rook (obviously he can't count on any support by the Queen Rook, who is firmly locked in by the paralyzed Queen Bishop).

The odd-looking move P—KB4 is designed to prevent Black's occupation of the center with a Knight. And the reason, in turn, for this is that White's flank attack could be effectively countered with a thrust in the center. The Pawn at KB4 also is designed to serve as a guardian for a White Knight at K5.

White intends to get his King Rook into the act by the zig-zag move R—B3—R3. He also plans on pushing his King-side Pawns forward to dislodge Black's Knight at KB3, which guards KR2. If all goes well the attack should succeed.

If all goes well. There's the rub.

If the player on the Black side of the board is on to White's plan he should have no trouble in taking the mortar out of the stone wall. It must be conceded, though, that the player who is unfamiliar with the Stonewall is quite likely to find himself in a bad way.

Suppose, for example, Black plays the following quite logical-looking moves:

1	P—Q4	P—Q4
2	P—K3	N—KB3
3	B—Q3	P—K3
4	N—Q2	QN—Q2
5	P—KB4	P—B4
6	P—B3	. . .

With this move White creates the escape route for his Bishop. It can now, if attacked, retreat to B2 or N1 and still strike along the same diagonal. One of the

big weaknesses of the Stonewall becomes apparent: P—KB4 creates a backward King Pawn.

6	. . .	B—Q3
7	KN—B3	O—O
8	O—O	N—K5

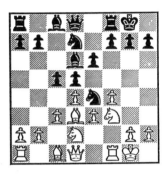

DIAGRAM 391

Position after 8 . . . N—K5

9	N×N	P×N
10	B×P	P—B4
11	B—Q3	. . .

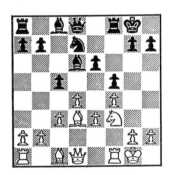

DIAGRAM 392

Position after 11 B—Q3

Now White will play N—K5, bring his Queen to R5, move his Rook in that zig-zag motion to R3 and push on. If Black defends with N—B3 White will shove his King-side Pawns forward to dislodge the Knight, whose position will be untenable. And if Black tries to break through the center, White will exchange Pawns, freeing his Queen Bishop, which will give the Queen Bishop and Queen Rook a chance to get into the fracas.

Now let's look at what might happen if Black were wise to White's strategy:

1	P—Q4	P—Q4
2	P—K3	N—KB3
3	B—Q3	P—B4
4	P—QB3	N—B3
5	P—KB4	B—N5
6	N—B3	P—K3
7	O—O	B—Q3
8	Q—K1	. . .

(To release the Knight from the pin.)

8	. . .	O—O
9	N—K5	B—B4

DIAGRAM 393

Position after 9 . . . B—B4

And Black equalizes. White must exchange Bishops and his King Bishop, the spearhead of his attack, disappears. The improvement found by White has been further improved, but by Black. Sic transit gloria chess.

The Indian Systems

The Indian systems are by far the most complex and difficult of all openings—King's Pawn, Queen's Pawn . . . any pawn. Aside from the involved positions that result, the principal reason for their difficulty is that the player who uses them must know dozens of other, less involved systems. Why? Because the Indian systems transpose all over the place. And the player who knows how to transpose a mediocre line into one that gives him all the advantages is way ahead of the game (and certainly way ahead of his opponent). One line, for example, may transpose into a sort of reverse Ruy Lopez, where Black is the attacker. If Black can do this, White is through.

The Indian Systems usually divide into three main lines: the Nimzo-Indian-Queen Indian; the Gruenfeld-King Indian; and the Old Indian. In addition, some off-beat variations crop up from time to time. The three main divisions are characterized, respectively, by the moves:

1	P—Q4	N—KB3
2	P—QB4	P—K3, P—KN3
		or P—Q3

Black's object in playing N—KB3 is twofold:

1—He avoids (or tries to avoid) Queen's Gambit lines.

2—He gives himself extreme flexibility. That is, without a committing Pawn move, he is free to adopt, at any favorable time, a line that is most advantageous.

We will not go into the Indian systems because such an excursion would be pointless without prior knowledge of the many lines into which the Indians can transpose. If you should meet 1 . . . N—KB3 over the board you are advised to play it by ear, to rely on the general rules and principles of opening play and to try to be as logical and careful as possible. If you choose a correct move each time it is your turn, you can't go too far wrong—and you will learn a great deal in the process.

Gambits

We will conclude our study of openings with a look at the true gambits—openings in which a Pawn, sometimes more, is sacrificed for the sake of rapid development and a good position. Unlike some of the lines we have examined, the sacrificed Pawn is given up without hope of a quick recapture. Material is traded for time or space or both.

Before going into some gambits, though . . .

STOP!

And try your hand at:

Self-Testing Quiz No. 17

(a) *In the following position (which arises out of a QGD by transposition) White has the move. Black has just played P—QN4, attacking the Bishop. White expects Black to follow through with P—N5, which will attack the Knight, and White would like to play N—K4 in reply. In view of this, how should White retreat his Bishop now?*

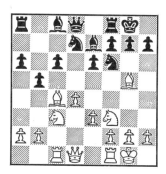

DIAGRAM 394

(b) *In the following position White has just played P—KR4, attacking the Black Bishop. Black tries to get out of his difficulties with Q—R4ch. What White move will cost Black a piece?*

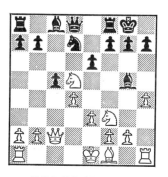

DIAGRAM 395

(c) It is Black's move in the following position. He can, with one move, tie White up in knots. What is the move?

DIAGRAM 396

Back to gambits.

The merits of gambits have been debated at length in all sorts of chess forums. But ours is not to do and die—ours is to reason why. And our reasoning runs along lines like this: a gambit is neither better nor worse than any other opening, though it may be worse for the gambiteer if he is not sure of his ground. In an ordinary opening, the player who loses his way or stumbles may find himself in a cramped position or defending where he should be attacking, or giving up the center. In a gambit, the player whose steps falter may find not only one or more of these situations prevailing, but he will also find himself behind in material.

Ergo, when you play a gambit, play it for all it's worth.

THE EVANS GAMBIT

The Evans, introduced almost 150 years ago by one Captain W. D. Evans, is an offshoot of the Giuoco Piano. It is characterized by the move 4 P—QN4, which offers the sacrifice of the Queen Knight Pawn in hopes of a quick development.

DIAGRAM 397

Position after 4 P—QN4

Does it work? The answer depends upon two things: which line is adopted by the players, and who the players are. If White chooses an aggressive line he may well launch a rapid and effective attack. But if Black knows what he is about he can take the sting out of the attack without too much trouble. Here are some typical lines in the Evans:

1	P—K4	P—K4
2	N—KB3	N—QB3
3	B—B4	B—B4
4	P—QN4	B×P
5	P—B3	B—R4
6	P—Q4	P×P
7	O—O	. . .

White gives up a second Pawn for the sake of a superior development.

7	. . .	B—N3
8	P×P	P—Q3

DIAGRAM 398

Position after 8 . . . P—Q3

The idea seems to be working. White is considerably ahead in development; he has two pieces posted on excellent squares; he has castled and even his undeveloped pieces (except the Rooks) have open lines along which to operate. Black has a way to go before he can castle; he has only a bare foothold in the center (compared to White's two central Pawns) and his King Bishop is not on its best square.

Looks are deceiving, though. Black is far from out of the picture. With the right kind of play he can still equalize. (Or, put the other way, with the wrong kind of play by White, Black can equalize.)

A game played in 1861, for example, continued this way:

9	P—Q5	N—R4
10	B—N2	N—K2

(Not 10 . . . N×B, for this would only be followed by Q—R4ch, which would even the material score and cost Black time.)

11	B—Q3	O—O
12	N—B3	N—N3
13	N—K2	. . .

All these Knight maneuvers are rather foreign to the Evans Gambit, which is essentially a tactical game, rather than a positional one.

13	. . .	P—QB4
14	Q—Q2	P—B3
15	K—R1	B—Q2

White is playing much too passively. With all those open lines he ought to be building up an attack. Black takes advantage of White's misguided skirmishing to capitalize on the rather weak White Queen side.

| 16 | R—B1 | P—QR3 |
| 17 | N—K1 | . . . |

(Still maneuvering.)

| 17 | . . . | B—N4 |

DIAGRAM 399

Position after 17 . . . B—N4

White's laconic play has given Black a chance to press a Queen-side attack. The pay-off will come quickly, with Black's pushing of his Queen Bishop Pawn, the resultant opening of the file and its capture by the Black Queen Rook.

Having seen what the wrong approach can do, let's take a look now at the right approach. We'll go back to the position two diagrams back (after 8 . . . P—Q3), but we'll proceed from there in a different way, starting with—

9	N—B3	N—R4
10	B—N5	P—KB3
11	B—K3	N—K2
12	P—KR3	. . .

The prevention of a pin of the King Knight is not a waste of time here.

| 12 | . . . | B—Q2 |
| 13 | B—N3 | . . . |

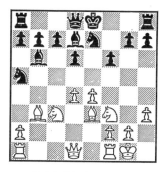

DIAGRAM 400

Position after 13 B—N3

White has the upper hand and should win without trouble. His center Pawns have not only remained strong, but they also threaten to move forward. All pieces are aggressively posted and ready to set themselves up in enemy territory.

Probably the strongest line for White is the one in which Black mistakenly plays 7 . . . P×P instead of the more usual 7 . . . B—N3. This gives Black three extra Pawns, but it also gives White a magnificent development with overwhelming attacking potential. The variation, in fact, is known as the Compromised Defense, because Black has compromised himself so badly and obviously.

The game can then continue as follows:

8	Q—N3	Q—B3
9	P—K5	Q—N3
10	N×P	. . .

DIAGRAM 401

Position after 10 N×P

White regains one of his three Pawns. Notice that he is threatening N—N5 with its resulting assault on Black's KB2.

| 10 | . . . | P—N4 |

Black tries to deflect the attack. He could also try (with equal lack of success) 10 . . . B×N. This would bring on 11 Q×B; and Black can now try 11 . . . P—N3, which would be followed by P—K6, or 11 . . . KN—K2, which would be followed by 12 N—N5,

O—O; 13 B—Q3 and the end is in sight. Or he could try 10 . . . KN—K2 which might be followed by 11 B—R3, O—O; 12 N—Q5 and the attack rolls on.

11	N×P	R—N1
12	Q—K3	N/N1—K2
13	Q—K2	. . .

White threatens to capture the Black Queen at once with N—R4.

13	. . .	Q—R4
14	B—R3	. . .

DIAGRAM 402

Position after 14 B—R3

Black's prospects are dim indeed. White can bring his Rooks to the center and put on the pressure. Black's cramped position makes any decent defense almost impossible. He has a lost game.

The best line for Black in the Evans begins with 6 . . . P—Q3, instead of 6 . . . P×P. (And there seems to be something of a moral here: the more Pawns Black grabs, the worse his position becomes; the fewer he takes, the better off he is.)

The merits of P—Q3 are obvious. With this move Black opens a line for his Queen Bishop, maintains a Pawn in the center, and—most important—deprives White of another tempo-bonus. A typical continuation might be:

7	Q—N3	Q—Q2
8	P×P	B—N3
9	B—QN5	. . .

(A waste of time. White is giving away what he won earlier.)

9	. . .	N/N1—K2
10	P×P	P×P
11	B—R3	Q—N5

DIAGRAM 403

Position after 11 . . . Q—N5

Black's chances are more than even. His pieces are all mobile and the immediate threat of Q×Pch can force White to compromise his position.

KING'S GAMBIT

The King's Gambit is characterized by the moves 1 P—K4, P—K4; 2 P—KB4. The object of White's second move is to gain control of the King Bishop file (after forcing it open, of course) and then to launch an attack against Black's weak point, his KB2. Secondarily, or primarily, depending on White's approach to the rest of the game, P—Q4 becomes possible immediately after the acceptance of the gambit with 2 . . . P×P. (First, however, White must take steps to prevent Q—R5ch by Black.)

One of the oldest lines for White—it has fallen into disrepute since the advent of "modern" chess— is the Muzio Gambit, a continuation that runs this way:

2	. . .	P×P
3	N—KB3	P—KN4
4	B—B4	P—N5
5	O—O	. . .

DIAGRAM 404

Position after 5 O—O

White offers a piece. The effect, since the gambit was introduced more than 400 years ago, is always sensational. On those rare occasions when it is played in a tournament it invariably evokes sharp in-drawings of breath from the audience, and muffled cries of "the Muzio—he's playing the Muzio!" This may be a result of the general feeling that the Muzio is unsound and is designed only to throw one's opponent off guard psychologically.

But sound or not, the Muzio invariably leads to chessboard fireworks.

5	. . .	P×N
6	Q×P	. . .

Some players, a while back, tried to push a good thing too far, playing 6 B×Pch and sacrificing not only the Knight and Pawn, but a Bishop too. After 6 . . . K×B; 7 Q×P, P—Q3; 8 Q×Pch, N—B3; 9 P—Q4, N—B3, however, Black was able to regroup his forces effectively enough to be able to take advantage of White's material inferiority.

6	. . .	Q—B3
7	P—K5	Q×P
8	P—Q3	B—R3

Attack and defense involving the Black Pawn at B5.

9	N—B3	N—K2
10	B—Q2	

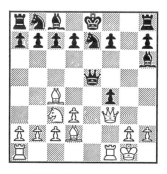

DIAGRAM 405
Position after 10 B—Q2

White, despite his sacrifices, has the initiative. He threatens QR—K1, driving off the Black Queen, followed by N—Q5, instituting a powerful King-side attack.

Black can improve his play with 6 . . . Q—K2, rather than 6 . . . Q—B3. The game might then proceed as follows:

7	P—Q4	N—QB3
8	Q×P	B—R3
9	Q×Pch	Q×Q
10	B×Qch	K—Q1
11	P—B3	B×B
12	R×B	. . .

DIAGRAM 406
Position after 12 R×B

White's sacrifice of the Knight is now paying off, but for Black. By forcing or finding exchanges, Black makes that initial sacrifice more and more costly to White. White's only real compensation is his powerful center. He will have to play well, though, to make it swing the balance against Black's superior forces.

The Muzio is certainly the best-known of the many gambits that stem from the King's Gambit. But better known still is the King's Gambit itself—just the plain King's Gambit, with no further sacrifices thrown in.

Here is a line in which Black quickly equalizes:

1	P—K4	P—K4
2	P—KB4	P×P
3	B—B4	P—Q4
4	B×P	Q—R5ch
5	K—B1	N—KB3
6	N—QB3	B—QN5

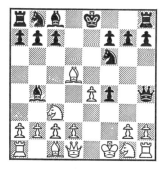

DIAGRAM 407
Position after 6 . . . B—QN5

Black has seized the initiative, and his lead in development is impressive; his Bishops have open lines and he is ready to castle. White is suffering from the cramps and has little room for maneuvering.

But there are plenty of better lines for White. For example:

3	N—KB3	P—Q4
4	P×P	N—KB3

(Not 4 . . . Q×P; 5 N—QB3, for the retreat of the Black Queen gives White a chance to speed his development at the expense of Black's time.)

5	N–B3	N×P
6	N×N	Q×N
7	P–Q4	B–K2
8	P–B4	Q–K5ch
9	B–K2	B–KB4
10	O–O	N–B3
11	R–K1	O–O–O

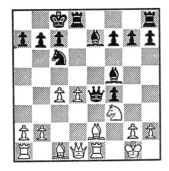

DIAGRAM 408

Position after 11 . . . O–O–O

Chances are about even. But White can improve his game still further by playing 9 K–B2 instead of 9 B–K2. White can then follow this with 10 P–B5, securing the initiative and giving him excellent chances for attacking.

BLACKMAR GAMBIT

We'll end this chapter with a quick look at a gambit that grows out of a Queen's Pawn opening—the Blackmar Gambit. It can backfire as in the following moves:

1	P–Q4	N–KB3
2	P–KB3	P–Q4
3	P–K4	P×P
4	N–B3	. . .

DIAGRAM 409

Position after 4 N–B3

Black can get much the better game here by continuing to accept Pawns. As, for example:

4	. . .	P×P
5	Q×P	Q×P
6	B–K3	Q–KN5
7	Q–B2	P–K4
8	N–B3	B–N5

DIAGRAM 410

Position after 8 . . . B—N5

Playing 5 N×P doesn't improve White's game. Therefore his best line is to avoid the situation entirely. As for example:

| 1 | P–Q4 | P–KB4 |
| 2 | P–K4 | . . . |

(What goes on? Is this the same opening? Yes—by transposition. Or, more correctly, the opening in which Black plays 2 . . . N–KB3 is the Blackmar by transposition.)

| 2 | . . . | P×P |
| 3 | N–QB3 | N–KB3 |

Here White can play 4 B–KN5, recovering the gambit Pawn, or 4 P–B3, which leads to a complicated game that runs in channels offering about equal chances to both sides.

| 4 | B–KN5 | P–B3 |

If Black tries to steer the game into the earlier version by playing 4 . . . P–Q4, he will regret it. For example: 4 . . . P–Q4; 5 B×N, KP×B; 6 Q–R5ch, P–N3; 7 Q×QP, Q×Q; 8 N×Q and Black not only loses an extra Pawn, but also leaves himself exposed and vulnerable on the King's side.

5	P–B3	Q–R4
6	Q–Q2	P–K6
7	B×P	P–K4
8	P×P	Q×KP
9	O–O–O	P–Q4
10	B–KB4	Q–B4
11	R–K1ch	. . .

And White has a strong initiative and a position full of potential for a King's-side attack (see diagram 411, page 161).

The survey of openings has been, admittedly, all too brief. If it has done these two things, however, it will have achieved its aim: (a) If it has given you even the barest hint of the wealth of possibilities—the almost

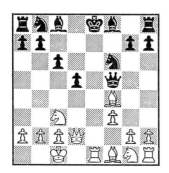

DIAGRAM 411

Position after 11 R—K1ch

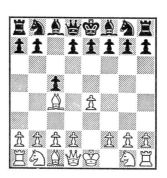

DIAGRAM 412

Position after 2 B—B4

unbounded wealth of possibilities—that can be explored in the first dozen-odd moves. (b) If you have formed from studying these few openings and variations an idea of the basic principles of sound opening play.

It ought to have been apparent too that one side can emerge from the opening with a great advantage only if the other side has played poorly or chosen an inferior line. With good play in a good variation chances should be just about even as the opening melts into the middle game. The line of play that leads to an advantage for White should be avoided by Black, if possible, and vice versa.

Suppose, however, that you meet an opponent who either knows nothing about openings or, knowing something about them, chooses to ignore regular lines of play. Suppose he tries to throw you off by playing way out in left field somewhere?

If you have learned your openings thoroughly and know, say, a total of 1,182 variations of 87 standard openings by heart—right out of the book—you are sunk. You will lose your head, founder, try something desperate and then be checkmated or lose your Queen.

If, on the other hand, you have a firm grasp of the principles of opening play you should be able to demolish anyone who tries to throw away the book.

Here, for example, is something you (as Black) might possibly meet.

| 1 | P—K4 | P—QB4 |
| 2 | B—B4 | . . . |

You have opened with the Sicilian and your opponent has replied with a move that just can't be found in the books. (True, B—QB4 can be played by White after a while; but there is no variation—no recognized variation—in which this is White's second move.) What do you do?

You consider. Your objective is control of the center. Your tactical object in playing 1 . . . P—QB4 was to prevent P—Q4 by White (never mind your stra-

tegic object of opening and occupying the Queen's Bishop's file: this is a tactical problem). Can you now force White out of the center?

He doesn't want to part with his Bishop. So:

2	. . .	P—K3
3	P—Q4	P—Q4
4	P×QP	P×P

And White must now lose time. Suppose, further, that he tries to wriggle out with, say 5 B—N5ch. You can reply B—Q2, forcing him again to move his Bishop. If he elects to capture your Bishop, the recapture will develop you, not him, and you will be three tempos ahead; you also will have a piece developed (the piece that recaptured) and he will not.

If White tries to protect his Queen Pawn (after 1 P—K4, P—QB4; 2 B—B4, P—K3) with 3 N—QB3, you can follow through with 3 . . . N—KB3 and still come out ahead.

And suppose now that your opponent (this time you're White) plays 1 . . . P—KN3 in reply to 1 P—Q4. What do you do? You occupy the center with 2 P—K4, then consolidate your position with developing moves. Your opponent will lose time and space, and eventually you will be able to convert these, if necessary, into material.

The victory need not be quick. It is only the experienced master who can punish an opponent swiftly for mistakes. You build slowly, establishing firm control of the center, forcing your opponent into a bind, tightening the screws, moving forward. Then—and only then—can you (rather, should you) launch your final attack.

It will pay off. If you have played well and your opponent poorly; if you have developed properly and your opponent improperly; if you have used time well and your opponent has wasted time—if all this has happened you are bound to cash in. If, to your surprise, you find your opponent has ignored all the rules and has still won, then you must look carefully at what you have done: perhaps you too, in your haste to make justice triumph, threw away the rules.

Chapter Nine

PLAYING AT ODDS

HAVING GONE THROUGH eight chapters in which you have been assailed on all sides with warnings and advice about the inexorable logic of chess, you come suddenly to a chapter on odds. Don't be dismayed. We are not about to introduce the throw of the dice into the game (though for hundreds of years chess, was, in fact, played with dice determining which man was to be moved). We don't mean gambling odds; that is something you will have to work out among yourselves.

By odds we mean handicaps.

Why handicaps?

Because if you sit down—you, a beginner—to play someone whose knowledge and experience are five times greater than your own you deserve some kind of compensating advantage. Without such an advantage your chances would be nil. Not only would you have no hopes of winning, but in all likelihood you would not even learn from your experience. How can you learn when the game is over before you know what has hit you?

Therefore, odds.

If your opponent has only a slight edge over you (this is easy enough to determine: you play, say, seven games on even terms: if he wins all seven in less than fifteen moves each the advantage is a great one; if he wins six out of seven and takes twenty moves to beat you his advantage is not so great; if you win five out of seven you offer him the odds) he may offer you the odds of move and draw.

Move and draw odds means that you have White (the move) and that if the game is a draw it counts as a win for you.

Other odds are, in the order of handicap:

1. The move.
2. Pawn (the stronger side removes one Pawn, usually the King Bishop Pawn).
3. Pawn and Two (the stronger side removes one Pawn and the weaker side is allowed two moves before his opponent, playing Black, moves).
4. Knight Odds (the stronger player has White but plays without his Queen Knight).
5. Rook Odds (the stronger player has White but plays without his Queen Rook. Because of the weakening of the Queen-side, however, White is permitted to start with his Queen Rook Pawn at QR3 instead of QR2).
6. Rook and Knight Odds (the same conditions prevail as in Rook odds, but the stronger side also does without his Queen Knight).
7. Queen Odds (the stronger side plays without a Queen).
8. Capped Pawn Odds (the stronger side contracts to give mate with a specified Pawn, usually the King Bishop Pawn. If he mates with any other man he loses. If he loses the capped Pawn, of course, he loses too).

Other combinations are sometimes given—Queen and move, for example, or Rook and two. Sometimes, too, a man other than a Pawn may be capped: the stronger side can, for example, contract to give mate with a capped Knight or capped Rook (the name capped derives from the practice of placing a "cap" on the contract piece to make it distinctive).

There is one further form of odds that is rarely used. In this form the weaker side is allowed to make as many moves as he wants before his opponent moves. There is only one restriction: the odds-taker must not place any of his pieces beyond his fourth rank. It is quite possible to arrange the men in such a way that mate becomes possible soon after Black makes his first move. This is not likely to happen, however, because anyone accepting such odds would not (or should not) know how to set up a mating net.

In games at odds it is customary, though not compulsory, for the player who gets free moves in the beginning to keep his pieces confined to his first four ranks. In odds involving the Rook it is customary for the player giving the Rook odds to retain the right to castle as though his Rook were still there.

If you accept Pawn odds it would be a good idea to remember that in exchange for his Pawn the stronger side will have an open file for his King Rook. Against a weak player the open file can be decisive. Perhaps you had better not accept Pawn odds. You can decline with a polite, "thanks a lot, but I'd just as soon not take advantage of you," or something of the kind.

Here is an example of a game at the odds of Pawn and Two. It was played in 1795 between Philidor and a gentleman named Atwood. Philidor, playing Black, removed his King Bishop Pawn.

1	P—K4	. . .
2	P—Q4	P—K3
3	P—KB4	P—Q4
4	P—K5	. . .

White used his two moves to set up a Pawn fort in the center. But he tried, on his third and fourth moves, to get too much of a good thing. It was not a wise strategy to lock the center; this gave Philidor, the strongest player in the world at the time, a chance to shift the action from the center to a wing.

White would have done better, after 1 P—K4; 2 P—Q4, P—K3, with a developing move such as N—QB3.

4	. . .	P—B4

DIAGRAM 413

Position after 4 . . . P—B4

The Pawn structure is now, in effect, that of a Queen's Gambit Declined with colors reversed.

5	P—B3	QN—B3
6	N—B3	Q—N3

Philidor, in shifting his Queen to the Queen's side, elects to make this the field of action. He is calling the tune, despite having given his opponent a free move and an extra Pawn.

7	B—Q3	N—R3
8	Q—N3	P—B5

The push is on. Philidor will infiltrate the Queen's wing.

9	Q×Q	. . .

The only possible answer to the Pawn fork.

9	. . .	P×Q

But, as you see, the Queen exchange has done White no good. It has, in fact, opened another file for Black's pieces, and the Queen Rook is ready to move.

10	B—B2	P—QN4
11	P—QN4	B×P

White, the unknowing amateur, is offered a Bishop. He should not accept it, but should gallantly—and prudently—try to catch up in development and mobility. He doesn't.

12	P×B	N×NP

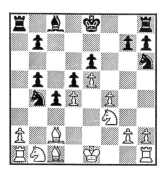

DIAGRAM 414

Position after 12 . . . N×NP

And now White sees the error. Unless he does something about it, Black will now play N×Bch, forking King and Rook. White does the only thing he can think of.

13	K—Q2	. . .

(13 B—Q1 might have been more effective. It certainly could not have been much worse.)

13	. . .	N×B
14	K×N	P—N5

The Pawns march on.

15	B—Q2	R—R5
16	P—KR3	. . .

White realizes his hopes are dim on the Queen's side. He starts a diversion on the other flank.

16	. . .	R—B1

The absence of the King Bishop Pawn gives Black an open file, which he now proceeds to utilize.

17	P—N4	N—B2
18	N—N5	N×N

Forcing open this file.

19	P×N	R—B7

And the King Rook joins in the invasion.

| 20 | P—R4 | P—N4 |

Philidor demonstrates that doubled Pawns, in the hands of a master, can be powerful weapons. By contrast, watch what happens to White's doubled Pawn on the King Knight file.

| 21 | P—R5 | P—N6ch |
| 22 | K—N2 | . . . |

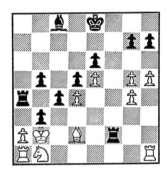

DIAGRAM 415

Position after 22 K—N2

22	. . .	P—N5
23	P—N6	RP×P
24	KRP×P	B—R3

The master takes the trouble to save his Bishop, though he probably could have won just as easily without it.

| 25 | R—R8ch | K—Q2 |

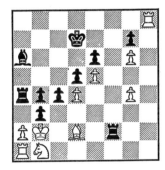

DIAGRAM 416

Position after 25 . . . K—Q2

At this point White resigned. He saw the hopelessness of his position. For example:

26	R—N8	P×P
27	R×Pch	K—B3
28	R×P	R×Bch
29	N×R	P—B6ch

and it is all over.

What lessons can the odds-taker learn from this game?

First and most obvious is the fact that the odds-taker is what he is because his opponent has an edge in technique and this must not be forgotten. The weaker side must not be fooled into thinking that his material or temporal advantage makes him the stronger player. Obviously it does not; it simply helps to equalize. If the odds are fair they put the players on a roughly equal footing. Sharp play is called for to maintain that equality.

Second, when the odds of a Pawn are given the odds-taker must act decisively to offset the advantage of the open file. He must try, if possible, to force an exchange that will plant one of the stronger side's Pawns on the open file, blocking it.

Third, he must not at once ease the tension in the center, thus giving the stronger side the freedom of choosing another field of action. How obvious this mistake is can be seen from the final position in the game above: the center Pawns remained unmoved. By locking the center with 4 P—K5 White gave his powerful opponent a free hand instead of occupying him with mobile action across the board.

Fourth, it is up to the odds-taker to attack. He must be the aggressor wherever and whenever possible. And he must not let the initiative slip from his hands. A stronger player who has the initiative is a sure winner.

Here is a game played at Knight Odds. The odds-giver was the famous Paul Morphy, the taker someone named Maurian. The game was played in New Orleans in 1857.

(Remove White's Queen Knight)

| 1 | P—K4 | P—K4 |

(It has been said that Morphy never played 1 P—Q4 and that, in fact, he had nothing but disdain for Queen's Pawn openings.)

| 2 | P—KB4 | P×P |

The King's Gambit Accepted, which is not a very advantageous opening for Black under normal circumstances. Against Morphy it is chessboard suicide.

3	N—KB3	P—KN4
4	B—B4	P—N5
5	P—Q4	. . .

Morphy offers a second Knight, turning the game into a sort of super-Muzio Gambit. His nonchalance—or his hauteur—must have been disconcerting to the amateur facing him across the board.

5	. . .	P×N
6	Q×P	P—Q4
7	KB×P	P—QB3
8	B×KBPch	. . .

The inimitable Mr. Morphy gives up still another piece—though the sacrifice is a very temporary one.

8	. . .	K×B
9	Q—R5ch	K—N2
10	B×P	. . .

DIAGRAM 417

Position after 10 B×P

The only piece Black has moved is his King! Hardly the right way to go about winning.

10	. . .	B—K2

A weak and pointless move. If Black hopes to get out of his difficulties (hardly likely at this point, but nevertheless worth trying) he ought to play vigorously, like a man, not a mouse.

11	O—O	. . .

That open file again.

11	. . .	Q×Pch

At last a manly move. And a lot of good it does!

12	K—R1	Q×KP
13	QR—K1	Q—N3

Giving up too easily. Black should, before this and certainly now at the latest, have tried to bring his Rooks into play. Possibly N—B3, attacking the White Queen and freeing the Rook, would have given him more of a chance. White, remember, is two pieces down; if Black can in any way force more exchanges his material advantage may count for something.

14	R×Bch	K—B1

(Not N×R, which would be followed by B—R6ch and then mate.)

15	B—Q6 dis ch	

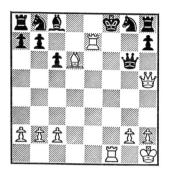

DIAGRAM 418

Position after 15 B—Q6 dis ch

Black resigned here. It is not only too late, but disastrous as well, to play N—B3 now. For this would be followed by R×Nch, Q×R; Q—K8mate. Or R×Nch; K—N1; R×Q; P×R; Q×Pch, K—B1; R—K8mate.

The same comments made on the Philidor-Atwood game apply here. The odds-taker played passively instead of vigorously. He gave up the initiative too easily; he allowed open files to work for the stronger side; he did nothing to develop aggressively.

Here's another game by the boy genius of New Orleans. This time Morphy plays without his Queen Rook, and without having his Queen Rook Pawn at QR3. His opponent—the game was played in New Orleans in 1858—was an unnamed amateur.

1	P—K4	P—K4
2	N—KB3	N—QB3
3	B—B4	N—KB3
4	N—N5	. . .

Morphy's tremendous advantage in ability permits him to break rules left and right. Break No. 1: he moves his Knight twice in the opening.

4	. . .	P—Q4

His opponent plays vigorously. Has Morphy underestimated the enemy—or overestimated himself?

5	P×P	N×P
6	N×BP	K×N
7	Q—B3ch	K—K3

Morphy's play, by any normal standards, is unsound. Still, he plays on, confident of victory.

8	N—B3	N—Q5

DIAGRAM 419

Position after 8 . . . N—Q5

9	B×Nch	K—Q3
10	Q—B7	. . .

And here the amateur makes a slight mistake—enough to give Morphy the chance he needs to insure his winning.

10	. . .	B—K3

Seemingly vigorous. But not vigorous enough. The amateur should have tried Q—K2, not only forcing a retreat, but instituting a valid counter-attack as well.

11	B×B	N×B
12	N—K4ch	. . .

From now until the end the amateur's King gets no rest.

12	. . .	K—Q4
13	P—B4ch	K×N
14	Q×N	Q—Q5
15	Q—N4ch	K—Q6
16	Q—K2ch	K—B7
17	P—Q3ch	K×B
18	O—O mate	

DIAGRAM 420

And what do we learn from this game?

First, Black would have been better advised to have castled as soon as possible. This would have nipped White's plan right then and there.

So, you say, White would have found another way. True enough—but we're only saying what Black might have done; we're not saying it would have worked against Morphy (nothing seemed to work against him).

Then, Black made that one really bad slip. His seemingly powerful move was not powerful enough. The player who is given odds must use his material advantage, whenever possible, to launch attacks (or, in this case, a counter-attack).

And, finally, his defense was inadequate. Had he, for example, played 14 . . . K—Q5 instead of 14 . . . Q—Q5 he might have had more of a chance. Try it yourself and see.

Finally, a game played at Queen odds. The master who played at this handicap was Cochrane; the place was London, the time the early 1800's.

1	P—K4	P—K4
2	P—KB4	P×P

The King's Gambit seems to have been a favorite with odds givers. And, most of the time, the odds takers have accepted the gambit. Is there a moral here?

3	B—B4	Q—R5ch
4	K—Q1	. . .

(Not 4 P—N3 of course, for this would be followed by P×P with a devastating discovered check threatened.)

4	. . .	B—B4
5	N—KB3	Q—Q1
6	P—Q4	B—N3

What the amateur does not realize is that his Pawn is a powerhouse. He ought to be taking steps to push it on, instead of retreating.

7	B×P	. . .

And that is the end of his powerhouse and of his chances.

7	. . .	P—KB3

A timid and weakening move.

8	P—K5	. . .

Cochrane, on the other hand, understands the power of the Pawn.

8	. . .	N—K2

Another weak move. Even with a Queen to the good an amateur cannot afford to play in this wishy-washy way against a strong player.

9	P×P	P×P
10	N—B3	QN—B3
11	R—K1	. . .

DIAGRAM 421

Position after 11 R—K1

Look at that position. Black's pieces are tripping all over each other. The Queen's Bishop might just as well not be on the board. The Rooks are staring at the back of their Pawns' heads. The Queen doesn't have a move at her disposal. And White? Every piece except his Queen Rook has open lines and points aggressively at the opponent's home territory. Now watch the minor pieces weave a mating net.

11	. . .	B—R4

A useless attempt to pin the Knight. White blithely —and quite correctly—ignores it.

12	N—K4	B×R

White is now down a Queen and Rook. So what!

13	N×Pch	K—B1
14	B—R6 mate	

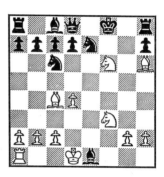

DIAGRAM 422

Let this be a lesson to you. Given odds, take advantage of it. If you have a material advantage, press it. Attack when you can, defend vigorously when you must. Don't waste moves. Don't cramp yourself. And don't make the mistake of thinking you are the better player.

Chapter Ten

ANNOTATED GAMES

AND JUST WHAT is an annotated game?

It is a game in which the author (or annotator, if you prefer) comments on the moves. He may say "a brilliant move"; or "not the best"; or "in 1822, in a similar position, Glabonovsky played 47 . . . N—N7, with a better position on the Queen's flank." He may also—and this is the usual meaning of annotation— give a series of alternative moves showing what might have happened.

In essence, these alternative moves are nothing more than a string of if-I-do-this-then-he-does-this-and-if-I-then-do-this-he-then-does-this'es. The more alternatives given, the "deeper" the analysis. Players who can go through this process while actually playing over the board are known as "deep" players (in contradistinction to players who eat too much and are known as "wide" players).

There are thousands upon thousands of books of annotated games. We will confine the analysis here to pointing out principles or to showing more obvious alternatives and what they might lead to. We will also keep historical annotation to a minimum.

We have selected three very different types of games for this chapter.

Game 1 was played by two rank amateurs—woodpushers, or maybe not even woodpushers.

Game 2 was played by a master and a talented amateur.

Game 3 was played by two of the best players in the history of chess.

A Battle of Blunders

1	P—K4	P—QB4
2	N—KB3	N—QB3
3	P—Q4	P×P
4	N×P	N—B3

So far everything is "by the book." This is not hard even for the most inexperienced player; all he has to do is memorize these first few moves. Now, however, Amateur A leaves the book.

5	P—KB3	. . .

DIAGRAM 423

Position after 5 P—KB 3

It is hard to figure out just what White had in mind. Perhaps he thought this a good way to protect his King Pawn. By itself, the move is not too bad; at any rate it is not a move that leads at once to an irreparably bad position. No doubt it does protect the King Pawn. But what it does not do—and this is important in the Sicilian—is prevent . . . P—K4.

Perhaps White had read about the so-called Moscow Variation (1 P—K4, P—QB4; 2 N—KB3, P—Q3; 3 P—Q4, P×P; 4 N×P, N—KB3; 5 P—KB3) and figured he would be one-up on Black because Black could not play . . . 5 P—K4, having played 2 . . . N—QB3 rather than 2 . . . P—Q3. But even if this were good reasoning (which it is not; . . . P—K4 is quite playable and quite effective now), the Moscow Variation, he should have realized, is not a good one for White.

5	. . .	P—KN3

Alas, Black, almost as bad a player as his opponent, fails to see how effective 5 . . . P—K4 would be. Instead, he elects to fianchetto his Bishop. He—we figure—had originally planned to play the Dragon Variation and, come what may, he will play it.

But maybe we aren't giving credit to player B. This move, in addition to preparing for the fianchetto, also deprives the advanced White Knight of the square KB5 as a retreat should Black now elect to play . . .

P—K4. This would be pretty shrewd. Let's see what happened.

6 P—QR3   . . .

No comment is needed here. Besides, the only really applicable comment would probably be unpublishable.

6 . . .   **B—N2**

At least Black is being consistent. He pursues his Dragon.

7 P—KN4   . . .

The fifth Pawn move in a total of seven moves. If you can deduce White's reasoning you are no doubt a first-class mind reader. This move irreparably weakens the King side, creates a backward King Bishop Pawn, threatens nothing, develops nothing and invites all sorts of invasions.

7 . . .   **P—K3**

Black is not playing brilliantly, but at least he is playing conservatively. At this rate, developing nicely, playing cautiously, he ought to be able to build up (slowly, to be sure) a good game, especially if White cooperates by making nonsensical moves.

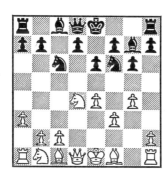

DIAGRAM 424
Position after 7 . . . P—K3

8 N—QB3   . . .

At last White develops a second piece. But his timing is way off. By playing 8 . . . P—Q4 now Black could effectively tie up White's game. For example: 8 . . . P—Q4; 9 P—K5 (which is probably what White would reply), N—Q2. This would unmask the fianchettoed Bishop and would leave Black free and flexible, White in a bind. Black, however, sees only the Dragon Variation. He continues by the book.

8 . . .   **P—QR3**

The move is not as bad as White's 6th. True, more effective moves were at Black's disposal; but this has the tiny virtue of a) preventing B—QN5 and b) preparing a Queen-side Pawn advance. Inasmuch as White has weakened his King side, though, Black ought to be getting into action there. (Incidentally, the move . . . P—K4 now would be able to lock the center and free Black for action on the King's wing.)

9 P—KB4   . . .

This is the move that finally gets the lead out of Black's pants. He sees a chance for a gain in material.

9 . . .   **N×NP**

DIAGRAM 425
Position after 9 . . . N×NP

Black's reasoning, no doubt, is this (and it isn't half bad): If White plays 10 Q×N, I will play 10 . . . N×N and come out a Pawn ahead. Pretty fair for a beginner. But White doesn't oblige that way. He obliges in another way, instead.

10 P—K5   . . .

White read somewhere that the move P—K5 is effective in the Sicilian. But the move—and he obviously hasn't the faintest idea of this—is good only under the right circumstances at the right moment. Incidentally, this is White's seventh Pawn move. Now Black gets pushing.

10 . . .   **Q—R5ch**

Pretty good. Black correctly sees that White cannot interpose and will have to move his King to Q2 (moving it to K2 would lead to mate almost at once, and even White sees this).

11 K—Q2   . . .

So Black wins at least a Knight, because the White King now cuts off the protection of the N/Q4.

11 . . .   **N×N**

Black is now a Knight and Pawn to the good, has a strong attack going and is trying hard to play brilliantly. White plods along, continuing to bungle.

12 B—K2 . . .

Even without looking very hard it is easy to see how wrong this move is. Of course there are not many good moves left for White, but there are some that would, at least, prolong the game a bit. Perhaps White was hoping to pick off the Black Knight at his N4 this way. A better move would have been 12 N—K4, for example, which would have had, if nothing else, the merit of preventing Black's next move.

12 . . . **N—KB7**

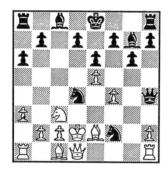

DIAGRAM 426
Position after 12 . . . N—KB7

The Knight forks Queen and Rook. White, already a piece and a Pawn down, is through. But he shouldn't have to be through in one move. It was only natural, though, that he should top off his brilliant game with the one move (sorry, there were two moves) that leads at once to mate. He cuts off his King's one remaining escape square (K1) with Q—K1. Perhaps he thought he was pinning the Knight. Some pin! He could also have mated himself with R—K1, but that was too hard to think of. Here is the denouement:

13 Q—K1 **Q×BP mate**

There is a moral in this little game: Even a rank beginner (which obviously Black was) can win quickly and, in what is apparently brilliant style, against someone who plays against himself. White almost unerringly picked the worst move in each of the last three moves of his game. And most of the preceding moves were Pawn moves which—as you now know so well—are weakening and dangerous. It took a lot of goading to get Black to see the glaring weaknesses on White's King-flank. When he finally did see them, though, he was able to take advantage of them; they—the weaknesses—were beyond repair.

A Battle of Wits

So much for the play of two novices. Now let's look at a game between a master and a talented amateur. The odds, of course, are heavily in favor of the master, who has years of experience behind him. He can tell at a glance when weaknesses appear. The amateur can see weaknesses, too, but he may have to search for them. The master knows almost without thinking how to capitalize on a weakness; the amateur must give the matter heavy thought.

The game is instructive in that it shows how weaknesses develop and how they can be exploited. The game selected is, like the game of the two beginners, a Sicilian Defense. The master was George Koltanowski, a specialist in blindfold and simultaneous play, playing White; the Black pieces were handled by a man named Kearns. The game appears in Koltanowski's book *Adventures of a Chess Master.*

1 P—K4 **P—QB4**
2 P—QN4 . . .

This is an off-beat variation known as the Wing Gambit and has the advantage of being little known. Before continuing with the game we might make a few sage observations about the psychology of chess:

When a master plays against a master he plays cautiously, taking, as a rule, fairly well known lines and playing the board, so to speak. But when a master engages an amateur he can afford to get off the beaten track, knowing that the odds are against the amateur's being able to refute his moves in a drastic and telling way. In such cases the master is playing his opponent rather than the board. He is banking to a certain extent on being able to confuse his opponent. He believes—and usually he is right—that his opponent will become flustered and quickly lose his way. Koltanowski, in addition to being a master chess player, is also a pretty fair psychologist.

2 . . . **P×P**

Black can do reasonably well here by playing 2 . . . P—K4, freeing a diagonal for the King Bishop and introducing the element of tension into the game, which so far is rather calm, if odd.

3 P—QR3 . . .

At a game in the Hastings Tournament of 1946-47, Abrahams played 3 B—N2 against Aitkens. The game continued with 3 . . . P—Q4; 4 P×P, Q×P; 5 P—QB4 (usually an effective move against the Sicilian, but not in this context), Q—K5ch; 6 N—K2, B—B4 and Black had a won game.

3	...	P—Q4
4	P—K5	...

The move 4 KP×P would lead to a rather different but still quite lively game. It would bring out Black's Queen and open lines more quickly.

4	...	N—QB3
5	P—Q4	P—K3

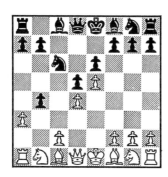

DIAGRAM 427
Position after 5 . . . P—K3

White, with his 5th move, and Black, with his 5th, lock the center. White has in effect, announced his intention of operating on the King's wing. Black's chances, as you know from the brief discussion of the Sicilian in Chapter 8, lie on the Queen's wing. Both are willing to keep the center frozen and to try their luck on their respective flanks. Had Black played, instead, 5 . . . Q—N3, the center would have remained fluid, the Queen's-wing attack might have gathered momentum earlier and Black might have had better chances.

Notice that, like Amateur A in the previous game, Koltanowski is making an excessive number of Pawn moves. But unlike Amateur A, Koltanowski has a plan in mind. He is also counting on his opponent's making a not-too-good move. And, likewise unlike Amateur A, Koltanowski will know what to do about that not-too-good move.

6	P×P	B×Pch
7	P—B3	B—B1

Black undoubtedly would have done better with 6 . . . N×NP. But his position is already compromised. And White, as you see, has an open file for his Queen Rook and a solid Pawn chain to break the board into fields of action.

8	B—Q3	...

White places a Bishop in an aggressive position, especially in view of his intention to wage war on the King's wing.

8	...	N/N1—K2

Black is putting himself in a bind, not very judicious against a master.

9	N—K2	...

DIAGRAM 428
Position after 9 N—K2

The surprising thing (it is not really surprising; White has made some not-of-the-best moves and has wasted time) is that White, for all his Pawn moves, is better developed—much better—and has a considerably freer game.

9	...	P—KN3
10	O—O	B—N2
11	P—KB4	...

This is the trumpet that announces the coming Kingside attack in earnest. Black should now give everything he has for a rapid Queen-side attack. Instead, he obliges White by creating weaknesses on the King side. His development, though not positively bad, is negatively so; it is mechanical and unseeing.

11	...	O—O
12	P—KN4	P—B4

This move, intended to free his pieces and unlock the center, works in reverse; it gives White the wedge he needs to crack open the King's wing.

13	P×P e.p.	R×P

The recapture with the Rook takes some of the momentum out of White's attack but leaves the King's defenses shot full of weaknesses.

14	N—Q2	Q—B2
15	N—B3	B—Q2

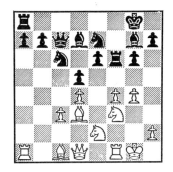

DIAGRAM 429

Position after 15 . . . B—Q2

| 16 | **Q—K1** | . . . |

White prepares to swing the Queen over to the King's flank to join in the fray.

| 16 | . . . | **R—B2** |

Black now intends to double Rooks on the half-open King Bishop file.

| 17 | **B—K3** | **P—KR3** |
| 18 | **Q—R4** | **QR—KB1** |

The battle is about to be joined. White's pieces are concentrated for the attack; Black's for the defense.

| 19 | **K—N2** | **B—B3** |

DIAGRAM 430

Position after 19 . . . B—B3

20	**Q—R3**	**N—R4**
21	**N—K5**	**B×N**
22	**BP×B**	**R×R**
23	**R×R**	**R×R**
24	**K×R**	. . .

Black probably felt it was safer to exchange heavy pieces and lessen the strength of White's attack. The strategy, however, is faulty, because the attack is just as strong or, worse, stronger than before. The King

Rook Pawn, for example, is lost; with its fall will go Black's hopes.

| 24 | . . . | **P—KR4** |
| 25 | **P×P** | **N—B4** |

DIAGRAM 431

Position after 25 . . . N—B4

| 26 | **B×N** | . . . |

Also playable, and quite strong, was 26 P×P.

26	. . .	**KP×B**
27	**P×P**	**B—N4**
28	**Q×P**	**B×Nch**

A desperation move and not worth much.

| 29 | **K×B** | **Q—B5ch** |
| 30 | **K—B2** | **Q—B2** |

No time to pursue these pointless checks. Black must get his Queen back to the defense.

| 31 | **B—R6** | **resigns** |

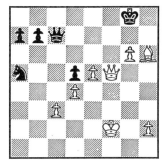

DIAGRAM 432

Position after 31 B—R6

There is not much Black can do to stop mate. For example: 32 Q—K6ch, K—R1; 33 Q—K8 mate. Anything Black tries for his 31st move will only lose his Queen for him. Even—and this is, at this point, a preposterous "even"—if Black could exchange Queens, he has a hopelessly lost end game.

So far you have seen:

(a) A game in which, though both sides played poorly, one side—White—played so very poorly that he was checkmated before the middle game had been reached. This game illustrated the dangers of making pointless and haphazard moves, even against a novice.

(b) A game in which both sides played well, but one side not well enough. Here, having made no outright blunders or really bad moves, the weaker player was able to stay with it until well into the middle game (he almost made it to the end game). But the weaknesses he allowed to develop on the King's wing, coupled with his having acquiesced in the locking of the center, led to his defeat.

A Battle of Brains

Now, to finish, we'll show two chess giants at work—Alekhine and Capablanca (and you'll still find arguments today about which was the greater, or about which of the two was the greatest chess player ever known). No blunders in this game, no slips, no booboos. It goes right straight through to the end game; and only there does Capablanca err, ever so slightly, giving Alekhine the tiny edge he needs to force a win.

The game was one of those in their Buenos Aires match in 1927. The opening is a sort of off-beat Queen's Gambit Declined by transposition, with Alekhine playing the White pieces.

1	P—Q4	N—KB3

This move of Black's (see Indian Defenses, Chapter 8) is a flexible one; depending upon White's reactions, he can transpose into any number of favorable lines. Alekhine, however, wants to stick to the QGD and plays accordingly.

2	P—QB4	P—K3
3	N—QB3	P—Q4

The opening is now a genuine QGD, despite the odd beginning.

4	B—N5	QN—Q2
5	P—K3	P—B3
6	P×P	. . .

For this move see the discussion in Chapter 8 of the Cambridge Springs Variation.

6	. . .	KP×P

This is one occasion on which the principle of capturing toward the center must be ignored. The capture with the King Pawn, ordinarily, gives a temporary advantage in space that calls for extremely aggressive and accurate play to maintain. The capture with the Bishop Pawn (also ordinarily; you will see this game takes some extraordinary turns) tends to give Black troubles with his Bishop in that the Pawns turn out to be on the wrong-colored squares.

7	B—Q3	B—K2
8	KN—K2	. . .

The first of several off-the-beaten-path moves. The more usual continuation, 8 N—KB3, leads by transposition of moves to the Cambridge Springs Variation.

8	. . .	O—O

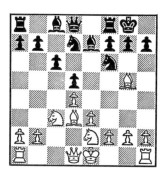

DIAGRAM 433
Position after 8 . . . O—O

9	N—N3	. . .

White begins maneuvering to regroup his forces. He intends to post the Knight at B5, then move up his King-side Pawns. At this early stage, however, the plan is still only a strategic conception; the tactical considerations are far from firm. And anything can happen.

9	. . .	N—K1

Black, too, aims for a regrouping of forces. He takes his cue from White, intending to permit no uncompensated weaknesses.

10	P—KR4	. . .

White, with this move, commits himself. He cannot castle short now—the Pawn formation being too weak on that flank—and he is not yet able to castle long.

10	. . .	N/Q2—B3
11	Q—B2	. . .

White could now castle long, if it were safe to do so. But Black has kept himself highly mobile and castling long might prod Black into launching a Queen-side flanking movement.

| 11 | . . . | B–K3 |
| 12 | N–B5 | . . . |

Carrying out one objective.

| 12 | . . . | B×N |

Black has no intention of allowing White to keep a Knight posted in that aggressive position.

13	B×B	N–Q3
14	B–Q3	P–KR3
15	B–KB4	R–B1

Black, having regrouped, now broadcasts his intentions to swing the scene of action to the Queen's wing.

DIAGRAM 434
Position after 15 . . . R–B1

| 16 | P–KN4 | . . . |

White wants to keep things boiling over on the King's wing. Notice that, not having castled, his King Rook is still in a position to take advantage of the opening of the King Rook or King Knight file.

| 16 | . . . | N/B3–K5 |

The old principle: the best way to meet a flank thrust is with a counter-thrust in the center.

| 17 | P–N5 | . . . |

Threatening to wrench open a file.

| 17 | . . . | P–KR4 |

Black stops the opening of the file, but loses a Pawn in the process.

18	B×N/K4	N×B
19	N×N	P×N
20	Q×KP	. . .

DIAGRAM 435
Position after 20 Q×KP

Black is now a Pawn down. However, he has succeeded in freeing the game considerably and he remains quite mobile.

| 20 | . . . | Q–R4ch |

The object of this move is not simply to harass White, but to force an exchange of Queens and, then, to invade White's territory by way of the Queen Bishop file, which will be forced open by the Queen exchange.

| 21 | K–B1 | Q–Q4 |

White is forced to accept the exchange.

| 22 | Q×Q | P×Q |

The Queen Bishop file is now open, with Black occupying it.

| 23 | K–N2 | . . . |

White must resort to "artificial castling" to connect his Rooks.

| 23 | . . . | R–B7 |

Invasion.

| 24 | KR–QB1 | KR–B1 |

Black cannot capture White's Queen Knight Pawn because the loss of time would outweigh the material advantage. White would get a chance to invade by way of 25 R—B7—Q7 and then would be able to double Rooks. The threat is too great.

25   R×R   . . .

Here White disregards the principle of forcing your opponent to make the first capture on an open file. Though he loses control of the file by so doing he has compensation in this: Black no longer has doubled Rooks on the file. And, since White's King Bishop Pawn is protected by the King, it remains only to protect the Queen Knight Pawn.

25	. . .	R×R
26	R—QN1	. . .

DIAGRAM 436

Position after 26 R—QN1

Despite the presence of a hostile Rook on his second rank, White has the edge. His King is more mobile than Black's and—of course—he has the extra Pawn. One of the hardest things in chess to do, however, is to win a won game.

26	. . .	K—R2

Black gets his King into play.

27	K—N3	K—N3
28	P—B3	P—B3
29	P×P	B×P
30	P—R4	K—B4

The Kings, as you see, precede the Pawns, depriving their counterparts of space.

31	P—R5	R—K7
32	R—QB1	. . .

White, a Pawn up, can afford to give up a Pawn for the sake of a more aggressive posting of his Rook.

32	. . .	R×NP
33	R—B5	. . .

DIAGRAM 437

Position after 33 R—B5

33	. . .	K—K3
34	P—K4	. . .

Even at this late stage the move P—K4 remains a powerful one. If now Black plays 34 . . . P×P, White can play 35 P—Q5ch, forcing Black to Black's Q2 or B4. White then can recapture (after 35 . . . K—B4 by first playing 36 P—Q6 dis ch) and get two united passed Pawns. Black, however, sees the pitfall.

34	. . .	B×P
35	R×P	B—B6
36	R×P	P—R3
37	B—B7	B—K8ch
38	K—N4	R—N7ch
39	K—R3	R—KB7
40	K—N4	. . .

Certainly not 40 K—N3, followed by 40 . . . R—QB7 dis ch.

40	. . .	R—N7ch
41	K—R3	R—KB7
42	P—B4	R—B6ch
43	K—N2	R—B7ch
44	K—R3	R—B6ch
45	K—N2	. . .

We can offer no rational explanation for these time-consuming moves. It is possible both men were anxious to enter a new time period in the tournament to be able to take more time in the later stages. Obviously Black can gain nothing by these constant checks.

45	. . .	R—B7ch
46	K—N1	R—QB7

The action resumes.

47	B—N6	R—B5

DIAGRAM 438
Position after 47 . . . R—B5

DIAGRAM 439
Position after 53 . . . R—B5

| 54 | **K—B5** | . . . |

And the principle of bringing the King up ahead of the Pawns.

| 54 | . . . | **B×P** |

Black's only real hope lies in the two Queen-side Pawns. He tries to turn them to account. But White is too resourceful.

| 55 | **R—R7ch** | . . . |

Had White played 55 B×B, Black could have followed with 55 . . . R—B4ch; 56 K—N4, R×R; 57 K×R; 58 P—R6 and the passed King Rook Pawn would be unbeatable.

55	. . .	**K—B3**
56	**B×B**	**R—B4ch**
57	**K—K6**	. . .

White not only gets out of checks, but also grabs territory from the Black King, assuring his passed Pawns of a march to the eighth rank.

| 57 | . . . | **R×B** |

Black tries to recover a Pawn. White could protect it with, say, R—K5ch, but after . . . K—B3 White's Rook would be rendered less mobile. White, however, finds a brilliant way to protect the Pawn.

| 48 | **K—N2** | . . . |

At first glance this move seems baffling. But look: If Black now plays 48 . . . R×P, White follows with 49 K—B3, R—B5 (or N5 or R5); 50 R—K5ch and the Black Bishop is lost.

48	. . .	**P—N3**
49	**R—K5ch**	**K—Q2**
50	**P—R5**	. . .

The Rook check at K5 now works because the White King is in a better position. (A move such as 48 K—N2, in which a subtle change of position effects a major change in potential, is known in high-class chess parlance as an "intermezzo.")

| 50 | . . . | **P×P** |
| 51 | **K—B3** | . . . |

White prefers to use his King, rather than his Rook, to stop the passed Pawn. For if R×P, then . . . R×P and White's united Passed Pawns are wrecked.

| 51 | . . . | **P—R5** |
| 52 | **R—R5** | . . . |

The principle of attacking a Pawn from the rear.

| 52 | . . . | **R—B6ch** |
| 53 | **K—N4** | **R—B5** |

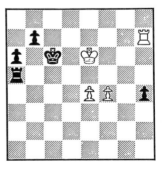

DIAGRAM 440
Position after 57 . . . R×B

Black has an extra Pawn, but it does him no good because White has much the superior position. White's King is beautifully posted to run interference for the Pawns; Black's King Rook Pawn can be taken almost at will. Black's only real resource is the pair of passed Queen-side Pawns. But he will not have time to use them.

58	P—B5	R—R6

To try to halt the Pawns from the rear.

59	P—B6	R—KB6
60	P—B7	P—N4
61	R—R5	. . .

White will interpose his Rook to see the Bishop Pawn through.

61	. . .	P—R6

Note the vital importance of time. He who makes it to the eighth rank first wins.

62	R—B5	. . .

This forces the issue.

62	. . .	R×R
63	P×R	. . .

DIAGRAM 441
Position after 63 P×R

Not 63 K×R, for this would give Black a chance to deprive White of territory. This, in turn, would force White to maneuver. And this, in turn, might give Black the extra move he needs to reach the eighth rank in time.

63	. . .	resigns

If Black plays 63 . . . P—R7, White follows with 64 P—B8/Q, P—R8/Q; 65 Q—R8ch, K any; 66 Q×Q.

And there you have it. A game between two amateurs with a one-two checkmate resulting from hideous blunders; a game between a master and a talented amateur, in which small weaknesses are exploited and lead to an untenable position in the middle game; and a game between two greats in which slow, sure play and a couple of brilliant moves keep the game teetering until the very last moment.

Chapter Eleven

THE MAD, WONDERFUL WORLD OF CHESS

NOW THAT YOU have diligently worked your way through the chapters on tactics, openings, end games, middle games and what not; now that you have studied carefully and thought out all the problems; now that you have spent all this time learning chess when you could have been out making money or spending it; now that you have done all this—what are you going to do?

You could, of course, keep right on reading and studying and thinking; there are thousands upon thousands of books you could buy (see the list of books a few pages on) to take you through the advanced beginner, intermediate, advanced intermediate, advanced, advanced advanced and out-of-this-world stage of erudition. And you could do this right in the comfort of your own home. There is nothing wrong with this approach to chess, especially if you have always had a secret desire to be a hermit or a lighthouse-keeper.

Or you could venture into the world of chess-nuts—abandoning your home and job to follow the tournaments; spending your life savings to go to international tournaments in Yugoslavia and Melbourne; subscribing to periodicals in Ukrainian, Serbo-Croatian, Italian and Rumanian to learn who is going to play whom in which city and when; fighting the State Department for visas to Communist countries so you can stand outside a Hall of Socialist Labor Heroes in 20-below weather to follow the games because no tickets were left by the time you got there. Others have adopted this approach and they probably would be delighted to have a chance to tell you of its pleasures. But visiting hours at the asylum are booked well in advance; you will have to make your reservations now for next year.

Then there is postal chess (about which more later in this chapter). You could be patriotic and decide to subsidize the Post Office Department, reducing the annual postal deficit by playing a thousand opponents at once and putting five-cent stamps on your post cards when only four cents is required. Not only would this keep you busy night and day answering your opponents, but you might even get your picture on a postage-due stamp when you die, and thus become immortalized.

Or you could make chess a hobby for your spare time—possibly even forgo your weekly golf sessions to make it down to the local chess club—playing perhaps a dozen games a week, maybe even half a dozen by mail. You could subscribe to one or two periodicals and buy a chess book now and then to keep up with theory. You might even buy a good inlaid chessboard and a set of hand-carved chess men to go with it. And you might play in a tournament once or twice a year for the fun of it and, perhaps, to win an official rating and improve your game.

Let's assume you love your family, want to hold on to your job and your savings and are disinclined to be a recluse and that the last course therefore appeals to you. How do you go about making chess your hobby?

If you live in a major metropolitan area—New York, Chicago, Los Angeles, Pittsburgh—or even in a minor metropolitan area, all you have to do is look around for a chess club. The Yellow Pages of your telephone directory, for example, will list them (under "clubs"). If you don't find any there, write to the U.S. Chess Federation, 80 East 11th Street, New York 3, N.Y., and ask for the name and address of the nearest chess club. If there is none in your area you can start one. Before you do, though, you might want to know what a chess club is, what it offers and how it works. Here, then, is a portrait of a fictitious, but perfectly plausible, chess club.

The Middletown Chess Club meets Tuesdays and Thursdays at 8:30 P.M., except during July and August, when it meets only every alternate Thursday. It used to meet at members' homes, but recently its reserve fund got large enough to permit it to rent a large room in a veterans clubhouse. It's also on the waiting list of organizations that would like rent-free facilities in the village recreation hall; it ought to make it in about three years.

The club started out with six members but, by way of advertising—a small ad in the hometown newspaper and word-of-mouth—now has thirty-three members, including a dozen hard-core types who do most of the work and never fail to show up. The dues are reasonable: $10 a year, including $5 for annual individual membership in the U.S.C.F. Out of this the club has managed to buy three dozen chessboards and sets and a dozen chess clocks. It also subscribes to several periodicals and buys books for a circulating chess library.

It's a rather informal group, this chess club. The "business" end of the meeting—when it takes place at all—is usually short, except once a year when new officers are elected; the treasurer gives a quick rundown of how things stand, occasionally making a recommendation for a fund drive, occasionally reporting enough of a surplus to make a purchase of a book or something. Most of the members, including the treasurer, grow impatient at business meetings; they come down to the club to play chess or kibitz, not to talk business.

The club runs a continuing ladder contest to rate its members. The "ladder" gets its name from the rating board that hangs on the wall; the current club champion is at the top of the ladder. If he is beaten, his name plaque—a tongue depressor with his name on it—will be moved down and his opponent's plaque hung up in its place. This keeps the interest high. The club is even thinking of awarding a permanent trophy to the member who manages to stay on top for six months.

Despite its official status and the glory it brings, the ladder game is not the biggest drawing card. That honor belongs to the skittles games—the offhand, unofficial, well-kibitzed games that go on hour after hour at every meeting. As often as not the post-mortems that follow these games are longer than the games themselves.

"So you think you could have got me if I'd played Rook to Rook 4 there, huh? Let me show you. Here, Rook to Rook 4, now whadda you do?"

"So! I put pressure on your isolated Queen's Pawn. You couldn't have defended it. And with your Queen's Pawn gone where would you have been? Luck, it was just luck you played your Bishop where you did. You thought I was going to attack your Queen so you got it out of there."

"Just a minute, just a minute. He had a mate in three. You didn't see it? You musta been blind. Like this—Knight takes Pawn check; Pawn takes Knight. Queen to Queen 8 check; King to Rook 2 . . ."

They're still talking the game out when they're walking to their cars. To be continued.

Once in a while the club decides to invite a master to give a lecture or a simultaneous exhibition. Then the club takes an ad in the paper—sometimes it gets free publicity by treating the event as a newsworthy item and getting the paper to carry a story—and outsiders show up for the meeting to hear or play against the master. If enough non-members come down, at $2.50 a board, the club realizes a profit. Even when it doesn't, though, it is well worth it because—aside from the members' having had a chance to play the master—the club sometimes gets new blood from these affairs.

The non-members become members and everybody is happy.

Sometimes, too, the club buys a bloc of tickets to a big tournament in a near-by city. And sometimes it buys a bloc of tickets to something that has nothing to do with chess: a road company production of a Broadway play, for example, or a visiting opera troupe.

Twice a year the members have a family day. In the summer they organize a picnic, wives and children invited. And in December they have a big Christmas party for members and families.

But mostly they play chess.

This, then, is a more-or-less typical chess club. Actually dues range from $2 a year to more than $25. And many clubs play tournaments with other clubs. Some even get their top-board men together as a team and compete in national and regional team events.

If a chess club appeals to you, then, and there is none around, you can organize one. The biggest problem will be getting members. Try your place of business for a starter. Drop in on non-chess clubs—the Kiwanis, the veterans groups, the P.T.A.'s—and scrounge around. When you enlist someone, have him do the same, and spread the word along to family and friends. You can get the ball rolling with as few as six people.

You don't have to have officers or even regular meeting days; you can meet when it's convenient for the six of you, and where it's convenient. What's the difference as long as you get to play chess? Once your membership gets respectably large you can start to think about the more formal aspects—the election of officers, the collecting of dues and setting of meetings; the enrollment in the Chess Federation.

As for tournaments, you don't even have to belong to a chess club to play in them. All you have to do, as a rule, is pay an entry fee (usually no more than a couple of dollars) and show up on time.

Tournaments—club, inter-club, regional, zonal, national and so on—are listed in the two principal American chess periodicals, Chess Review and Chess Life (for information on how to get copies see the list of further reading, page 182). Many of these tournaments are run under U.S.C.F. sanction. If you play in them you will get an official Federation rating (these run from Class C on up through Class A, then Expert and Master ratings). In your first sanctioned tournament you will, of course, be playing as an unrated player; you will emerge from the tournament with a score and a rating equivalent to your best performance against a rated player. If you draw with a Class B player, for example, you are given his rating. If you beat a Class B player you are given his rating plus 50 points. The points required for the official Federation classes are as follows:

Class C .... under 1600 points
Class B .... 1600 to 1799 points
Class A .... 1800 to 1999 points
Experts .... 2000 to 2199 points
Masters .... 2200 to 2399 points
Senior Masters ..... 2400 points and up

Beyond this are the ratings conferred by the Fédération Internationale des Echecs (International Chess Federation), which are grandmaster, international grandmaster and world champion.

For figuring your score once you have attained a rating see the chapter on FIDE rules.

In non-sanctioned tournaments you will, usually, be playing only for fun or glory. Some, however, offer prizes such as trophies, books, chess sets or cash. (U.S.C.F. tournaments also offer prizes, in addition to ratings and such things as the title of U.S. Open Champion)

Some tournaments are for invited participants only, such as the U.S. Chess Championship (not to be confused with the U.S. Open Championship, which is, as the name implies, open to all comers) and the interzonal play-offs. These, too, are listed in the chess periodicals. Here you get a chance to see the masters in action and if you're inclined to spectator sports this may be your cup of instant tea. You are not allowed to kibitz, however, and may be escorted quite forcibly from the tournament room if you try to offer unsolicited advice to the masters and grandmasters.

In the big cities there are, in addition to regular clubs, things called chess parlors. These are commercial establishments at which you pay, say, 15 cents an hour for the privilege of using the facilities. Here you will meet the coffeehouse type of player. Do not let his looks deceive you.

Lots of coffeehouse players look like, and some are, bums. But this does not necessarily mean they are woodpushers (this is a term with which you must become familiar if you are to play chess; a woodpusher is to chess what a divot-digger is to golf. No—more. A woodpusher is the lowest of the low—a schlemiel, a man who knows all the answers when he is kibitzing and none when he is playing). On the contrary, coffeehouse players look the way they do because they do not buy clothes; they buy books of tournament play; they look the way they do because they are so engrossed in the strength of their Pawn position that they do not notice the thick, black coffee dribbling down the front of what might once have been a reasonably decent second-hand vest; they look the way they do because they take time to shave only when they have run out of opponents.

Some coffeehouse players are house men. Approach them with caution. They will play you for stakes and you will have to thumb a ride home. They may offer you a deal: if you win its costs you nothing to play, if you lose you pay not only the 15-cent-an-hour tab, but a bonus to boot.

Do not be deceived by the house manager, either. If you drop in for a game and he asks you what your strength is and you tell him you are not bad, not good, maybe fair, he will tell you he's sorry he has only strong players around, but wait, wait, someone your strength may drop in any minute. And sure enough, ten minutes later a seedy-looking character will stroll in and the manager will tell him to sit down he's got for him an opponent. And this not-bad, not-good, maybe-fair player will then proceed to play the pants off you.

The best way to cope with coffeehouse players is to become one yourself. You don't have to do it full time, though; you can assume the role perhaps once a week, finding your oldest, most moth-eaten sweater, splashing coffee on it, taking care not so shave too closely (if at all) and then strolling into the chess parlor in your best nonchalant fashion. Don't plunge right into a chess game, though. Establish yourself first by kibitzing volubly, using such standard insults as schlemiel, imbecile, potzer (= wood-pusher) or nincompoop. After a while you will be recognized and invited to play.

When you do sit down, don't be timid; that will stamp you at once as an outsider and, win or lose, you will not be made to feel that you belong. No, you must be forthright in your denunciations of every move your opponent makes—and especially of the time he takes to make his moves—and even more forthright in your proclamations of your own infallibility. When you make a move, do not lift the piece delicately and place it with finesse upon the board. Rather, grasp it firmly, slam it down as though you intended to smash it to powder, and say "Hah!" If, in error, you move right into a mate-in-one; show concern, but not dismay. Turn the board around, start setting up the pieces for a new game and congratulate your opponent on his immense good luck. Offer to buy the next round of coffee to celebrate his first victory in years and, no doubt, his last. Do not, however, fail to tell him that you lost only because you had developed—no doubt from lack of sleep—a sudden cataclysmic headache. For this you must always carry a small box of aspirin so you can pop a couple into your mouth, sit back and say "in two minutes I'll be all right—then poof! you are mate."

If your style is right (never mind your game, it doesn't matter too much) you will be in. You will, from then on, never have to wonder where your next game is coming from.

What happens, though, if you live too far from the nearest chess parlor to make it there and back without arousing the suspicions of your wife (or husband, ladies)? Then you take up correspondence chess.

To do this all you need is a supply of post cards (file cards will do; you need only affix a 3-cent stamp to it to turn a file card into a post card) and something to write with. And opponents. The first items you can get in a stationery store. The second calls for something else.

If you know a chess player who is willing to correspond you can start without further ado. If you don't, or if you want to play more than one or two games at a time, you must go through a postal chess organization. There are about 100 such organizations in the U.S. and all will welcome you. You join, ask for games and the organization will set you up in a tournament (fees range from nothing to about $3.50, depending on the organization and the type of tournament). To get you started, here is a sadly incomplete list of postal chess clubs, with some pertinent data about each:

Chess Review: This is a magazine published in New York, not a club. However, it has a postal chess department through which you can get opponents. There are three kinds of tournaments: Class Tournaments, which are four-man events in which each player plays two games—one as White, one Black—against each of the others. The entry fee is $1.25. Prize Tournaments, which are seven-man events in which each entrant plays White against three opponents and Black against three. The entry fee is $2.50. First prize is $6.00, second is $3.00, both in credit good for the purchase of books or chess equipment from Chess Review. Golden Knights Postal Championships, which are seven-man qualification tournaments, the final winner getting a respectable cash prize. See Chess Review for details. The magazine's address is 134 West 72nd Street, New York 23, N.Y.

Correspondence Chess League of America: This is the official North American affiliate of the International Correspondence Chess Federation. By playing through the C.C.L.A. you can earn an official correspondence chess rating. Dues are $5 a year, which entitles you to a subscription to the monthly magazine, The Chess Correspondent, one of the best chess magazines published anywhere. The League can book you for any number of different kinds of matches and tournaments, ranging from off-hand challenge matches (two-man affairs that lend themselves to grudge fights) to the big Grand National for the correspondence chess championship of North America. Entry fees range from 50 cents to $3.00, again depending upon the kind of event. To join or to get more information write to Dick Rees, C. C. L. A. Secretary, 816 South Cecelia Street, Sioux City 6, Iowa.

Courier Correspondence Chess Club: This club is connected with the U.S.C.F. and offers official U.S.C.F. postal-play ratings. Dues are $3 a year (physically handicapped persons are given membership and games at no charge) and include a subscription to The Chess Courier. Entry fees are 50 cents and $1.00. For further information write to Virgil M. Kimm, P.O. Box 104, Terryville, Conn.

Knights of the Square Table: This is a real far-out organization that is dedicated as much to fun and friendship as to chess. Dues are $2 a year, which includes a subscription to Nostalgia, a monthly something-or-other that calls itself the only illiterate chess magazine in the world. Entry fees range from nothing to about $1.50 and all entry fees go back to the participants in the form of cash prizes. The club also offers non-chess games through the mails, such as three-dimensional tic-tac-toe, Go, and some you may never have heard of. Interested? Write to Bob Lauzon, 151 West Jefferson Road, Pittsford, N.Y.

If you join any of these organizations, or one of the many others, and find yourself playing ten or a dozen or fifty or a hundred games at one time, you will need more than post cards and a writing tool. You will also need postal chess recorders. These are cardboard or plastic chessboards with flat chess men; you can put them in looseleaf albums or stack them or hang them up. If you try to keep track of your games on regular chessboards you will find no room left in your house or apartment for such useful things as beds, chairs and tables. Postal chess recorders can be purchased through any postal chess organization.

A warning about postal chess: This, too, can become habit-forming. If it does, you will have no time left for anything else. (One man in California some years ago ran up the staggering total of 1,100 simultaneous games. We've often wondered how he managed to avoid writer's cramp.) The average postal chess player—if there is such a thing—apparently plays about thirty games at once. Since not all opponents answer at the same time, of course, he doesn't have to ponder thirty moves with each mail delivery; the thirty games seem to distribute themselves nicely over the week.

There is one more area in which you can enjoy chess. This is problem-solving. It has little relation to live chess, except, of course, that the rules for moves, etc., are the same. This is a pastime suited to people who, for example, do a lot of traveling on trains or plains: they whip out a problem and proceed to work away at it. It makes the time pass nicely. It is also an excellent therapy for the shut-in, for the same reason. Problem-solvers do not mix with chess players, and vice versa.

This brings to an end our thumbnail survey of the world of chess. If you would like to know more there are always other books. Here, then, is a short list.

FURTHER READING

PRIMERS AND GENERAL WORKS

CAPABLANCA, J. R., *A Primer of Chess* (New York: Harcourt, Brace, 1921). Supposedly a beginner's book, but actually for the somewhat more advanced player.

CAPABLANCA, J. R., *Chess Fundamentals* (New York: Harcourt, Brace, 1921). A sort of sequel to the Primer, going into tactics and strategy in more detail.

FINE, REUBEN, *Chess the Easy Way* (New York: David McKay). A thoroughgoing presentation of general principles by one of this country's leading players and theoreticians.

LASKER, EDWARD, *Chess Strategy* (New York: Dover, 1959). Not really a work on strategy, but nonetheless an excellent work on general principles. Written in the easygoing, witty style for which Edward Lasker is noted.

LASKER, EMANUEL, *Common Sense in Chess* (New York: David McKay, 1946). An old stand-by that may not be up to date but that is, nevertheless, full of instructive ideas.

NIMZOVICH, ARON, *My System* (London: G. Bell & Sons, 1957). A witty, sometimes sarcastic presentation of chess principles. Not for the beginner. This is the volume that caused an uproar in the world of chess; it stated the principles of the hypermodern school. An excellent section on Pawn play and "overprotection," Nimzovich's notorious—and successful—system.

RETI, RICHARD, *Modern Ideas in Chess* (London: Bell). A survey of the development of chess technique from Anderssen to modern times. This and the Nimzovich book are the two testaments of hypermodernism.

TARRASCH, SIEGBERT, *The Game of Chess* (New York: David McKay, 1959). One of the best all-around works ever written. Clear, lucid explanations of fundamental principles and a fine collection of annotated games to illustrate them. A bit outdated on openings, but nonetheless valid.

ZNOSKO-BOROVSKY, E., *How Not to Play Chess* (Buffalo: Sterling, 1959). An analysis of the faults to be found in amateur chess and advice on how to overcome them.

BOOKS ON OPENINGS

BARDEN, LEONARD, *A Guide to Chess Openings* (Princeton: Van Nostrand, 1957). One of the newest and best books on opening play. Lucid explanations.

FINE, REUBEN, *The Ideas Behind the Chess Openings* (New York: David McKay, 1957). A thoroughgoing study of the reasoning behind a potful of various openings and variations.

FINE, REUBEN, *Practical Chess Openings* (New York: David McKay). The companion to the above volume. A big and worthwhile reference work.

HOROWITZ, I. A., *How to Win in the Chess Openings.* (New York: David McKay). Analysis of popular openings. Well illustrated with diagrams.

KORN, WALTER AND COLLINS, JOHN W., *Modern Chess Openings* (London: Pitman, 1960). The "Bible" of

openings. The latest edition is the ninth. Gives variations and byplays on almost any opening you can think of. A "must" book.

BOOKS ON THE MIDDLE GAME

CHERNEV, IRVING AND REINFELD, FRED, *Winning Chess* (London: Faber & Faber, 1959). An excellent survey of tactics. Profusely illustrated and well written.

EVANS, LARRY, *New Ideas in Chess* (New York: Pitman, 1958). Not really new ideas, but certainly new ways of presenting ideas. Well planned, well executed and quite lucid.

FINE, REUBEN, *The Middle Game in Chess* (London: Hollis & Carter, 1953). The best book there is on general principles and specific applications. Out of print but worth hunting for.

HOROWITZ, I. A., *How to Win in the Middle Game* (New York: David McKay). General principles clearly illustrated with examples from play.

REINFELD, FRED, *How to Force Checkmate* (New York: Dover). Problems and solutions to master combinations.

ZNOSKO-BOROVSKY, E., *The Middle Game in Chess* (New York: David McKay). A classic work by a great master and teacher.

BOOKS ON THE END GAME

CHERNEV, IRVING, *Practical Chess Endings* (New York: Simon & Schuster, 1951). A basic reference work.

FINE, REUBEN, *Basic Chess Endings* (New York: David McKay). The end-game equivalent of *Modern Chess Openings* and, like this book, a "must" for your library.

ZNOSKO-BOROVSKY, E., *How to Play Chess Endings* (Buffalo: Sterling, 1959). A companion to the other Z-B volumes.

COLLECTIONS OF GAMES

ALEKHINE, ALEXANDER, *My Best Games of Chess* (London: G. Bell & Sons). Two volumes, covering the years 1908-23 and 1924-37. Annotated by Alekhine, these are a mine of information for the advanced player. A third volume, put together after Alekhine's death, covers the years 1938-45. It was annotated by the great British player-teacher C. H. O'D Alexander. Also for the advanced player.

BARDEN, LEONARD AND HEIDENFELD, W., *Modern Chess Miniatures* (London: Routledge & Kegan Paul, 1960). A collection of 161 short and brilliant games.

CHERNEV, IRVING, *1000 Best Short Games of Chess* (New York: Simon & Schuster). The same sort of thing as the Barden-Heidenfeld book, only bigger.

FINE, REUBEN, *Lessons From My Games* (New York: David McKay, 1958). Fine annotates some of his great games.

KOTOV, A. AND YUDOVICH, M., *The Soviet School of Chess* (New York: Dover). 128 fully annotated games of Soviet players, who are the best in the world.

LASKER, EDWARD, *Chess Secrets* (New York: David McKay). A collection of Lasker's games with the greats of his day (which includes today), annotated. Anything by Lasker is well written; this book—more a volume of memoirs than a simple collection of games—is no exception.

MARSHALL, FRANK J., *Marshall's Best Games of Chess* (New York: Dover, 1960). Formerly called "My Fifty Years of Chess." A collection of games notable for their slashing attacks, brilliant sacrifices and traps.

NAPIER, W. E., *Paul Morphy and the Golden Age of Chess* (New York: David McKay, 1957). A collection of games in which the hero is the great Morphy. A biography, too.

RESHEVSKY, SAMUEL, *Reshevsky's Best Games of Chess* (New York: Dover, 1960). A collection annotated by the man many consider the finest chess player America has ever produced.

The Book of the New York International Tournament of 1924 (New York: Dover, 1961). A re-issue of one of the most famous tournament books ever published. The notes are by Alekhine, one of the participants. Edited by Herman Helms.

BOOKS ON PROBLEM-SOLVING

BOUWMEESTER, HANS, *Modern Endgame Studies for the Chess Player* (New York: Pitman, 1959). A collection of 101 composed studies.

HOWARD, KENNETH S., *The Enjoyment of Chess Problems* (New York: Dover, 1961). A presentation of the fundamental principles of problem composing.

HOWARD, KENNETH S., *How to Solve Chess Problems* (New York: Dover, 1961). A collection of problems and explanations of the technique of solving them.

TROITZKY, A. A., *Chess Handbook of 360 Brilliant and Instructive End Games* (New York: Sterling, 1961). Just what the title says.

MISCELLANEOUS

ABRAHAMS, GERALD, *The Chess Mind* (London: Penguin, 1960). A brilliantly written work by a man who is a psychologist-philosopher as well as one of Britain's strongest chess players. Did you ever wonder how a chess master thinks—what makes his mind tick? Here's the book for you.

"ASSIAC," *The Pleasures of Chess* (New York: Dover, 1960). A witty collection of this-and-that by a great British chess columnist. Fine reading for idle moments.

CHERNEV, IRVING AND REINFELD, FRED, *The Fireside Book of Chess* (New York: Simon & Schuster, 1949). Anecdotes, short stories, problems, quizzes, games and whatnots for the chess fan. Cartoons, too.

HARKNESS, KENNETH, *Official Blue Book and Encyclopedia of Chess* (New York: David McKay, 1956). Want to know all the FIDE rules? How to organize a tournament? How to score a tournament? How to play chess with 18 Pawns and no Queen? How to conduct a chess club meeting? Then you ought to have this book. An indispensable reference work for chess clubs, a highly desirable one for individuals.

HAYDEN, BRUCE, *Cabbage Heads and Chess Kings* (London: Arco, 1960). More stories, anecdotes and curiosa for the chess enthusiast.

LASKER, EDWARD, *The Adventure of Chess* (New York: Dover, 1959). A charmingly written collection of essays, including a history of chess, stories about famous players professional and amateur, and a short primer.

REINFELD, FRED, *The Treasury of Chess Lore* (New York: Dover, 1951). Another collection of stories, amusing incidents, anecdotes and assorted trivia that chess buffs find fascinating. Includes Edgar Allan Poe's solution of the famous mystery of the chess automaton.

BOOKS FOR CHILDREN

WEART, EDITH AND BRUSSEL-SMITH, B., *The Royal Game* (New York: Vanguard). An illustrated introduction.

WEISSENSTEIN, HELEN, *John and the Chessmen* (New York: David McKay, 1952). A primer disguised as a story.

PERIODICALS

British Chess Magazine. A fine, highly literate magazine, just the sort of thing you'd expect from the British. Games, analyses, reports on tournaments. No photos, but lots of meaty articles. Annual subscription (12 issues) costs $4 and can be ordered from the publisher. Address is 20 Chestnut Rd., West Norwood, London, S. E. 27.

Chess Life. The official publication of the U.S. Chess Federation. A year's subscription costs $4. But for another dollar you can join the Federation and have your subscription thrown in. Address is 80 East 11th St., New York 3, N.Y.

Chess Review. Already discussed under postal chess. In addition, it carries articles, reviews, features, quizzes, problems, analyses and stories. A year's subscription is $6. Address again is 134 West 72nd St., New York 23, N.Y.

The Chess Correspondent. Publication of the Correspondence Chess League of America (see section on postal chess). This is a slim magazine, but the articles are thick in content. Few frills. You get a subscription automatically when you join the League. Cost, including membership, for a year is $5. Address once more: 816 South Cecelia St., Sioux City 6, Iowa.

This is, naturally, only a very brief sampling of books and periodicals. You'll be able to find other books and magazines, though, through the pages of the ones listed here. And as you get to know your own needs and desires better you'll be able to pick from among those publications.

One final warning (we've been full of warnings, haven't we?): Don't let yourself fall prey to the chess-book mania. Those who do soon have to make every wall a built-in bookshelf. The mania is incurable once contracted, the only palliative being insolvency. Even that doesn't work. There are always credit cards.

Chapter Twelve

THE RULES OF CHESS

THE RULE BOOK of chess, though not nearly as long and involved and amended as the Rule Book of baseball, is nevertheless an impressive collection of do's, dont's and clarifications. The rules are formulated by the Fédération Internationale des Echecs and are, theoretically anyhow, binding on anyone who plays the game.

Most of the rules concern the running of tournaments, scoring, the pairing of players and related things. A great many of the rules are more-or-less technical and would be of interest more to judges than to chess players. Be that as it may, here is an extract of the FIDE rules.*

Articles 1 through 6 deal with the setting up of the board, the arrangement of the pieces, the moves of the pieces, the method of capturing and other items with which you already are quite familiar.

Completion of a Move

ARTICLE 7

A move is completed:

(a) in the transfer of a man to a vacant square, when the player's hand has released the man;

(b) in a capture, when the captured man has been removed from the chessboard and the player, having placed on its new square his own man, has released the latter from his hand;

(c) in castling, when the player's hand has released the Rook on the square crossed by the King; when the player has released the King from his hand, the move is not yet completed, but the player no longer has the right to make any other move than castling;

(d) in the promotion of a Pawn, when the Pawn has been removed from the chessboard and the player's hand has released the new man after placing it on the promotion square; if the player has released from his hand the Pawn that has reached the promotion square, the move is not yet completed, but the player no longer has the right to play the Pawn to another square.

* The following extracts are from Kenneth Harkness, *Official Blue Book and Encyclopedia of Chess* (New York: McKay, 1956), published for the United States Chess Federation, and reproduced here with the permission of the publishers.

Why all this fuss and bother about releasing a piece and putting it down and so forth? Because, in tournament chess, especially, and even offhand chess, "taking back" the move is not quite cricket. After all, the winning or loss of a game—and, in serious play, of a tournament or match—may hinge on one move. As for the elaborate conditions surrounding castling, they are necessary because if a player decides to castle but moves his Rook before his King, the move could be construed as a Rook move at that point. But, since the King can legally move only one square at a time, it is obvious that if the player moves his King two squares he intends to castle and to castle only. No ambiguity there.

Before the adoption of the FIDE rules chess tournaments were chaotic affairs in which the judges had to decide, sometimes at the outset, sometimes as the tournament went along, which set of rules to use (and there were many, each of several countries having adopted its own). FIDE was organized in 1924 and five years later its council adopted the code. The translation from the original French to English was done by the British Chess Federation and this version was adopted by the National Chess Federation of the United States, then the U.S. affiliate of FIDE; later, the National and American Chess Federations merged to become the U.S.C.F.

The Touched Man

ARTICLE 8

Provided that he first warns his opponent, the player having the move may adjust one or more men on their squares.

Except for the above case, if the player having the move touches one or more men, he must make his move by moving or capturing the first man touched which can be moved or captured.

No penalty is entailed if the opponent does not claim a violation of this rule before himself touching a man, or if none of the moves indicated above can be made legally.

In tournament play a man who intends to adjust a

man says "j'adoube," or its English equivalent "I'm adjusting." This is to be on the safe side. The rule says no penalty is entailed if the opponent does not claim a violation; it does not say the opponent can't claim a violation.

Illegal Positions

ARTICLE 9

1. If, during a game, it is found that an illegal move was made, the position shall be reinstated to what it was before the illegal move was made. The game shall then continue by applying the rules of Article 8 to the move replacing the illegal move. If the position cannot be reinstated, the game shall be annulled and a new game played.

2. If, during a game, one or more men have been accidentally displaced and incorrectly replaced, the position shall be reinstated to what it was before the displacement took place and the game shall be continued. If the position cannot be reinstated the game shall be annulled and a new game played.

3. If, after an adjournment, the position has been reinstated incorrectly, it shall be re-established to what it was at the adjournment and the game shall be continued.

4. If, during a game, it is found that the initial position of the men was incorrect, the game shall be annulled and a new game played.

5. If, during a game, it is found that the board has been wrongly placed, the position reached shall be transferred to a board correctly placed and the game shall be continued.

Seems odd to include these last two rules. After all, anyone who feels strong enough to enter a tournament is not likely to put his Knights where his Bishops ought to be, or to play with a dark square at the lower right. Still, the legal mind being what it is, all possibilities are taken care of.

Article 10 deals with the rules of check—when a King is in check, how he gets out, etc. Article 11 deals with the conditions necessary to victory (a game is won through checkmate or when one player resigns). There is no need to burden you with the stiff-language version of what you already know.

Drawn Game

ARTICLE 12

The game is drawn:

1. When the King of the player who has the move is not in check, but such player cannot make any legal move. The King is then said to be "stalemated."

2. By agreement between the two players.

3. Upon demand by one of the players when the same position appears three times, the same player having the move each time. The position is considered the same

if men of the same kind and color occupy the same squares. The right to claim the draw belongs exclusively to the player:

(a) who is in a position to play a move leading to such repetition, if he declares his intention of making such a move;

(b) who is in a position to reply to a move which has produced the repeated position.

If a player makes a move without having claimed a draw in the manner prescribed in (a) and (b), he loses the right to claim a draw; the right is restored to him, however, if the same position appears again, the same player having the move.

4. When a player having the move demonstrates that at least fifty moves have been made by each side without the capture of any man, or the movement of any Pawns.

This number of fifty moves may be increased for certain specific positions, provided that this increase in number and these positions have been clearly established prior to the commencement of the game.

The use (or abuse) of Section 2 came in for a good deal of adverse criticism in recent years. When several hundred people paid hard cash to see a tournament, and the grandmasters played a dozen or fifteen moves and then agreed to a draw, several hundred people were justifiably entitled to feel they had been shortchanged. But there was more to the criticism than that; a draw readily agreed to after so few moves does not provide a true test of ability. These draws could seriously affect the outcome of a tournament. If, for example, a man who had no chance of winning agreed to draw with a good friend, while the favorite was playing a tough opponent, the good friend could gain half a point for nothing, putting him closer to the top, or even putting him in first place. No question about it; this was not very sportsmanlike.

There is a rule that a game has to go thirty moves before a draw can be agreed to. This rule was dropped, for a while, however, and while it was off the books all sorts of "grandmaster draws" were agreed to. An outcry from the chessgoing public brought about a move for the revival of the rule, and it went back into effect in 1963.

Section 3, though it is a newly worded section, is still somewhat confusing and has led to several disputes. A new revision undoubtedly will be made. Notice that the draw by perpetual check is covered by this section.

The fifty-move rule is intended to keep games from going on forever, which could happen, say, in a Bishop-and-Knight ending. The player who does not know how to force mate with Bishop and Knight, but who theoretically has a won game, can refuse to give up. Better study that Bishop-and-Knight ending again.

Tournaments and Matches

The remaining rules—Part Two—concern tournament and match play. They were drawn up by a committee headed by Kenneth Harkness and are given in their entirety in Mr. Harkness' book *The Official Blue Book and Encyclopedia of Chess*. Here are some extracts from those rules:

PART ONE: GENERAL RULES

Eligibility of Entrants in tournaments co-sponsored by an affiliate of the U.S.C.F.

5. Every member of the U.S.C.F. is entitled to enter every open tournament upon payment of the entry fee, unless the tournament is limited to a particular class of players, such as the U.S. Junior Championship and the U.S. Women's Open Championship; and—

(a) As of the date on which the first round begins, every player in an individual tournament must be a member in good standing of the U.S.C.F., and every team in a team tournament must represent an affiliate in good standing of the U.S.C.F.

(b) An eligible player has entered the tournament when he has paid the entry fee.

6. An entrant who is not present within one hour after the time specified for the start of play in the first round, and has not informed the local Committee or the Director that he will be late for the first round or will be present to play in subsequent rounds, is assumed to have withdrawn, and the Director has the right to admit any eligible entrant to fill the vacancy. If it be so filled, a new game is started. . . .

PART TWO: TOURNAMENT REGULATIONS

INTERPRETATION OF ARTICLE 6 (CASTLING MOVE)

9. A player who castles by moving the Rook before moving the King, or by moving the King and Rook simultaneously, should not be penalized for his infraction of the Laws unless he repeats the offence in another game. The Director should warn the player that he is breaking the Laws of Chess. If the player repeats the offence, after being warned, the Director may use his discretionary power to impose a penalty.

INTERPRETATION OF ARTICLE 12, SECTION 2

10. It is unethical and unsportsmanlike to agree to a draw before a serious contest has begun. The Director must use his discretionary power to penalize any player who repeatedly fails to respect his duty toward the tournament organizers and the chess public by agreeing to short draws.

INTERPRETATION OF ARTICLE 12, SECTION 3

11. The procedure of claiming a draw under Article 12, Section 3, of the FIDE Laws shall be as follows:

(a) The Player who is in a position to play a move producing the third repetition of the position should say, "I claim a draw," and write the move on his score sheet. The player should not make the move on the board.

(b) The player who is in a position to reply to a move which has produced the third repetition of the

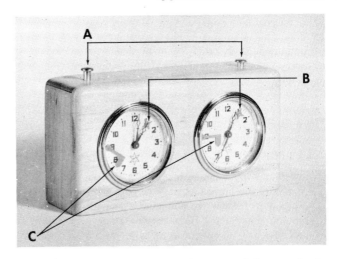

A Chess Clock: A player punches one of the two knobs (A) as he finishes making his move. This stops his own clock and starts his opponent's. The "tickers" (B) show which of the two clocks is running. When a player has used up an hour, the flag (C) drops.

position should say "I claim a draw," but make no move on the board.

(c) In either of the situations described in (a) and (b) above, making a move on the board must be interpreted as waiving the claim of a draw; but the right to again claim a draw is restored to the player if the same position appears again, the same player having the move.

(d) If, in either of the situations described in (a) and (b) above, the player claims a draw and then makes a move on the board, he has waived his claim of a draw, but his opponent may accept and validate the claim, provided he does so before touching a man . . .

RECORDING OF GAMES

12. In the course of play, each player is required to record the moves of his game in a clear and legible manner on a score sheet furnished by the Director . . .

TIME LIMIT

15. Unless specified otherwise in the tournament program, each player must make 50 moves in the first two and one-half hours registered on his clock, and the number of moves that he must make shall be increased by 20 for each additional hour so registered . . .

THE CHESS CLOCK

17. Control of each player's time is effected by means of a clock equipped with special apparatus for the purpose. The clock has an attachment which stops the player's clock and simultaneously starts the opponent's clock. Each clock should have a "flag" which indicates the moment at which the minute hand of the clock is pointing vertically upward.

The chess clock is a fairly recent innovation. Until it came into use chess tournaments were timed in all sorts of odd ways, including not at all. Many a tournament, in fact, was won by the player with the best *sitzfleisch;* he simply outsat all his opponents.

A chess clock is really nothing but two clocks linked together. One runs while the other is shut off. The player who has just moved punches a button on top of the clock; this stops his own clock and sets his opponent's clock in motion. When his hour is up a "flag" pops up on his clock; if he hasn't made the specified number of moves he loses on time forfeiture.

Timing the Game

STARTING CLOCKS AT BEGINNING OF SESSION

19. With the exception of any game or games postponed by consent of the Director, all the games of each round must start at the time specified for the commencement of the round. When the Director gives a signal to start play, each player who has the Black men must start his opponent's clock. If a player with the Black men is absent, his opponent must start his own clock. If both players of a game are absent, the Director or an Assistant Director starts the clock of the player with the White men.

COMPLETING THE LAST MOVE

21. Upon the execution of the prescribed number of moves, the last move is not considered as being completed until after the player has stopped his clock . . .

INTERRUPTED GAMES

24. If a game must be interrupted because of some situation for which neither player is responsible, the clocks shall be stopped until the situation has been adjusted . . .

ADJOURNMENT PROCEDURE

27. Upon conclusion of the time prescribed for play [a session may last four or five hours; this is an arbitrary rule adopted, usually, prior to the tournament or match], the Director goes from board to board and checks the number of moves that have been made in each unfinished game; and at each board where the prescribed number of moves has been completed, the Director gives an envelope to the player having the move, and instructs the said player to seal his move.

Each player who has been instructed to seal his move must write his next move in unambiguous notation on his score sheet, place his and his opponent's score sheets in the envelope furnished by the Director, seal the envelope, and then stop the clocks . . .

Upon the envelope must be indicated:

(1) The names of the players;

(2) The position immediately before the sealed move;

(3) The time used by each player;

(4) The name of the player who has sealed the move and the number of that move;

(5) The date and time of resumption.

The envelope must be delivered to the Director, to be retained by him until the game is resumed.

RESUMPTION OF AN ADJOURNED GAME

28. The procedure in the resumption of an adjourned game is as follows:

(a) The position immediately before the sealed move is set up on the chessboard, and the time used by each player at the time of adjournment is indicated on the clocks.

(b) The envelope is opened only when the player having the move (the player who must reply to the sealed move) is present. That player's clock is started after the sealed move has been made on the chessboard.

(c) If the player having the move is absent, his clock is started, but the envelope is opened only at the time of his arrival.

(d) If the player who has sealed the move is absent, the player having the move is not obliged to reply to the sealed move on the chessboard. He has the right to record his move in reply upon his score sheet, to place the latter in an envelope, to stop his clock, and to start his opponent's clock. The envelope should be placed in security, and opened at the time of his opponent's arrival.

(e) If the envelope containing the sealed move at the time of adjournment has disappeared, and it is not possible to re-establish, by agreement of the two players, the position and the times used for the adjourned game, or if, for any other reason, the said position and said times cannot be re-established, the game is annulled, and a new game must be played in place of the adjourned game.

CONDUCT OF THE PLAYERS

36. (a) During play the players are forbidden to make use of notes, manuscripts, or printed matter, or to analyze the game on another chessboard; they are likewise forbidden to receive the advice or opinion of a third party, whether solicited or not.

(b) No analysis is permitted in the playing rooms during play or during adjournment.

(c) Players are forbidden to distract or annoy their opponents in any manner whatsoever.

Other rules have to do with the duties of tournament directors, the imposition of penalties, the naming of deputies for blind players, special rules for the handicapped, the election of juries to hear appeals and the pairing of players in tournaments, as well as with breaking ties and scoring.

All in all the rules are rather complete; they try to take into account all the conflicts that could arise at a match or tournament. But chess players are ingenious, especially when it comes to playing for high stakes or high titles, and situations constantly arise that cannot be straightened out by appeal to the rules. It's very trying on the judges and referees, and results in conferences to amend the rules.

Local and regional chess organizations frequently have their own rules in addition to those of FIDE and the U.S.C.F. And there are special rules, too, for such things as candidates' tournaments.

The candidates' tournament takes place every three years. The participants are the winners of interzonal tournaments and certain others who have earned the right to try for the world championship.

There are also special rules formulated by the International Correspondence Chess Federation for postal chess, and these are almost as involved as the FIDE rules. In some cases, because of the peculiar problems of postal chess, they're even more complex than the FIDE rules.

Then, of course, there are the rules formulated by two players over the board. Such as: If I make a mistake I can take back my move but if you make a mistake, tough! Or, We'll play until 10 o'clock, but if you're winning we'll keep going until 11, or until you make a mistake and I win.

Don't forget, too, the unwritten laws; they are fully as important as the more formal rules. Here are some of those unwritten laws; study them carefully:

1.

2.

3.

4.

There are others, of course, but space does not permit our listing them all.

QUIZ ANSWERS

QUIZ NO. 1

(a) The Bishops are where the Knights should be and vice versa on both sides of the board. Also, the Black Queen and King have their placcs reversed.

(b) The Black Rook.

(c)

DIAGRAM 442

QUIZ NO. 2

DIAGRAM 443

QUIZ NO. 3

(a) The White Knight can capture the Bishop on the Black square.

(b) The Black Rook can capture the White Knight; the Black Bishop on the White square can also capture the White Knight. And the Black Knight can capture the White Knight.

(c) Yes. The White Pawn two squares above the White Queen can capture the Black Knight diagonally to the right of the Pawn.

QUIZ NO. 4

(a) By moving the White Knight to the square directly above the King, thus shielding him from the attacking Rook.

(b) No. The White Bishop is protected by the White Knight. By capturing the Bishop the King would be moving into check, which is illegal. But did you notice that the King can capture the White Pawn and by so doing move out of check?

(c) By capturing the White Queen with the Black King. Capturing the Rook with the Bishop would do no good; the King would still be checked by the Queen.

QUIZ NO. 5

(a) The Black King can castle King-side. He cannot castle Queen-side because his own Knight is in the way. The White King cannot castle at all. On the King side he has already moved his Rook (which is not on its initial square); on the Queen side he would have to move to a square controlled by the Black Bishop on the Black square.

(b) Yes. The White Pawn on the square directly above the Black Knight can capture en passant. If the White Pawn did this the board would look like this:

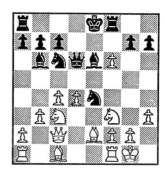

DIAGRAM 444

(c) Yes. The Black Queen can move one square diagonally to the right, attacking the King along the file. The King could not escape to the squares at his

189

right because they are controlled by the Black Rook. The escape squares are occupied by his own men. No White piece could interpose and the Black Queen could not be captured. The final position would be:

DIAGRAM 445

QUIZ NO. 6

(a) 1—Q2   (b) 1—Q7
     2—QB2   2—QB7
     3—K7   3—K2
     4—KB5   4—KB4

(c)

DIAGRAM 446

QUIZ NO. 7

(a)

DIAGRAM 447

(b)

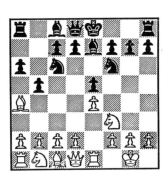

DIAGRAM 448

(c) 1 B×KP, N/Q2×B (or N/2×B or N/Q×B)

(d)

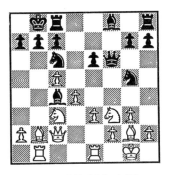

DIAGRAM 449

QUIZ NO. 8

(a) Black can play 1 . . . P—Q4, which will contest White's control of the center and, at the same time, give Black a pawnhold there. He can also play 1 . . . N—KB3, which, though it does not occupy the center, prevents White from playing 2 P—K4, which would give White a powerful central position.

(b) Black has wasted time by moving his Knight twice.

(c) White. He has a centrally posted Knight, a powerful Pawn at K4 and an aggressive Bishop at KN5. Black's pieces are already somewhat cramped and he does not have a foothold in the center.

(d) Black has not castled. White is about to launch an attack directly on the exposed King.

(e) Black should play . . . N—QB3. This would develop a piece and, at the same time, force White to waste time by retreating his Queen.

QUIZ NO. 9

(a) By playing 1 B×N. Black's Queen Bishop Pawn is pinned and cannot capture the Bishop. White therefore wins the Knight and eliminates the Fork.

(b) White can play 1 N—Q7ch. Because of the priority of check, Black will have to attend to his King, giving White the opportunity to capture the Rook.

(c) White can play N—B7ch. The Black KNP is pinned and cannot capture the Knight. From there it is only a few moves to mate.

(d) Black can play B—K7ch. The White King cannot capture the Bishop and, on his next move, Black can take the Rook.

(e) 1 . . . B—Q2; 1 . . . N—Q2; though this, of course, is dangerous.

QUIZ NO. 10

(a) White can play 1 N—K7ch and follow it with 2 N×R.

(b) Black plays 1 . . . P—N4. This threatens mate on next move, R—N8. To stave off mate, White must lose his Queen to the Pawn.

(c) 1 P×Pch, winning the Black Queen.
2 N×Pch, winning the Black Queen.
3 The play could run like this:

1 N×Q	R×Q
2 R/QB×R	B×B
3 R—K7ch	

White has won a Rook for a Bishop and will mate in short order.

(d) 1 . . . Q—Q2 pins the White Rook. 1 . . . K—R1 also would prevent the discovered check.

QUIZ NO. 11

(a) No. If he plays 1 . . . R×Q White could reply 2 R—Q8 dis ch and mate.

(b) The best move for Black is 1 . . . resigns. Because:

If 1 . . . K—R1
  2 B×Pch and the Black Queen falls
If 1 . . . K—B1
  2 B×Pch and the Black Queen falls
If 1 . . . Q×N
  2 B×Pch and the Black Queen falls

(c) Black's best move is to resign.

QUIZ NO. 12

(a) Three. For example: 1 R—KR5, K—Q1; 2 R—K5, K—B1; 3 R—K8 mate.

(b) 1 K×B. This forces a draw because the two Knights are unable to force a mate.

(c) No. The White King would then be stalemated.

(d) By playing 1 . . . B—K6. White then has only one move left, 2 K—N1. This is followed by 2 . . . B—K5ch; 3 K—R1, B—Q5 mate.

(e) Mate in one is 1 Q—B1 mate. Stalemate in one is 1 Q—Q3, which would leave Black no legal moves.

QUIZ NO. 13

(a) 1 R—N8 (this "wastes time"; the Black King must now move, abandoning the Bishop. Mate follows).

(b) 1 K—Q7. This is followed by 1 . . . K—N4; 2 K—Q6 and Black is in zugzwang. If White plays 1 K—Q6, Black replies 1 . . . K—N4 and it is White who is in zugzwang.

(c) 1 . . . K—N5. This is followed by 2 K—Q6, K—B5 and White is in zugzwang.

(d) Yes—he can draw with 1 K—N1. This move fulfills the conditions discussed in the section on Philidor's drawn position.

(e) Black can intercept the passed White Pawn on its way to the Queening square with 1 K—Q7; he also has united Pawns to Black's isolated Pawns.

(f) 1 . . . P—Q7. If White replies with R×R the Pawn will Queen.

QUIZ NO. 14

(a) 1 P—QN4, forging a Pawn chain.
1 P×P, opening the Queen Bishop file for Rook and Queen.

(b) Force: Black is behind a Knight and a Pawn.
Space: Black observes 12 White squares; White observes 8 Black squares.
Time: White has 6 visible tempi; Black has 2.
King Safety: Both Kings are unsafe.

(c) 1 . . . Q—R5ch. White would have to get out of check and Black would play 2 . . . Q×B.
Force: Black is still (temporarily) a piece and a Pawn behind.
Space: Black observes 15 White squares; White observes 8 Black squares.
Time: Black has 3 visible tempi; White has 6.
King Safety: Black's situation is superior.

(d) N—N7, on the principle that holes should be occupied.
N×B if Black replies P×N, he loses the Pawn, weakening the King's protection, and allows White to double his Rooks on the King file.

(e) Black has backward Pawns at QN2, KB3 and KR2. There are holes in his lines at QN3, K3, KB4 and R3. White has a backward Pawn at Q3 and weak doubled Pawns on the King file. But White has a semi-open file for his doubled Rooks. Force is equal, White has an advantage in space; his position (except for his

Queen, which is en prise) is better. If it is his move he can get his Queen to safety and have much the superior position.

(f) Yes. (Schlechter played 1 N×BP. Then if 1 . . . R×N; 2 R×R, R×R; 3 Q—K8ch, winning)

QUIZ NO. 15

(a) 1 P—K5. This locks the center for action on a wing. It also blocks Black's Queen Pawn, reducing the effectiveness of Black's fianchettoed Queen Bishop.

(b) 2 B×Pch. If Black doesn't play 2 . . . K×B you are a Pawn ahead. If he does play 2 . . . K×B, then 3 N—N5ch. Black cannot play 3 . . . B×N because of 4 P×Bch, opening the King Rook file and threatening mate almost at once. So 3 . . . K—N3 (not 3 . . . K—N1; 4 Q—R5, again threatening mate); 4 Q—Q3ch and the attack is too strong for Black to counter.

(c) 1 . . . Q×P, for this would be followed by 2 B×Pch, winning Black's Queen.

(d) N×Nch followed (after B×N) by an attack with the Queen, Rook and Bishop on the castled King's position.

(e) First N/N1—Q2 to keep a Knight at B3; then a thrust in the center to keep White busy there and to forestall action on the King's wing.

(f) Black's Rooks command open files and the King Rook bears down directly on the castled King's weak KR1. Black can play 1 . . . R—R8ch. What follows (this is from an actual game between Lasker and Blackburne) is 2 K×R, B×B; 3 N×B, N—B7ch; 4 K—N1, N×Q and Black is ahead in material and still positionally better off.

QUIZ NO. 16

(a) 2 . . . P—Q4 is logical. If 3 P×P then 3 . . . P×P and the symmetry (and hence the balance) is maintained. 2 . . . N—KB3 might also work out. If 3 P—K5 then 3 . . . N—Q4 and Black, though cramped, may be able to consolidate.

(b) 1 P—K4; 2 P—Q4; 3 N—KB3; 4 N—QB3; 5 B—QN5; 6 O—O; 7 B—K3; 8 Q—K2; 9 R—K1; 10 QR—Q1. The Bishops might also be posted at N5, the Queen at Q2. All pieces bear on the center and observe enemy territory. All is in readiness for attack.

(c) 1 . . . P—Q5 will do it nicely. It will lock the center, prevent Black's playing N—QB3, tie up Black's Queen Pawn and restrict his King Bishop.

(d) B×N, loosening the position.

(e) No. It may prevent B—N5, but it gives White a free hand in the center.

QUIZ NO. 17

(a) He should play 1 B—Q3, to protect the Knight when he gets to Q4. If White plays B—N3, he will be unable to play N—K4, the play being 1 B—N3, P—N5; 2 N—K4 N×N and White ends up a piece down.

(b) 1 P—QN4. If Black retreats the Queen, White plays P×B. Black must then take time to parry the threat of Q×RP mate, giving White a chance to get his threatened Knight to safety.

(c) 1 . . . N—K5 (if 2 N×N; 3 B×R).